The Disabled Church

The Disabled Church

Human Difference and the Art of Communal Worship

Rebecca F. Spurrier

FORDHAM UNIVERSITY PRESS
New York 2019

Visit us online at www.fordhampress.com.

Library of Congress Cataloging-in-Publication Data

Names: Spurrier, Rebecca F., author.
Title: The disabled church : human difference and the art of communal
  worship / Rebecca F. Spurrier.
Description: First edition. | New York : Fordham University Press, 2020. |
  Includes bibliographical references and index.
Identifiers: LCCN 2019028504 | ISBN 9780823285532 (hardback) | ISBN
  9780823285525 (paperback) | ISBN 9780823285549 (epub)
Subjects: LCSH: Public worship. | People with disabilities—Religious
  aspects—Christianity. | People with disabilities—Religious life.
Classification: LCC BV15 .S68 2020 | DDC 264.0087—dc23
LC record available at https://lccn.loc.gov/2019028504

Printed in the United States of America

21 20 19   5 4 3 2 1

First edition

for Sacred Family Church
and
for Silas

TEXTUAL DESCRIPTION OF THE
COVER ART AND TITLE

The image on the front cover is a photograph by Cindy M. Brown of a room where Sacred Family artists weave together during weekly day programs. In the center of the photograph is a painting of a loom by a Sacred Family Artist (used here with permission). The loom is rendered in dark green on a bright red background and sits on a black floor. Next to the loom is a small brown table on which are piled cones of thread and a smaller table loom. The painting hangs on a cream-colored brick wall that sits over an actual table on which are piled cones of thread of various sizes and colors—red, gold, green, purple, aqua, white, multicolored. A manual bobbin winder is in the center of the table with scissors beside it.

The dominant colors of red and green in the cover and title are reminiscent of the bright reds and greens of the cover of Nancy L. Eiesland's book *The Disabled God*, which is referenced by this book's title, *The Disabled Church*. The title is not a description of Sacred Family Church but rather an argument for the transformation of the Christian church.

CONTENTS

For three years I am known as the person who wanders around Sacred Family Church with a notebook and a voice recorder. One spring morning a congregant calls me to her and asks me to record her skills in my research notebook. Before I begin, Lillian makes sure that I write down the date: "March 11, 2014." She then asks me to record this list:

I can do hair.
I write poems.
I can sing.
I can fight.
I can sew.
I can paint.
I can dream dreams.
I have visions.
I can see things that aren't there.
I see invisible people.
I can do makeup and nails.
I can have good sex.
I'm a librarian.
I can dress—fashion dress—model gowns.
I'm a good lover.
I can tell fortunes.

Lillian's description of herself and the playfulness of the moment lead her to use her fortune-telling skills to tell me about myself. I like talking to Lillian. I am fond of her witty company. She has shared some heartbreaking stories from her life with me, but she also makes me laugh, and I share with her stories about my life. I offer her my hand. She takes it and carefully runs her finger along the lines in my palm, talking to me while she does: "You'll have a long life. You'll have two children: a girl and another baby." And then as she runs her fingers along my fingers: "You are mysterious, curious, nosy, feisty; your husband likes you and you like him and there's the band to prove it."

"You're feisty too," I comment.
"Yeah, but I'm not nosy," she replies.

As a participant observer at Sacred Family for three years, I am both observer and observed; I participate in the representation and construction of my own identity and the identity of others. Accepting Lillian's self-identification as a fortune-teller requires me to reflect on the kind of fortune she predicts for me and the way she sees me—a future that involves both great love and my characteristic "nosiness." Indeed, my friends and those closest to me would confirm Lillian's description of me. If I were to make a list of skills like Lillian did, I would probably list this as one of the things I do in any place where I happen to be: I ask questions.

While Lillian is the only fortune-teller I meet during my research, her interest in my husband and future family is a common point of inquiry and fascination among the people of Sacred Family. I became engaged and then married during the time of my research, and so the most frequent questions I field are about my spouse: what he was doing that day, how did I meet him, and when was he going to come visit Sacred Family with me again. Because Sacred Family is a place that welcomes many visitors throughout the week, on occasion I brought friends and my spouse to join us in Sunday or Wednesday worship. Many Sacred Family congregants expressed their pleasure in being able to meet people close to me and especially to meet my spouse. And I experienced it as a privilege to introduce these friends and family to a place that had impacted me in profound ways.

Attraction is difficult to predict or dissect. There is a mysterious quality to the way that any particular person or place catches our attention and elicits a desire for future engagement. I could say that my relationship with the congregation about which I write in this book was love at first encounter. My nosiness was born of attraction. I visited Sacred Family my first month in Atlanta, having learned about it from another student. Almost twelve years later, I find myself returning again and again. Although my own role and relationship with the church have changed over time— intern, regular attender, researcher, occasional attender—my desire to be woven into the ever-changing community that is Sacred Family persists.

My attraction to Sacred Family was both unexpected and unsurprising. Sacred Family was not only a place where it was fun to spend time and where I had enjoyable and thought-provoking conversations with people like Lillian; it was also a place where people like Lillian claimed the beauty of their lives and cared for (and fought with) one another in experiences of pain and distress. From a young age I had lived among extended kinship networks that were practices of faith and mutual care rather than blood ties or biological bonds; I had long been interested in countercultural communities that testify to human beauty and mutual care. Sacred Family appeared to me as one of those communities.

It was also a place that made profound sense to me in light of other communities in which I had actively participated. Prior to my arrival in Atlanta, I volunteered for six years in the country of Ukraine with a Christian organization called Mennonite Central Committee. My work in Ukraine connected me with a number of Ukrainian organizations and groups that supported people with disabilities and mental illness: a group of local women who were advocating for families with disabled children; a home for the elderly that took in people of different ages who had been abandoned by friends and relatives; and a group of church women who regularly visited patients at a local psychiatric hospital. Simultaneously, my experiences with Orthodox, Baptist, and Mennonite liturgies in Ukraine prompted an interest in the power of worship and liturgy. When I arrived in Atlanta, Sacred Family was a place where the presence of disabled people in Christian worship provided me with fresh ways of thinking about what it is that Christians do when they worship God together and why people with disabilities are vital for Christian worship.

Of course, attraction was only the beginning. Over time my interest in Sacred Family evolved into a deeper set of affections for and investment in the people who gather and the kinds of play, prayer, care, and protest that this community embodies. Affection prompted a desire for a more profound understanding of both the hope and the challenge of being this peculiar kind of congregation.

My desire for understanding, what Lillian called my nosiness, was instigated not only by the hopeful gathering of Sacred Family but also by the prophetic work of the Disability Studies Initiative at Emory University. A cross-disciplinary group of faculty and students, the DSI encouraged my conviction that disability is a vital and compelling lens with which to study and investigate all human embodiment as well as the political and social environments that shape assumptions about human abilities and relationships. Both Sacred Family and the DSI at Emory expanded my theological and liturgical imagination regarding the human person. Both Sacred Family and the DSI were places where my own body-mind was profoundly engaged in ways that were challenging, compelling, and life-giving to me.

Through these interactions, I began to dream of communities in which people with and without disabilities might flourish together and to claim my own responsibility to interrogate ableist assumptions in myself and others.

While I could have taken a number of paths to deeper engagement with Sacred Family, the path that fit best with my own emerging vocation involved ethnographic and theological research. My desire to learn the arts of research coincided with the habitus of Sacred Family as a learning community. Sacred Family was a place that enthusiastically welcomed students from across Atlanta to "loiter" and learn from its intentional experiments in being a circle of friendship and support for people with mental illness as well as a church and an unconventional community. While I recognize the dangers and challenges of pursuing ethnographic research without knowing firsthand the experiences of mental illness or poverty of many Sacred Family congregants, my hope was not to study and represent the lives of people who were different from me but rather to study a community of people that I and people like me had and would continue to learn from, worship with, and join. I wanted to describe what made it possible to embrace a wide range of mental abilities and experiences, my own included, as central and irrepressible factors of Christian worship.

My hope, upon the completion of my research, was to continue spending significant time at Sacred Family and, even more, to have time with Sacred Family congregants outside of the formal time and space of church life. Consistent with some of the tensions I analyze in Chapter 3, I have found that the structure of my work time is often in tension with Sacred Family time. Still I continue to attend about once or twice a month on Wednesday evenings. I no longer carry a notebook or a recorder, and while the community at Sacred Family continues to spark my curiosity, I no longer maintain the breadth of interactions I sustained while I was researching or analyze every moment of participation in the community's life together. I go to pray and eat with people I have come to consider friends, even as I am still learning to be worthy of that name, and I go to make the acquaintance of newer people who have come to make Sacred Family what it is now. I go to encounter God, whom I worship in a particular way in the time and space of Sacred Family.

Sacred Family, like every living and breathing community, continues to change. New people bring new rhythms and new art forms even as the heartbeat of the community continues. Of all the changes that have taken place at Sacred Family since my research, the most painful involve the significant number of people who are no longer part of the creation of community there. I came to Sacred Family with questions about how Christian liturgy is and might be transformed by the presence of disability. I left with questions about how the social violence of urban spaces and the lack of safe and affordable living spaces affect the arts of Christian worship. I continue to be haunted by the memories of a group of people who were lost to the church during the period of my research. They drive my commitment to housing justice movements that are vital for the people with whom I spent time at Sacred Family. A significant number of the people I mention in this narrative have died. Others have moved to a new location or have been moved by family members or group home owners. Some stopped coming to programs, and I lost touch with them.

The last time I spoke with Lillian was in a hospital room. Still feisty, still full of life even at the threshold of death, she was a person I was glad to have known even for a brief time. I hope that she is pleased by this record of her skills and that others like her are honored by the ways they are represented and remembered in this work. Each of the congregants I write about here has left a profound mark on me. They are a part of my memories and my dreams. The anthropologist João Biehl writes of "an ethnographic venture" that "has the potential of art: to invoke neglected human potentials and to expand the limits of understanding and imagination—a people yet to come, ourselves included."[1] I cannot tell the future, my own or the lives of others, but I imagine and seek to understand a future world where people with skills like Lillian's and mine can expect to find a place to pray and dream with others and a life of great love in community.

A Sacred Family congregant participates in liturgy with bulletin, hymnals, prayer book, and hat. (Photo credit: Cindy M. Brown)

Disabling Liturgy,
Desiring Human Difference

The beauty is there, all over the church, on the inside,
right there on the inside of the church. . . . That's us,
that's the beauty, the attitude and the love and respect,
and showing respect and love and happiness.

—ROSE WILLIAMS, congregant at Sacred Family Church

A priest I know once described Episcopal liturgy as a dance. Processing, sitting, standing, setting the table for communion, and moving around the altar—all of these movements were a way of being caught up in something greater than herself, a mode of prayer and praise that was not solely about the words she was professing but also about an embodied unity with others in love to God. Over the years, I have come to know what she means. Although I initially felt awkward and inept, juggling prayer books and learning to sit, stand, and kneel at the appropriate moments, I grew used to the rhythms and became able to keep worship time with the rest of a community. I came to understand this priest's description of liturgy to extend to many kinds of worshipping communities, where a unity of movements, songs, cries, shouts, and silences becomes a dance whose rhythms guide each member to take their part.

Yet since 2006, I have become a regular visitor at an unusual church community in Atlanta, Georgia, whose worship calls into question these understandings of a well-choreographed dance of prayer. Sacred Family[1] is a church in which more than half the congregants live with diagnoses of mental illness; many of them come to the church from personal care homes or independent living facilities. Here the dance of the Sunday Eucharist often seems dissonant or disjointed. Some people stand for the hymns and the gospel reading as the prayer book instructs. Some people sit with their bodies folded over into their laps for most of the service. Some wear dresses and suits, and some wear sweatpants and never take off their coats. Some people sing all of the hymns, and some do not sing at all. During the prayers of the people, a congregant inserts his own needs and concerns before he is called upon to do so. A woman reads her own poetry softly to herself. One congregant flips through a travel magazine during the eucharistic prayer. Another negotiates with his neighbor for a cigarette. People walk in and out, disappearing from a pew for a time only to reappear in the same seat or in another. Even in the long amen after the eucharistic prayer, someone's voice bursts forth with an "Aaaa" before the rest of us begin to sing. Whenever one worships God at Sacred Family Church, there is someone who is doing it differently.

"What do you need in order to have *church*?" liturgical theologian Gordon Lathrop asks to begin his study of the holy people called to worship God.[2] He describes how holy people in all their diversity gather weekly around central symbols of Christian liturgy—a day set apart for the reading, praying, and preaching of Scripture and the meal of Christ.[3] The people gather to share food and stories and to remember the poor.[4] He suggests that these symbols invite difference by means of "a strong center and an open door" through which all are welcome. The open door is a symbol of access by which the holy people come, bringing their own needs and gifts to the transforming work of the assembly in order to participate "side by side, in the concrete gifts of the mercy of God."[5] Sacred Family opens wide the church doors, and yet the central elements and the participation in the symbols of Christian worship raise questions rather than supplying clear markers of unity. Not everyone is awake for the Scripture reading. Not everyone pays attention to the sermon. Not everyone goes forward for the meal. Even the collection highlights the differences between poor and wealthy, as some congregants dig coins from their pockets and others lay folded checks and envelopes on the offering plate as it is passed.

Thus my question: What do you need in order to have a church that assumes difference at its heart? Sacred Family is not a communion of different people with similar capacities to read, pray, think, move, and love, but a gathering of people with and without mental disabilities who challenge assumptions about the bodies we call church. Sacred Family congregants embody the struggle of a church imagining people with disabilities as essential to its life and faith. They point to the gathering of difference itself as an act of faith: the belief that human beings in all their variety can enter through an open door to be held together through love rather than coercion or conformity to particular practices or beliefs. If, as disability theologian and sociologist Nancy Eiesland argues, a body is that which is being held together and enabled to act out,[6] how are the bodies at Sacred Family held together and guided into the rhythms of acting out this life together? What does divine love, spoken and embodied through the liturgical symbols of the Christian tradition, have to do with this holding and acting?

The central argument of this book is that Christian liturgy embodies consensual, nonviolent relationships that rehearse a Christian response to an encounter with the creative beauty of divine love, which makes possible belonging to a community through and across difference. It is not first or primarily the ability to grasp or articulate a set of ideas about God nor to conform to a set of normative practices. Rather, the liturgy of Sacred Family, choreographed with and through disability, reveals both the fragility of human connection that is requisite for any worship of God and the persistent beauty of this connection as the gathered ones find, create, and improvise access to one another and the divine. The unconventional arts of becoming church are key to a liturgical theology with and through disability. By artistry, I include the forms of interaction between people that highlight the ordinary works and pleasures of a disabled church.[7] Naming and recognizing these arts illumines both the beauty and the struggle that incorporating difference into the church as the body of Christ entails.

Exploring Sacred Family Church as a community of difference, I analyze the significance of embodiment in shaping a sacramental community. My research methodology was primarily ethnographic participant observation, with its attention to thick description and listening to a multiplicity of voices within a community. Here, I had in mind anthropologist João Biehl's "The Right to a Nonprojected Future," in which he argues that:

> Attending to life as it is lived and adjudicated by people on the ground produces a multiplicity of approaches, theoretical moves and counter-moves, an array of interpretive angles as various as the individuals drawn to practice ethnography. At stake is finding creative ways of not letting the ethnographic die in our accounts of actuality. We must attend to the ways people's own struggles and visions of themselves and others—their life stories—create holes in dominant theories and interventions and unleash a vital plurality: being in motion, ambiguous and

contradictory, not reducible to a single narrative, projected into the future, transformed by recognition, and thus the very fabric of alternative world-making.[8]

I also investigated this community through a threefold approach to theological aesthetics: an emphasis on the role of sensory participation in relationships with God and others, attention to the role of art in theological interpretation, and a focus on beauty as a theological category.[9]

But that is not all. For this work is a conversation not only among the community at Sacred Family with the theological categories it performs and creates, but also with disability studies and disability theology with their critiques of cultural and theological presuppositions about well-being and embodiment, and with liturgical theology with its emphasis on the gathering of Christians to worship God as a primary mode of knowing and loving God.[10]

Sacred Family as a Community of Difference

Sacred Family, founded in the late 1800s as a mission church, moved to its current location in Atlanta in the 1950s.[11] The racial integration of schools that took place throughout Atlanta's neighborhoods in the 1960s, as well as the effects of post-war white flight to the suburbs challenged Sacred Family, then a small and struggling white parish, as it did many other churches and communities. According to one story told around the church, it was in the early 1980s, after a series of changes in the neighborhood and conflicts over church leadership, when membership at Sacred Family had dwindled once again, that the parish faced imminent closure by the bishop.[12] The vicar at that time began inviting people he met in the neighborhood, many of whom lived in group homes. The church not only shared a weekly meal with those who visited but also welcomed them into the worship life of the community.

During the planning for the 1996 Olympics held in Atlanta, some advocates for people with mental illness became concerned about the increased vulnerability of those who spent time on the streets.[13] As part of an initiative by the Georgia Department of Human Resources to create safe spaces during the Olympic Games for local people with mental illness, Sacred Family began its day programs.[14] What started as a temporary response to possible stress and displacement during the Olympics has evolved into a set of programs known as the Circle of Friends, which involves both congregants who attend Sunday and Wednesday services and those who do not. Many of the Circle participants have been diagnosed with various forms of mental illness—such as schizophrenia, bipolar disorder, anxiety disorder, or cognitive illnesses due to aging. Some live with other kinds of disabilities. Many describe themselves as people whose lives have been affected by addictions and homelessness. Some of them have been incarcerated.

Most of those who come to the Circle have been affected by government and state policies that took effect in the 1970s and '80s when persons were released from psychiatric institutions with the anticipation that community-based supports would provide necessary resources for their well-being.[15] In place of government institutions, there emerged for-profit group homes, many of which cannot or do not provide adequate support systems for the people who live there, as I discuss further in Chapter 5. Church staff and lay leaders at Sacred Family speak of group homes as enmeshed in systems that frequently exploit the vulnerabilities of people who have few viable options about where or with whom to live. Those who work at Sacred Family understand part of their mission as ongoing advocacy to secure essential resources for good meals, safe housing, adequate medical care, and, above all, the right to belong to a religious community of mutual care and support. They believe that Sacred Family itself is one of these resources, a place for relationships that are life-giving and transformative. They also acknowledge the limits of what Sacred Family can do and be for those it gathers.

Relationships at Sacred Family are constituted through a wide variety of interactions and contexts. Different kinds of church services take place throughout the week: Tuesday and Thursday morning and noonday prayer; Sunday morning and Wednesday evening Eucharist; and the monthly music event known as Worship Live, which features both dancing and solo performances by community members. In addition to attending services, some members gather twice a week for the Circle (located at the church) to do woodwork and weaving, to paint, and to play bingo and do yoga.[16] Some sell plants from the greenhouse on second Saturdays of the warmer months of the year. Tuesday and Thursday mornings begin with breakfast, and all midweek services are followed by a shared meal, which is supplied either by Sacred Family or by other churches. After lunch, some members choose to stay for support groups for those with mental illness. Many Circle participants also share a life together outside the church, returning by van to the eight or nine group homes where they spend most of their time.[17]

*Ethnographic Methods and Assembling
the Pieces of a Theological Puzzle*

During one of my first interviews, Tanya, a young woman with mental illness, volunteers to speak to me about experiences at Sacred Family. She appears nervous, and as soon as we enter the interview space, she confirms that she feels anxious about taking part in the conversation. In line with my research protocols,[18] I assure her that she does not need to participate in this recorded discussion if she feels uncomfortable. I also give her the option to meet with me at another time when she feels more at ease.[19] Tanya insists that she wants to continue our conversation and that she likes being able to contribute in this way, even if she feels anxious. She thinks she might be the "missing piece of the puzzle" I need to understand this community.

Like Tanya, I imagine that all people at Sacred Family are missing pieces of a puzzle about the church as a beloved community that witnesses to divine beauty and justice in the world. I also investigate Sacred Family Church as one missing piece in a larger puzzle about how the broader Christian church not only feels obligation to include those with disabilities but also how it comes to desire the beauty as well as the struggle that human variation brings. Assembling these pieces of the puzzle requires that my readers imagine what it would feel like to be part of a community like this: the excitement, the confusion, the boredom, the laughter, the distress, the tenderness, and the exhaustion. As Eiesland writes, "An accessible theological method necessitates that the body be represented as flesh and blood, bones and braces, and not simply the rationalized realm of activity."[20] Ethnographic methodologies keep me grounded within my field of inquiry to record in field notes and to evoke for my readers what it feels like to be part of Sacred Family's everyday liturgy. In order to draw readers into the flesh and blood—the hope and the struggle—of lived experience at Sacred Family, I have chosen to convey my research in the present tense so that the reader might feel the immediacy of events and relationships.

As a participant-observer, I investigate the stated goals, descriptions, and explanations offered to me by different kinds of participants about the purpose and identity of the parish, but I also investigate the sounds, gestures, silences, and relationships that are as much a part of Sacred Family as that which is explicitly claimed for the church's identity. I include in my study the kinds of participation and non-participation that confirm or contradict this church's own explicit theological claims about what Sacred

Family is and does. Ethnographic methods encourage me to pay theological attention not only to the places most obviously associated with religious or theological identity but also to a range of relationships that happen across space and time when people gather at the church.

Ethnographic methods as well as ethnographic writing ground my theological interpretations in a close description of ecclesial life and of the social dimensions of Christian worship. Such descriptions bring to my theological writing an openness to multiple and, at times, disparate and diffuse interpretations of who God is and how God is working among those who identify as Sacred Family. By grounding my methodology and my writing in close and careful descriptions of particular times and spaces at Sacred Family, I offer a multi-dimensional, theological portrait that illustrates both the beauty as well as the ambiguity of this church's struggle to keep the doors open to all who seek a place at Sacred Family—and by extension in the broader Christian church.

Sacred Family's doors were opened to me long before my formal research and writing began. Sacred Family is unusual not only as a church that welcomes people with mental illnesses, but also as a site of education and training. The parish welcomes many students from medicine, theology, and other disciplines for experiential learning opportunities that last from a few weeks to a couple of years. A supervised internship program during my master of divinity degree introduced me to this parish six years prior to my formal study of it. Even after I completed the internship, I found it difficult to leave Sacred Family and often returned to visit. Whenever I encountered a theological or humanistic claim about proper virtue or worship, the faces of Sacred Family parishioners appeared in my mind, gently interrogating its premise.

How and why has Sacred Family inscribed itself so deeply on my theological imagination and the imagination of so many others who spend time there? As one woman, a volunteer for over thirty years, declared to me, "There's no other church like Sacred Family. . . . I don't think there's any place in the world you can say is as nice as Sacred Family; what do you think?"[21] There are many members of the parish and former interns who would confirm her sentiment. Through a research period of careful participant observation, I have sought to understand better both what makes Sacred Family unique and what it holds in common with other Christian churches and communities.

To understand and describe divine and human love manifest through difference at Sacred Family, as well as to study the forms which constrain or obscure such configurations of difference, I have spent three years of research at Sacred Family (one full-time and two part-time years). I have attended Sunday morning and Wednesday evening communion services and eaten meals with the community. I have also participated in Circle activities: gardening, art, games, socializing, yoga, and Bible studies. I have attended occasional events such as plant sales, Worship Live services, social outings, and visits to other church communities. I have visited personal care homes and independent living facilities, so that I have a sense of life at Sacred Family in relation to these other primary communities that affect relationships within the church. I have also conducted interviews with congregants, interns, and volunteers in order to hear stories shared less frequently in the day-to-day activities of the church. I have tested my own theories and assumptions about the community by inviting others to reflect on the categories I employ. As an ethnographer and a theologian, I both trust and evoke divine agency in calling and shaping the church, an assumption shared by many who gather as part of this community. I also listen to voices and observe behaviors that would counter these beliefs and assumptions, seeking both confirmation for and doubt about the approach I have used to describe and identify "Christian liturgy" at Sacred Family. I take seriously the woman who says she can feel the presence of God at Sacred Family and the man who sits at the entrance, refusing to go in for noonday prayer, because he "never saw Jesus in a church."

Like anthropologist Karen McCarthy Brown, I understand ethnography to communicate a particular, subjective truth that occurs in between a participant-observer and the people she is studying and, as such, to rely on the process of ethnographic research as a "social art form, open to both aesthetic and moral judgment."[22] Such an art form acknowledges that ethnographic methods rely on the creation and maintenance of human relationships that affect both researcher and those from whom and with whom she seeks to learn; thus, there is no clear boundary separating the ethnographer from those she studies. Even as I seek a truthful and accurate representation of the community and individuals with whom I spend time, I also help to create this representation through my interactions with others and through the history, knowledge, and experience I bring to this place.

Aware of the part I have played in Sacred Family, I describe my interactions within the narrative of this book so that readers can observe my participation in community life. I often use a first-person narrative both in field notes and in this chapter to remind myself and my readers of my active part in discovering, eliciting, selecting, and interpreting particular elements of Sacred Family's life together. Ethnographic research and theological inquiry are inherently subjective tasks, shaped by the stories, relationships, cultures, and resources of the writer, who captures partial memories from a particular time within an ever-changing place. Thus, ethnographic and theological narratives always include some characters and exclude others. By focusing on some parts of a story, they obscure others. Thus, we might think of this book as one brief chapter in the yet unfolding story of Sacred Family.

Parts of my story are animated by my identity as a Christian who has been going to church all her life. Although I am currently a member of a Mennonite church, I have worshipped with and deeply engaged churches of many different denominations throughout the forty-five years of my lifetime. I am also a temporarily abled, white, straight, cisgender, married, childless woman, who has not yet been diagnosed with a mental illness and who has never lived in poverty. I have spent time with communities advocating for people with disabilities and mental illness prior to coming to Sacred Family. I have also had friends and family members who have been diagnosed with psychiatric disabilities.

Occupying both insider and outsider positions, I follow ethnographically and theologically this church's movements and struggles. I do not offer Sacred Family as a model that should be replicated by other churches and faith communities, but as a window into the kinds of aesthetic frames and questions that a disabled church inspires. As I do so, I take my cue from the philosopher and theologian Jean Vanier, founder of a worldwide movement of intentional communities focused on core members with intellectual disabilities. When Vanier was asked to give a formula for the organization called L'Arche, he suggested that L'Arche is a sign not a solution, a movement to transmit a vision and a counterculture rather than an institution that is about successful replication.[23] Following Vanier's suggestion, I do not view Sacred Family as the ideal form a church or community should take. Rather, I maintain the vital significance of that to which Sacred Family points, for its desires and limitations tell us something about the presence and absence of God in community through disability. Sacred Family offers wisdom about the liturgical formation of faith communities that manifest divine and human beauty as a response to social violence.

I gathered information so as to represent accurately the encounters in which I took part, as well as to maintain the research forms that felt least intrusive to the community. I took psychiatric disability into account not only as a critical lens through which to interpret church community but also as an experience that might affect a process of informed consent. I built into my research protocols an awareness of possible mental distress or change. Because some congregants struggle to remember certain kinds of information, as often as possible I reminded those with whom I was speaking about my role in the community; this included not only congregants but also staff who sometimes asked me to take on volunteer roles. I made sure congregants were always aware that they did not need to respond to my questions and could choose to end, to put on hold, or to continue our conversation at a different time if they were feeling uncomfortable. Some congregants asked to speak with me but then changed their minds when I offered them the option not to speak. I tried to build in a flexible and sensitive approach to interactions that did not contribute to any anxiety that congregants might be experiencing and that also took into account dramatic fluctuations in the ways that people expressed themselves to me. I used a process of oral consent to help protect the confidentiality of those with whom I met individually in formal interviews, made sure they knew that what they shared would have no impact on their participation in the church or its programs, and made clear that those with whom I had formal interviews knew that they could come back to me prior to the completion of my research and ask me not to use any information they had shared.

I carried a digital voice recorder with me, taped all formal gatherings and interviews, and recorded some informal interactions. Some congregants were more comfortable with taking written notes than audio recording our interactions. Thus, there are numerous events and conversations that I recorded in a small notebook and then reconstructed through field notes. I give you, my readers, indications to these different forms of gathering information through the punctuation I use in the dialogues I recreate here. Quotation marks denote conversations where a recording or the pace of a conversation allowed me to capture the conversation verbatim. When I do not use quotation marks, I have reconstructed conversations from notes I have taken when I was not able to capture every single word. For these reasons, some conversations are written with the use of quotation marks and some are not.

Mental Illness through the Lens of Disability Studies

I come to the study of this community as a liturgical theologian who uses ethnographic methods and as a disability scholar. I am not trained as a mental health practitioner or as a psychiatrist. Thus, I attempt to describe behaviors and interactions within the parish as I observe them or as I hear them described rather than analyzing them through a medical or psychiatric lens.[24] For example, I describe genres of touch and what this touching evokes within community, rather than asking what mind-body processes lead a certain group to use touch rather than speech or how certain kinds of medications affect the embodied interactions of the community. In doing so, I assume the legitimacy of such forms of interaction and behavior. By drawing on my own experiences and the experiences of others who participate in or otherwise engage with this community, my primary interest lies in investigating communal experiences of church with and through disability. I seek to keep disabled and non-disabled people together as theological subjects within my field of inquiry rather than to turn to the disabled body or mind as an object of inquiry. At times, I explain both conventional and non-conventional forms of interaction when people in the community choose to explain behaviors for me, and I want to highlight their interpretations of themselves or one another.

I use disability criticism to consider the activities of persons with diagnoses that explicitly label them as mentally ill or as people with mental health challenges. Psychiatric disability is not a term that is deployed at Sacred Family, where mental illness or mental health challenge/disorder is more commonly used to refer to the experiences of many congregants. While some scholars might desire a clear distinction between disability and mental illness, much disability criticism emphasizes different forms of embodiment on a continuum rather than making hard distinctions between embodied experiences.[25] Three approaches of disability criticism are particularly helpful in thinking through the relationships that Sacred Family explicitly seeks to nurture and transform.[26]

First, disability studies and disability theology tend to emphasize the capacities and limitations of embodied minds as manifest through relationships with other people and places and through political, religious, and social assumptions about what it means to be human. That is, if I come to identify as mentally ill, I know this through cultures, environments, and discourses that give me that designation and that construct some behaviors as sane and others as crazy. Real suffering exists, and people desire that their bodies be transformed in light of this suffering. However, these desires and experiences of pain are inextricably enmeshed in social relationships and cultural representations through which people negotiate their own meaning and worth and receive care from others. Through these relationships and representations, we learn to identify the meaning of sickness and health, capacity and incapacity; we learn to name and understand our conditions, as well as to envision alternatives. Using the language of psychiatric disability, I identify two systems (psychiatry and law) through which persons at Sacred Family come to know themselves and others as normal or abnormal. To describe human life in these ways is both useful and limited.

Second, disability studies as a form of critical discourse emphasizes that in order to talk about a particular category of embodiment (woman, black, gay, poor, disabled, sick, mad) we must also think carefully about both the construction and the invisibility of its opposite. What kinds of behavior come to be designated as abnormal and through what relations to the normal? What sorts of descriptors, capacities, and aesthetics set apart the able bodied from the disabled, the mentally healthy from the mentally ill, the sane from the insane, the ordered mind from the disordered one? In particular, disability discourse highlights the normal as an exclusive and elusive category—one that often remains uninterrogated and, therefore, works against an affirmation of human difference. Given that every year one in five American adults experiences a diagnosable mental illness and over forty-five million Americans live with mental illness in a given year, disability studies raises vital questions about what constitutes a "normal" human life and whose lives are considered good lives.[27] Thus, disability studies provides a critical framework for understanding how mental illness, a common human experience, occupies an aberrational and stigmatized position.

Third, disability scholarship also tends to emphasize vulnerability, interdependence, accommodation, and bodily variation and change as part of what it means to be human. This emphasis stands in opposition to certain ideals of ability, health, wholeness, independence, progress, and normalcy that are unattainable or unsustainable over the course of a human life. While there are different forms and degrees of joy and suffering, all of us face radical changes in our embodied minds and relations with the world and with others throughout the course of our lives. Some disability theorists emphasize that if we live long enough, most of us will experience disability. Thus, mental illness is not an extraordinary fate that affects only a small number of abnormal people, but a condition that is shared among many or indeed most families and communities. Disability must be reckoned with as part of human life; it is not something from which we can isolate ourselves.[28]

I use the terms psychiatric disability, mental illness, and mental difference.[29] Mental illness is the terminology that the people I encounter at Sacred Family use most often; I use it as a description indigenous to the community and to the surrounding culture. Psychiatric disability places this community within a larger conversation about what disability means and provokes as it encounters the assumptions of normalcy and ableism.

The language of mental difference emphasizes the fact that a range of body-minds is present within any human community, even if particular mental differences come to characterize Sacred Family. By using a diversity of terms, I intend "to recognize the complex interactions among individuals, their illnesses, and the larger social contexts in which these are all embedded."[30] Thus, I work to keep multiple frames for identifying and understanding human persons and interactions in play.[31]

Disability and the Christian Church

In *The Disabled God*, Eiesland describes significant ways that the Christian church has harmed people with disabilities through inadequate theological models of disability. The church has done so in part by regarding disabled persons as props and instruments of theological inquiry rather than as "historical actors and theological subjects." Unjust theological interpretations have prevented the church from accessing the lives of persons with disabilities, as well as barring disabled persons from the symbols of the church. Such "carnal sins" of the institutional church reveal not only the fragility of human bodies but also the fragility of the church that claims to be a witness to God's love in the world.[32]

Eiesland identifies three such "carnal sins" that have prevented churches from accessing the lives and insights of people with disabilities. First, she argues that the church has tended to practice segregationist charity.[33] While congregations desire to help people with disabilities, they often maintain a safe distance between church members and those whose forms of embodiment might challenge their theologies and body practices. Charitable practices that focus on helping and healing individuals—those deemed dependent or needy—often obscure the broader questions of "political engagement and social inclusion." Second, the church has used persons with disabilities as examples of "virtuous suffering."[34] By highlighting their suffering as a means of divine work in the world, the church symbolizes disability as a temporary test to be endured for a spiritual reward. In such a theological framework, disabled lives provide others with inspirational examples of suffering and overcoming. Such theologies have been used to isolate people with disabilities and to encourage them to adjust to unjust circumstances. Third, the church has participated in what Eiesland calls the "sin-disability conflation," where a causal relationship between sin and impairment is implicitly or explicitly evoked.[35] Disabilities are associated with evil; they are not part of God's good intentions for the world, and thus persons with disabilities become evidence of the sinfulness of the created order that God seeks to heal and transform. Through these three critiques, Eiesland identifies what she sees as a persistent thread in Christian theology: persons with disabilities are "either divinely blessed or damned: the defiled evildoer or the spiritual superhero."[36] Such theologies fail to represent "the ordinary lives and lived realities of most people with disabilities."[37]

Sacred Family is a community that seeks to transform these carnal sins of the church into new relations with persons who are often excluded from ecclesial practices and theologies. Although the church explicitly promotes its Circle activities as part of its mission, it intentionally distances itself from a communal ethos that views persons with mental illness as recipients, rather than full participants, in community. In an older pamphlet written about Sacred Family entitled "WHO we are! WHY we are! WHAT we are!" I read this assertion:

> It seems so difficult for many to accept the fact that Sacred Family is not a Church with a program for the mentally ill. Just as we are not a church with a program for women or persons of differing races, cultures, or lifestyle preferences; we are likewise not a church with a program for the poor, the ill and/or the oppressed. **They are us**. We are one body. We are a church. They run for church office, serve on parish boards and committees and help lead our congregation in worship. We at Sacred Family do not differentiate between persons or types of persons. Together we respect the dignity of every human being as all are welcome and included in our community.[38]

In addition, a newsletter reporting on activities in the Circle describes the community this way: "We are not a community of staff and clients, or even staff and participants. We are a community in the tradition of mutuality. We are all participants, we all benefit from [the Circle] and we are all supporters and friends of one another."[39] Sacred Family does not speak of its parishioners as singled out for divine blessing, nor does it connect mental illness to discourses of evil and sin. Rather, congregants, interns, and volunteers explicitly and implicitly challenge other churches and communities to consider how they might become more welcoming to persons with mental illness and participate in the creation of communities of mutual support.

At the same time, like any community of difference that embodies a shape of communal interaction rarely found in the wider church or society, Sacred Family struggles to become a group that is not easily divided: into "us and them"; into people who have mental illness and people who do not;

into people who have money and people who do not; into residents of group homes (a greater percentage of whom are black) and leaders, church visitors and volunteers, and donors (most of whom are white). Church structures, liturgical practices, and patterns of administration regularly perform and perpetuate such divisions, for Sunday congregants who work during the week rarely attend the Circle activities or experience the relationships created there. Few people from group homes participate in the primary decision-making positions and committees of the church.[40] At the same time, these power structures affect the shape, the rhythms, and the meanings of community life together as well as performing what is considered the primary work of the church. A smaller group of persons who do not live in group homes is often asked to bear numerous responsibilities for the everyday running of buildings, meetings, congregational care, and fundraising efforts. Many of the home-owning, wage-earning congregants must find money to provide for the inclusion of persons from group homes and for sustaining community programs and meals.[41] Such asymmetries in care and responsibility for Sacred Family provide potential places of fragility and explicit divisions within the community. They raise questions about who and what is central to the work of the people that Christian liturgy assumes.

Eiesland argues that the church's ongoing conversion to a more truthful understanding of God involves "two-way access,"[42] so that persons who historically have been marginalized find themselves at the "speaking center" of their own lives in a community of grace and struggle and the community itself comes to understand God differently in light of the experiences of people with disabilities. She argues that it is not enough to make a physical space within a church building for persons with disabilities, but that the actual "body practices" of the church must be transformed.[43]

As a participant-observer at Sacred Family, I look for evidence of two-way access and I study forms that facilitate such bridges across difference. How do the community's body practices incorporate and make space for the differences of congregants? What kinds of relationships shape the possibility of shifting not only the speaking center but also the moving, dancing, sitting, walking, and reading centers of the liturgy? What forms of interaction resist the asymmetries of power that so easily divide faith communities, where hierarchies threaten and sometimes obscure the work and witness of Love? Conversely, what are the obstacles that prevent such a community from being held together and acting together as a communal body able to bear witness to divine love?

These questions are not only about justice for persons excluded from the church; they are also about the possibility that Christian communities will cut themselves off from experience of the infinite differences that illumine divine love and justice. When congregations fail to recognize persons with disabilities, they also fail to name God adequately. People with disabilities surface new truths about what it means to be in relationship with God and others, uncovering hidden histories of the Christian tradition.[44] Such embodied truths participate in an "insurrection of subjugated knowledges" that Eiesland describes as "the corporate enactment of the resurrection of God."[45] In other words, Christian churches need the wisdom and struggle of disabled lives to help them interpret anew their holy texts and body practices, their traditions of gathering, their symbols and sacraments, in order to grasp the latent truths suppressed through segregation and stigma. Thus, the title of this book is offered not so much as a particular name for Sacred Family Church as it is for the broader Christian church, an evocation of how the symbol of church would be transformed if the myriad and manifold lived experiences of disabled people were invited to transform the practices and theologies of the people of God.

The One and the Many in Christian Liturgy

To attend to the wisdom of disability within Christian community is to question what disability theorist Tobin Siebers calls "the ideology of ability"[46] or what theologian Thomas Reynolds describes as "the cult of normalcy."[47] It is to query assumptions about abled human capacities as prescriptive for gathering as church. It is to mine the implicit prerequisites for experiencing and manifesting love and knowledge of God and neighbor through prayer, praise, contemplation, and reflection. It is to ask about the subtle forms through which we isolate and elevate individual persons or devalue and obscure their differences through assuming their similarity with others in community.

Descriptions of Christian worship often assume an ideal worshipper, who is also an able-bodied, able-minded congregant capable of demonstrating that he is being shaped by God through the sacraments and Christian practices in a particular way.[48] If, as a liturgical theologian, I focus only on ideal individual capacities to perform and grasp Christian practices of prayer, interpretation of Scripture, and participation in communion, then I imply that certain people with disabilities lack the ability to be in relationship with God. Graver still, I imply that they lack the preferred abilities to participate in Christian worship in a way that reflects the depth of liturgy's symbolic meaning. For example, when a congregant from Sacred Family goes forward to take communion, grabs the wafer from the priest, dunks it in the wine, refuses to say "Amen," and rather than consuming it, brings it back to stick it in his pocket or in the prayer book, he becomes an unlikely exemplar of Christian community. While loving exceptions might be made for such a congregant who is unable to show the reverence or intentionality expected of him, such a person would not be conferred the implied status of ideal Christian practitioner. At the same time, other congregants might experience the presence of this congregant as central to their worship at Sacred Family. His presence might serve as an icon of the cherished differences that are essential to the worship of God at Sacred Family, even if he is not an ideal practitioner.

Focusing on an idealized, synchronized communal body often obscures the diversity of individuals, the forms by which the many congregants access a common liturgy, and the varied tones and textures throughout a gathered assembly. To describe a parish as an assembly capable of doing and being one thing is to obscure the full range of responses and experiences occurring throughout the liturgy and liturgies of the community. For example, when I note that the congregation at Sacred Family offers prayers of intercession together by responding in unison, "Hear our prayer," such language fails to conjure the group in the back right whose members appear to be sleeping. It also fails the two individuals in the front right who eagerly desire to insert the names of their beloved family and friends into the formal prayers we are reciting. Worship at Sacred Family is different depending on where and with whom I sit and stand. Such differences matter not only to the prayers that are offered but also to a theological understanding of a beautiful liturgy as pleasing to God. Those with whom I worship contribute to a theological aesthetic of a communal body even if they seem to be utterly disengaged or disruptive to others.

Theologian Min-Ah Cho writes of the urgency of attending to the divergent responses of those who are present:

> The weakness of the believers at the margin, their "flaws" and "crooks" are precisely the nudge that their power lodges, as they reveal the illusion of the homogenous institution. Even though these individuals seem passive and guided by established norms, each of them is an agent that brings divergent plurality to the institution and alters its conventional determinations. Without the individual bodies, the body of Christ remains dormant and fails to incarnate.[49]

Cho emphasizes what may be lost when we elevate the communal response over the individualistic one. The many may obscure the one; but the one is always affected by the ones around her. Her worship is informed by the bodies that open or obstruct her way into the church, the individuals who border and nudge her thanksgiving or petition or lament. Thus, the quest for a liturgical theology that captures the "divergent plurality"[50] of Sacred Family includes a frame that holds the individual difference and communal action in dialogue, interanimation, and tension.

Theological Aesthetics through Embodiment, Art, and Beauty

Theological aesthetics affords a nuanced yet dynamic way to attend to dimensions of difference and interdependence present within a communal body through individual bodies. Attending to bodies, to sensory experiences, and to the performance arts evoked by clusters of individuals within the church helps me to recognize the possibilities of difference. At the same time, it refuses to elevate individual capacities as the ideal for those who come in through the open door of the church.

Likewise, when I contemplate communal interactions at Sacred Family, in all their ambiguity, the word *beauty* comes to mind; the way that beauty, in all its culturally constructed and often very conventional forms, calls forth attention and invites some shared word or comment of appreciation or curiosity. I consider this word *beauty* not only in relationship to the ostensible pleasures of an ecclesial gathering but also to all of the sensory experiences that evoke disgust or confusion in this community: body odors and disheveled clothing; the way some people eat their food; some people standing very close to others and staring; someone's condescending words to another; and someone else's expressionless face. Are these beautiful too, or ugly, or neither? What makes someone or something beautiful, and for whom? Why do some people or parts of a liturgy seem beautiful to me and others do not?

According to theologian Edward Farley, Christian theological language has often neglected beauty as a lens through which to consider a relationship with the divine as well as to trace the process of redemption. Fearful of idolatry and concerned that beauty is a superficial distraction from the ethical dimensions of faith, Christians have paid insufficient attention to beauty as a way to describe the Christian life.[51] Reflecting on the absence of an aesthetic dimension in his own theological writing, Farley observes, "It was as if the most concrete way in which human beings experience their world—namely, their emotional participation in surprising, interesting and attractive events—had no place in the world of faith."[52] What might it mean, he asks, to take seriously this dimension of faith and beauty.

Farley distinguishes the "aesthetic" as an immediate relation to beauty mediated through embodied experience from "aesthetics" as a theological consideration of the arts.[53] Thus, he articulates two approaches to the relationship between Christian faith and human embodiment: theological aesthetics attends to the relationship between religion and the arts, and a theological aesthetic reflects on beauty's role in the life of faith. Both require discernment of embodied practice and response. Both involve attention to the sensory experiences of faith, to the way it feels to be faithful.

Farley argues that discerning a theological aesthetic begins with the beauty in "redemptive transformation," which he describes as a life moving from unfreedom to new freedom through transcending oneself toward another in need. Made in the image of God, humans are freed by God for a transcending turn in which freedom and compassion are non-competitive. Beauty is found in the faith of one who is called to respond to another: a theological aesthetic tracks the shape of this faith, its desires and hopes for "ethical self-transcendence" in a relationship with another through divine grace. It looks for the beauty inherent in such a relationship and tracks the sensations that a life of such hopeful turning to another arouses in them.[54]

For Farley, beauty, as a theological term, marks the lived experience of one's outward turn to another, a turn both passionate for another and restrained by the needs of the other. As we turn to the ones who call to us, through their need for us to turn, we become beautiful, and the turning arouses our interest and desire in the beauty of another. A theological aesthetic thus implies an inherent sweetness, an eroticism to asceticism: a faith in the pleasures of the disciplines of loving God and another. Beauty in this sense "means the inevitable grace of a living body as it movingly negotiates the world of space, place, time and gravity."[55]

In an alternate analysis of the aesthetics of Christian doctrine, theologian Serene Jones also articulates two approaches to theology: one analyzing the category of beauty (a theological aesthetic, using Farley's definition) and another offering a more detailed analysis of "what particular features of something—an idea, an object, a person—make it appealing (or not) to us" (a theological aesthetics). This second level of analysis should focus on "the qualities of a given topic or object—its form, shape, texture, proportions, feel, sound, color, and so forth." Giving an example of the aesthetics of a Christian understanding of creation, Jones asks: "What does creation look like when we see it in our mind's eye: what does it taste like, what colors appear when we hear the term; what memories do we associate with it; what kind of music does it play?"[56] This kind of theological analysis connects with the affective connotations of Christian discourses. To explore the meaning of a Christian doctrine, we begin by asking: Does it make one fearful or indifferent, or does it elicit passion or desire?[57] Jones, like Farley, suggests a different approach to evaluating faithfulness to Christian belief, one that traces the subtle patterns of embodied relationships within and among human persons.

I begin by using theological aesthetics as an analytic tool, with attention to both sensory descriptions of bodies in space and time and to the artistries of relationships that constitute the parish of Sacred Family. I remain as close as possible to the affective responses and embodied interactions that constitute the space, time, form, and names of Sacred Family—the qualities of the given congregation and the associations to which they give rise. I hope to turn my readers from fear or indifference to desire for the kind of community that Sacred Family hopes for and imagines. In doing so, I also propose an understanding of art forms, broadly conceived, as a helpful frame for describing the unities and coherence of Sacred Family's practices with attention to the nonconformity of human differences. I illustrate how an expansive weeklong liturgy is created with and through configurations of individuals in ongoing, flexible, imaginative, and collaborative forms that exist alongside assumed rituals of Christian worship (offering spoken and sung prayers, listening to God through scripture and a sermon, reciting the creed, participating in communion, silence).

At the same time, I also use a theological aesthetic as I evaluate these forms and the relationships they help to create through the lens of beauty as a theological and ethical category. I want to argue for a theological criterion of beauty as a means of assessing the communal life of Sacred Family: its hopes and fragilities, its strange humor and its suffering, its cohesion and incoherence, its consent to difference and its powerful hierarchies of ability, wealth, and race. Beauty, as a theological trace of consent to a shared liturgy, matters to an unconventional, disabled church community struggling to incorporate human difference into the heart of its gathering.

In choosing aesthetic/s as an analytic framework, I join a company of disability scholars and theologians concerned with how senses of the good and beautiful exclude many bodies from the desires of others. In the contrasts they establish, some definitions of goodness and beauty thwart desire and, instead, conjure up disgust, revulsion, or fear in the wake of strange difference. At the same time, disability scholars and theologians emphasize the potential of the arts as catalysts for altered experiences of difference and for the transformation of human perception to new understandings of what it means to be beautiful. They maintain the hope that "rare beauty" might be allowed to do the works of justice in the world.[58] Aesthetic concerns can be said to serve justice insofar as they probe the heart of stigma. Philosopher and theologian Sharon Betcher asks: "What 'rites of passage' make sharing of this everyday world and our urban neighborhoods possible among bodies with whom we do not always share taste, smell, or cultural resonance?"[59] She goes on, "To find a place of equanimity, of deep love and insight about the world, humanity, and our urban situation will require the navigation of disgust, fear, and pain otherwise than by encultured avoidance."[60] Betcher describes the vocation of Christians who seek to transform the aesthetics of public life through intentionally navigating and occupying the streets of a city.[61] In turn, I pursue the aesthetic encounters offered by a church's liturgy: through the places it creates and sustains and through the persons who navigate and occupy it.

A turn to theological aesthetic/s also marks the work of scholars who consider the subtle ways that oppression moves through the guise of the well-intentioned and charitable congregation. For these theologians, an emphasis on aesthetics invites witness and reflection on power, stigma, and violence without proclaiming solutions that further obscure the structures through which certain bodies, minds, and lives are idolized over others.[62]

I find a particularly helpful example in scholar of religion and humanist Anthony Pinn's reflection on the significance of arts for theologies that take human bodies seriously. In *Embodiment and the New Shape of Black Theological Thought*, Pinn argues that black theologies, in their quests for liberation from unjust systems, often exit certain normative hierarchies only to reinscribe harmful constraints through other exclusive definitions of a good human life. Thus, he argues that when black religious communities seek freedom from the pervasively racist ideologies and institutions of North American cultures, they often force worshippers to identify themselves through other rigid and reductive categories that fail to account for the complexity of human beings: certain definitions of black and white, cults of domesticity and notions of masculinity, descriptions of good and evil, and even distinctions between human and non-human. Pinn argues that the task of theology is not to fix and confine bodies but to move with them, finding new ways to keep embodied lives visible in relation to the social and religious definitions that identify them. Theologians must engage in this task without pretending to escape the discourses within which we all live and move.[63]

Pinn broadens the discourses in which theology moves by turning toward the public arts. He analyzes resources for black theology in photography and hip-hop, in the blues, and in abstract expressionism. He regards these art forms as an interrogative rather than prescriptive mode of struggle. Interrogative art both keeps individual particularity perceptible and troubles the rigid categories through which embodied lives seek expression. In doing so, some art communicates a genre of "creative disregard" that respects religious forms and institutional norms while also calling them into question, sometimes playfully, sometimes angrily, sometimes mournfully.[64] Pinn's work raises provocative questions for a community like Sacred Family, which not only seeks to exit the practices of charity, segregation, and stigma, but also desires justice for congregants who live without adequate resources and community support.

At the same time, there is a danger that Sacred Family as a liturgical community exits certain harmful relations only to reify other stigmatizing identities. For example, on Sunday mornings, those who can read and participate fully in the explicit liturgy of the community and those who cannot read and participate in such ways are set apart from each other. Every Sunday I watch some members refuse to engage the two to three books we use to worship, and I watch others who at first engage with the texts but then stop somewhere in the middle of the service, apparently giving up or growing disinterested. Still others keep the books open without singing or reading. While Sacred Family is intentional in offering forms of community life in which everyone can take part, there are also occasions on which some people are invited again and again to do what they seemingly cannot or will not. The refusal to comply with expected forms of full and active liturgical participation implies and creates alternate forms of engagement. Still the explicit request to comply persists. Disability scholars Sharon Snyder and David Mitchell critique a rehabilitation approach to persons with disabilities that reinforces a "persistent historical attention to formulations of disability as excessive functional deficit." They ask, "What is the psychic toll of repetitiously attempting to perform activities beyond one's ability?"[65]

While Pinn turns to public art forms outside the institutional church to address this question, my intention is to extend a definition of artistic forms and to think them from within the community. How does a church keep mental difference visible, audible, and palpable without dismissing it as distraction or deviation from the common good? What I find most surprising and arresting at Sacred Family are the artistries of interpersonal connections that make community life not only possible but also joyful. There is a performance art in the creativity of interactions that enable a frame for difference to emerge from Sacred Family's liturgical choreography. I choose the phrase art form rather than the word practice to highlight the differences that arise within the congregation rather than to evoke regular actions or responses of worshippers. Such art forms seem to complicate categories of exclusion and practices of condescension, and these in turn obscure the lively and perplexing differences of people in the church. These forms also illumine how congregants creatively regard and disregard expectations or anticipations, turning them into something new. For example, where worship leaders often assume what liturgical theologian Siobhan Garrigan calls "the myth of the single acting agent"[66] (e.g., "Will everyone please turn to page 121 in the hymnbook?"), there are ways in which people at Sacred Family question these ideals of uniform liturgical ability.

One man, who is almost blind, walks and plays bingo with the help of another woman who leads him around. I observe the two of them walking one in front of the other, her large frame followed by his slender one with his hand resting on her shoulder. They have learned the rhythms and postures by which walking in tandem is possible, and they serve as a perceptible reminder that when everyone is invited to do something, some people might only respond as others move with them. These sorts of interdependent art forms do not dispel the normative habits through which Sacred Family orchestrates community life. However, they do keep visible, audible, and palpable the differences within community while at the same time transforming the possibilities for participation and access. Watching two people walk together or play bingo through the other's presence suggests an alternate response to a liturgy that assumes capacities either on the level of individuals or on the level of the whole community. To mark this as an art form, rather than as a reciprocal gift between two people or the relationship between a dependent person and an independent one, is to emphasize what is created through relationships in the community. Identifying artistries of social interaction draws attention to who is beside whom and what hope or harm might occur among them through their presence. Such new creations become possible within configurations of relationships that would be difficult to prescribe ahead of time, but that emerge over time from this community's life together. Such art forms have theological significance for a community that often claims God's presence and transforming love through sermon, song, and in conversation.

Dichotomies such as disability/ability, mentally ill/normal, leader/recipient of help, high-functioning/low-functioning, wealthy/poor, arrive by van/arrive by car powerfully affect Sacred Family's desire to be an inclusive community. These divisions obscure the complexities of a diverse group of people who, living out their faith, struggle with love and loss together.

Like other churches, Sacred Family participates in what theologian Mary McClintock Fulkerson calls obliviousness, "a form of not-seeing that is not primarily intentional but reflexive . . . [that] occurs on an experiential continuum ranging from benign to a subconscious or repressed protection of power."[67] For Fulkerson, the theological response to wounds of obliviousness involves accessing the embodied practices through which transformation occurs: "What is needed to counter the diminishment and harm associated with obliviousness is a *place to appear*, a place to be seen, to be recognized and to recognize the other." She sees this as "essential to a community of faith as an honoring of the shared image of God."[68] If embodied responses to ourselves and other people obscure their particularity and beauty from us, how is it that the church might become a "place to appear" to one another?[69] In light of my experiences at Sacred Family, I argue that such artistries of interpersonal relationships—performed through touch, through jokes, through gestures, through music, through stories, through paintings and tiny plants, through sitting together, through silence, through the struggle to name one's relationship to another—are key to answering this question. People appear to one another at Sacred Family insofar as these artistries bridge the socially and theologically inscribed categories through which disability and human differences are obscured. People create and manifest access to one another in their ways of inhabiting sacred space and time and in their patterns of naming their losses and desires together.

Furthermore, such artistries of social interaction are intimately involved with a theological understanding of beauty. In claiming beauty as theological, I intend the qualities of joy and pleasure that mark the possibility of non-violent transformation. Certain forms of oppression challenge Sacred Family's ability to name its life together as one of love through God. Certain mysteries of human pain and difference may also make it difficult to envision a communal transformation in which oppressive practices no longer operate. Such possibilities render necessary these artistries of difference as signs of love and hope for a community with psychiatric disability at its heart. To hold together a community like Sacred Family as a common relation is costly and requires hard work from many of its members, but where the Spirit of God breathes and animates, beauty ensures that such a journey is possible and even pleasurable. Thus, discerning beauty's presences and/or its absence is an important and even urgent theological task, one that Pinn describes as moving with bodies, noting their fluidity, and noting places where such movement is constrained or obscured.

A Liturgy in Five Movements: Gathering, Weaving, Disrupting, Naming, and Sending

To describe Sacred Family as a community of difference, I follow a liturgy through five movements. Describing worship through these five movements draws attention to the dynamic margins as well as the shifting centers of Christian worship. While each chapter explicitly focuses on one movement, a single chapter also highlights multiple movements. For example, the chapter on weaving also includes movements of disrupting and the chapter on sending turns a reader back to choreographies of gathering and arts of weaving. Thus, each chapter is, itself, woven of threads that run throughout the book, much as are the movements of the liturgy at Sacred Family.

Chapter 1 describes how those who gather understand their access to this church and community. Mapping different centers of interaction at Sacred Family, I explore their relationships to one another and make the case for a decentered liturgy that manifests activities and relationships outside the boundaries of the sanctuary and the prayer book. Decentering a liturgy emphasizes the central works of persons who might otherwise be deemed peripheral to its movements. It also requires a definition of a weeklong liturgy that does not confine common prayer to ritual actions within a church building but understands liturgy as communal work of/ for the people of God. Such work involves the multiple actions and relationships that a community might offer to God both within and outside the walls of a church building. Thus, Sacred Family offers clues to the significance of a consensual and non-coercive unfolding of sacred space.

In Chapter 2, I examine the arts of interdependence through which congregants weave one another into community, with a particular focus on three art forms: arts of gesture and touch, arts of silence and imagination, and arts of jokes and laughter. I consider the role of these unconventional arts both in inviting people with very different abilities to be present with and through one another and in keeping the doors of the church open. Encountering barriers to a common liturgy, congregants improvise access to one another through their artistries of social interaction. In doing so, they reveal such art forms to be essential to communal belonging premised on consent rather than on coercion.

In Chapter 3, by focusing on disruption as a common experience of liturgical time at Sacred Family I consider how this community makes time for these artistries of interpersonal connection. Arguing that disruption is a fluid category across difference, I examine how different senses of time, work, and pleasure disrupt anticipations about what it means to come to church. People whose lives are often disrupted by poverty and by loss of families, jobs, and homes navigate communal time differently than those who do not. I argue that consenting to share time together requires an experience of time as pleasure rather than as measured by obligation. Thus, pleasure disrupts an approach to "the work of the church" as efficiently accomplishing a set of objectives or worship practices for God.

In Chapter 4, I return to the arts of community by exploring a fourth art form, the arts of naming. I consider how this church as a "communion of struggle"[70] uses multiple ways of naming what it means to be human, Christian, and mentally ill, and how the church searches for adequate names to account for the differences and desires of community members. Finding a Christian theological method for understanding the church's struggle to name adequately the losses and recoveries congregants experience becomes important. The ongoing struggle for good names for consensual relationships at Sacred Family reveals the desire for such relationships. This struggle for good human names is, moreover, essential to a communal pursuit of the love and knowledge of God.

In Chapter 5, I explore the limitations the church faces in sending congregants to do the work it gives them to do—to love and to serve—within a segregated and increasingly gentrifying city. Given that, outside of the church, some of the congregants have lives deemed of little public worth, these limitations raise questions about the church's mission. Examining Sacred Family's past and imagining its future, I consider how structures of ableism, as they intersect with racism and poverty, challenge this church's abilities to imagine a common good for all of its members. Coercive relationships outside the time and space of Sacred Family trouble the consent to a shared liturgy and point to the importance of other shared spaces and times across a segregated city.

In the Conclusion, I return to beauty as a theological lens through which to understand the liturgy of Sacred Family and the mysteries of divine work in its midst. Indeed, Sacred Family's creative patterns of consent to shared time, space, and form, as well as the struggles to belong to one another that Sacred Family embodies, manifest a theology of beauty. Such beauty is revealed through the creation of space, time, and social forms for both human difference and manifold belonging.

Being Human, Becoming the Disabled Church

Ginny tells me a story about how she first became a part of Sacred Family. She came because she and her friends could no longer carry her disabled friend Belinda, for whom she provides care, up the seventeen steps and through the doors of another church they had lovingly attended for over ten years. Ginny came tearfully at first, grieving the loss of access to a church they could no longer attend together. She came alone the first time and then, the second time, accompanied by Belinda in her wheelchair. She became certain in just one Sunday that "the Spirit of God was there" and that they could find a home at Sacred Family. What happened that day is a story she repeats to me on several occasions:

> A guy who introduced himself as Orange Juice brought up bulletins and gave me a bulletin and handed one, *tried* to hand one to Belinda, and I said something like "Oh, thank you, she can't read." And he just looked at me with these beautiful eyes and said "Lady, you don't got to know how to read to need a bulletin." And I thought "Wow!" (She laughs.) He wasn't scolding me but he had *told* me. (Again laughter.) And then I notice that people are singing out of the wrong books, and the books are upside down, and it was quite all right. Then I began to hear the rhythm of Roy's voice always praying and somebody else who is no longer here always praying, and I began to see the rhythms.

Seven years later, she does not know what happened to Orange Juice, who no longer comes to the church. She still recalls him as a sign of the open door at Sacred Family, a gentle challenge and reminder about what she and her loved ones needed in order to worship God.

Thus, a third question: *Whom* do you need in order to have a church that assumes difference at its heart? Liturgical theologian Don Saliers declares that in worshipping assemblies "to meet God is to meet our own human lives in unexpected form, and to 'pray without ceasing' is the stretch of a whole lifetime—in season and out of season, in joy and pain, in fear and hope, in great gratitude and sorrow, in cries for justice and healing and in sheer ecstatic delight in the beauty of God."[71] The arts of becoming church, then, have to do with the possibility of meeting human lives in an unexpected form, so as to understand the ways these lives stretch our understandings of what it means to be holy, human, community, disabled, and mad. It is my hope that as you read this text you will meet your own human life in unexpected form in the strange rhythms of liturgy, lament, love, and struggle that is Sacred Family.

Sacred Family congregants gather at picnic benches to smoke together under a large oak tree. (Photo credit: Cindy M. Brown)

CHAPTER I

Gathering: Unfolding a Liturgy
of Difference

[T]urning to the liturgical tradition is not a turning away
from other sites of encounter with the Holy One. It is, rather,
a turning to all other sites with utmost passion and clarity—
but a clarity sharpened, deepened, and nourished by liturgy.

—TERESA BERGER, *Fragments of Real Presence*[1]

For both ethnography and liturgy, particular locations are essential to knowledge of human and divine others. As an ethnographer, I choose to occupy a particular place in order to participate in knowledge that I cannot grasp from a distance. As a participant in liturgy, I likewise inhabit a particular space in order to grasp an experience of the divine that I cannot obtain at a distance from those with whom I gather. Ethnography and liturgy both require access to a physical location, a space for gathering that facilitates the meeting of people with different backgrounds and experiences. Because difference matters to a faithful map of Christian liturgy, here I trace both my own paths of entry into the liturgy that is Sacred Family Church, as well as the access of those who count themselves a part of this community. This introduction to the repertoire of spaces at Sacred Family reveals how people from diverse backgrounds and with different kinds of abilities gather together within the physical location that is Sacred Family.

Liturgical theologian Gordon Lathrop identifies "assembly, a gathering together of participating persons" as "the most basic symbol of Christian worship." If "all the other symbols and symbolic actions of liturgy depend

upon this gathering,"[2] access to the assembly is imperative. From the perspective of people with disabilities, this access cannot be assumed or taken
for granted.[3] Access to common worship requires relationships and different ways of sharing time and space. Gathering different kinds of embodied
minds into a common space requires "two-way access," to and from the
church and to and from the lives of people with disabilities, so that each
informs the other.[4] In this chapter, I suggest that people with psychiatric
disabilities, once they are gathered into a common space at Sacred Family,
transform both an understanding of the borders of sacred space and the
isolation of a sacred space called the sanctuary. Disability differences
amplify liturgical spaces such as Sacred Family by requiring and creating
multiple points of access to the divine through a plurality of interconnected centers.

    To map liturgy at Sacred Family, I begin with the most recognizably litur-
gical of spaces: the sanctuary. The community gathers here for celebrations
of Holy Eucharist on Sundays and Wednesdays, and for morning and noonday prayer on Tuesday and Thursday mornings. Alongside the sanctuary, I
map other spaces of gathering, too, like the garden, the Circle hall, and the
smoking area. In doing so, I orient readers to the daily lives of people who
help to create spaces of encounter and to the interactions that characterize
each encounter. While these spaces and interactions may appear peripheral,
they are, in fact, essential to the liturgical fabric of Sacred Family.

A Point of Gathering: The Center of the Sanctuary on Sunday Morning

Mother Daria, a visiting priest at Sacred Family, shares with me an image
she has of the sanctuary on a Sunday morning. She has been a visiting priest
at Sacred Family for a year when we meet at a coffee shop to talk about the
congregation. As a young white queer woman, she embodies some of the
differences that Sacred Family gathers and affirms as part of its community.
Even so, she acknowledges the congregation's struggle to make room for
the differences of all people who come. Given this struggle, she offers me
a hopeful image of what it means to gather such a diverse group on a Sunday
morning. From her vantage point she witnesses the moment when the
Gospel is carried from the altar to the center of the sanctuary. Lifting the
holy book from the altar, the deacon walks with the book into the congregation. According to liturgical rubrics, which provide prayers and instructions
for this church's common worship, the congregation should respond to the
reading of good news by standing. The assembly rises and turns in their
pews to face the deacon as she reads.

From the front, Mother Daria witnesses different responses to this reading. In her words, "it is an amazing vision, because everybody is in a different place, some people are just sitting down, and facing in their own world, other people are turned toward the gospel being read, other people are like . . . everyone is doing something different and it is all okay, it all fits together. It's one of my favorite visions to watch." A multiplicity of responses symbolizes for her the meaning of Sacred Family: It is a place where difference is essential to common prayer.

Many Points of Access: Gathering Throughout the Week

Mother Daria's story exemplifies the faith of many who come to Sacred Family: a faith that human differences can be gathered and held, and that worship itself holds people together. When I worship in the sanctuary Mother Daria describes, I note the differences in people's abilities to read, to stand, to focus, to sing the hymns, and to follow a prayer book liturgy. Some people, in the back, are sleeping, and some, in the front, whisper to one another. The range of responses to the gospel reading—bored, resistant, reverent, enthusiastic—reflects the ambiguities of this congregation's faith and the diverse narratives that parishioners share with me.

Jack, for example, first came to Sacred Family Church for the food. A middle-aged white man living in a group home with other Sacred Family participants, he found the parish as many congregants do: by word of mouth. Housemates spoke about a place to go during the weekdays. I ask Jack how, a year after his first coming, he now describes Sacred Family to those outside the church. Jack responds:

> I would tell them that this is a church that is doing what the church is actually supposed to do, and that is reaching out to people with disabilities, whether they be mental or physical, and to become an intricate part in the community, and that's what they are to me. And I admit, when I first came—I still use tobacco—and I came just to eat and smoke because I was hungry. But after coming for a while and noticing the people in the garden and seeing what was going on around me, I started asking questions, and before you know it, I was a part of the church. But there are people who come just to eat and smoke.

> "Is that alright, you think?" I ask.

> "Yeah, that's alright." he said. "That was me for a couple of months."

Jack's story maps entry points into the landscape of Sacred Family. He references the smoking circle at the east entrance, a designated set of picnic benches and cigarette receptacles. Jack's story involves the Circle hall, where meals are shared. He also talks about the garden where Circle participants tend flowers and vegetables to sell and to eat, as well as to offer to God on Sunday morning along with the bread and wine for communion. In time, Jack is baptized in the sanctuary, and then a few months later, due to a series of hospitalizations, he is absent for many months. Occasionally, other members bring news of him to the church, reminding us of his absence. In Jack's story, as in many Sacred Family narratives, gathering happens not once, but over time in multiple ways as people leave and come again.

Aisha's story also highlights this multiplicity. A young black woman and a Circle gardener, she describes her initial encounter with the church as "a little bit forced because I was living in a group home, but the lady who was over the group home had us come here, and at first I wasn't very fond of the place to be exact."

"What made you not very fond of it?" I ask.

"We came into the eating area, and it had beautiful pictures on the ceiling, but it was limited space, and I figured that's the only place we can go, to be in that space outside or in the eating area."

"Did it feel cramped?"

"It did, and it was a whole bunch of people I didn't know. That's what I remember."

After leaving for about a year and a half because of a close relationship turned sour, she returned. She now comes to work in the garden, but does not attend services. She cites differences in her religious beliefs, differences with which she does not think everyone at the church would be comfortable.[5] I ask what keeps her coming back to the Circle in spite of her initial dislike of the church space and in spite of differences that distinguish her from other congregants. "I think it's the friendship. There are a lot of people who respect you as a person. I remember when I left the Sacred Family for about a year and I came back, they treated me like I was a celebrity. They yelled, and they were saying 'yay!' I was like, 'I didn't know you guys would miss me so much.'" Her return also has to do with a sense of peace she feels here as compared to other programs for the mentally ill that she has attended. "Sacred Family is peaceful. There isn't many fights. There isn't really many people arguing. There's just a whole bunch of friendship, and if not friendship, it's like your distant family. You don't really talk, but at least you know that people are there for you when you need them."

Aisha's narrative, too, reflects spaces and relations across the Sacred Family landscape that enable her presence here. The church space that initially felt crowded to her transformed into an experience of "distant family," who take note of her coming and going, even if she does not engage with everyone. The garden, which centers her time at Sacred Family, provides a space outside the dining hall and sanctuary where she tends to relationships with other gardeners. Although she does not feel comfortable sharing her own faith with everyone who gathers, she now describes her relationship to the community as one of peace rather than coercion. A consensual relationship to Sacred Family involves her ability to choose the spaces and activities in which she participates. Aisha speaks of the garden itself as a site of encounter with God. Recalling a teacher who nourished her appreciation for growing things, she describes her first encounter with the garden at Sacred Family: "When I first went into the greenhouse and started working, it was like the garden of Eden; I was in the right place." Aisha did not immediately access a "right place" at Sacred Family but discovered this place over time and through multiple gatherings. Finally, it was the garden rather than the sanctuary that created this possibility.

Like Aisha, Fiona recalls an initial gathering at Sacred Family as unintentional, something she may not have chosen. As a wealthy, middle-aged white woman and a church member with no mental health diagnosis, she remembers her slow conversion to this community. About fifteen years ago as a member at another parish, a Sacred Family volunteer invited her to a dance for Sacred Family congregants. She recalls the motivations that compelled her to accept the invitation:

> I was just getting to know people . . . I always like to make new friends, new church community. I thought: 'Okay, I'll come to the dance'. . . . I had no clue what this was. I thought it was a way to meet friends at St. Mary's, which is ultimate [wealthy Atlanta], and so I come down here and think 'holy moly!' That night I came and I brought Coca-Colas, and I had no idea what I was coming to and it really was quite different than my world, and it really captured me. And then I came down here (to Sacred Family) and after I got over the . . . not shock, well it was shocking right at first, but after I thought, 'what in the world,' then I was really interested in learning more and then I started volunteering.

I ask Fiona what captured and shocked her.

> Well, you know I'm a professional, wealthy, affluent, white woman that lives in Atlanta, Georgia, that lives an exquisite life, and so you come to Sacred Family, you come to a [church] that is in [this neighborhood],

which I didn't even know where it was, and it's like, okay, (she pauses), and then everyone here is . . . they look, they speak, they smell differently, clearly very, very different, because this is not from my world, so, just initially, it is very surprising to someone who lives in the village or the bubble that I live in. I was like: 'What? What the hell?' But not only negatively, just in . . . I wasn't . . . I didn't even know what Sacred Family was. . . . I think that it is not unusual actually because it's raw from our definition when you live in the bubble I live in.

"So what captured you?"

It captured me in so many different ways . . . after me getting over the shock and surprise, then I settled into [it]. This is the experience of coming to Sacred Family; it has been my whole life and still could be today: the very worst thing that could ever happen to me, to be homeless and to lose my mind—that would be my deepest fear of my universe, to be homeless and to lose my mind. And then you come here, and that's what this is, and I meet my fear, right there in my face, raw, staring back at me, touching me, looking at me, doing the hokey-pokey with me at the dance . . . because that was the first thing it was, a dance. That was my deepest fear, and then you settle into it and you take a breath, and you know, okay. And that's what captured me and hooked me. And the fear hasn't gone but it's . . . so I'm right here with [the fear] . . . because even from that first dance, it was fun. I didn't know anybody. Yeah, it was my deepest fear, but it was fun. . . . And I kept coming back, learning, and just being really interested, and interested in mental illness and poverty and learning about my friends here . . . I'm kind of embarrassed. This could be anybody. This could be my brother. This could be me. These are just my family here that suffers from severe mental illness and poverty. From where I sit, I often think, you know, what I have are resources and a support network that keeps me tethered to my bubble and my village, but it's real, I believe passionately, for all of us, fragile, and if you become ill and/or your resource network goes, anybody could be here. You could come from any walk of life. This could be me.

Fiona speaks of spaces in the city that are segregated, and at the same time, she speaks of these spaces as permeable because of the possibility of psychiatric disability. She imagines that she could end up on the street or in a group home if she were to lose her mind, her social network, and her material resources.[6] She enters Sacred Family through a dance hall in another parish and also through the sharing of hamburgers and Coca-Cola.

Fiona rarely comes on weekday mornings, when Aisha attends Sacred Family, but she describes Wednesday evening Eucharist and the suppers afterward as a place where she learns about spaces that exist outside of the bubble of white, abled wealth she describes as home. Fiona's first encounter reflects common reactions to mental illness and poverty on the part of those who visit Sacred Family. Whereas anxiety initially objectifies the people she encounters, turning them into shadows of her fears, through regular encounters with Sacred Family, she is able to perceive those who gather as persons, as family, rather than as projections of her fear. While she continues to grapple with her fear of mental illness and poverty, Sacred Family lures her into a way of inhabiting and creating community premised on dignity rather than fear. Fiona eventually becomes a Sunday morning regular; she later moves into a leadership position at the church. After that position ends, she disappears for a time.

Another leader in the parish, a young white man named Neil, recalls being gathered into life at Sacred Family when he was a seminary intern. He locates the time and space when his lines of identification crossed with those of Circle participants.

> My job [as an intern] was just to come and be with people. I thought that was the greatest thing ever . . . I wasn't a chaplain facilitating this prayer service, I was Neil, who was getting to know a host of people and in the process evaluating what my own hang-ups were and the ways I was preoccupied with myself that was damaging to others. . . . At the time, I was going through some very dark days myself. I was very depressed . . . I was in a bad place. I was drinking extremely heavily, I mean, shocking amounts of alcohol each day, and living just a very sad, depressed, and lonely life, and meanwhile coming to church here (He begins to laugh.).

"And it was a good place to come?" I ask. "How did you find it as someone who was feeling in a dark place?"

"And it was a very healing place to be." He tells a story to illustrate this claim.

> I missed a week of site work because I was hospitalized for psychiatric observation for suicidal ideation. So I just, I called in sick. I missed that week, and the next week I was back again. I was sitting out at the picnic benches drawing because I just love to draw . . . and the man sitting next to me is Jason, who in many ways is, or no longer is, but has been, one of the most significant sources of frustration in my

employment at Sacred Family. I would not say he is my nemesis, but if I had a nemesis, it would be Jason.

And so Jason said, 'We missed you last week. You weren't here.'
I said, 'No, I was out for the week.'
Then he asked, 'Well, where were you?'
I answered, 'I just, I wasn't feeling well. I didn't come in.'
Then Jason said, 'What was wrong? What was wrong?' (Neil uses his voice to imitate Jason's pestering voice.)
And I said, 'Well, I had made plans to kill myself, and instead of killing myself, I committed myself for psychiatric observation. And I was in the hospital.'
And he said, 'Which hospital were you in?'
Then I said, 'I was in [this] hospital.'
Jason said, 'Well, which room were you in?'
And I said, 'I was in the first room to the right.'
And he goes, 'Oh! The one with the huge plexiglass window?! The plexiglass observation wall?'
And I said, 'Yes, the one directly in front of the nurses' station where all of the family members just come in and sit and watch you, literally, watch you in this misery.'
And he said, 'Man, that's the best room in the house!'

Neil concludes the story:

> So, I just . . . that was a very clarifying moment for me. . . . Almost immediately my identification with people at Sacred Family changed radically. It wasn't me talking to a staff member about being a vegetarian, blah, blah, blah, but it was me chatting with Jason about the best room in the house for psychiatric observation. (He laughs.) That was a significant experience for me.

Jason does not display horror or pity for Neil's struggle; rather, his primary interest is in a shared experience of hospitals and hospital rooms. And Neil assumes that Jason can handle the full truth of Neil's story.

As I listen to Neil, I can easily imagine this conversation taking place at Sacred Family: two people sitting outside, side by side on a bench, each doing their own thing, while also engaging one another, their interactions both casual and intimate. As Neil's story illustrates, relationships are not always easy at Sacred Family; yet Neil finds it is possible to share aspects of his life that he may have withheld in another community, where stigma makes it difficult to talk about the struggles of mental illness. Neil's access to the church involves a bench where he and Jason sat together. And yet this space opens a common experience of another space, a shared connection to a hospital room.

Jack, Aisha, Fiona, and Neil narrate their initial gathering into the community as one that occurs both for and against their own desires. Points of access are mapped across the landscape of Sacred Family: a set of picnic benches where a common experience of suffering can be shared, the garden where Aisha and Jack work together, the Circle hall where all four have shared meals, the smoking area in front of the church, and a dance hall in another church building.

While the stories do not focus on worship services or the proclamation of the gospel, these access points could be interpreted as pathways that eventually lead congregants into the sanctuary, where the gospel is proclaimed. Jack, for example, begins with hunger for a meal, moves into the garden to work, and gradually becomes a member of the church. Fiona begins quite literally by dancing with her fear and later finds the fellowship of Wednesday evenings. But as I listen to the narratives and observe the choreographies of the dance that is Sacred Family, the gathering does not follow a linear progression or direct pathway. Rather, a series of centers— garden, art center, picnic tables, sanctuary, meal hall—are connected to one another. Each space allows for different assemblies of people to gather, and each space elicits different abilities and desires. The communal "We" of Sacred Family's congregation is diffuse, dispersed across a set of interactions and relationships.

From the perspective of Christian liturgy, it is plausible to view most of these spaces as peripheral or extracurricular. Smoking and playing bingo seem trivial in comparison with the gravity of gathering for prayer and praise in the sanctuary. Yet, in the narratives and interactions I observe, it is impossible to isolate the small, brightly colored sanctuary, for the spaces connected to it are the lifeblood of its work and imagination. Most congregants cannot imagine the life of Sacred Family without its weeklong liturgy and the many physical spaces these liturgical activities entail. During difficult discussions about the parish's budget, staff and lay leaders discuss the possibility of cutting Circle programs, but they quickly agree that such measures are inconceivable. The weekday activities are not accessories to a Sunday gathering but animate Sacred Family's worship and witness. These gatherings make Sacred Family a different kind of church.

When Fiona remarks, "I didn't know what Sacred Family was," she describes an enigmatic entity. Her first encounter with Sacred Family compels her to ask, "What in the world is this?" Questions like Fiona's provoke my study of this gathering: What is this? What makes this a church and not a social program for those labeled mentally ill? When I explicitly raise this question, congregants often point to activities within the sanctuary: prayer, sermon, hymn singing, communion, and worship. The sanctuary materially marks Sacred Family as a Christian church with its altar and icons of the Trinity, its sacred hymns and texts, its celebration of Christ's body in the Eucharist, its stations of the cross around the walls, and its images of the Holy Spirit descending on both sides of the door.

A vital center of gathering, the sanctuary at Sacred Family can also be the least accessible space. Walking up the steps (or entering along the side ramp and down a hall through another entrance), congregants enter a small space with rows of wooden chairs facing forward. Narrow passageways along the sides of each row and a narrow aisle do not offer much room for movement as parishioners walk in and out during prayer book services. Six texts surround each chair (hymnals and prayer books) while those who sit in each chair often struggle to read. In this Sunday sanctuary space, congregants from group homes never preach and rarely serve as lectors. They are usually welcome to respond as they are able but are often unable to participate as able-minded members do. The Sunday liturgical gathering accommodates disability, but anticipates the full participation of able-bodied, able-minded congregants.

In contrast, the Circle does not intentionally mark itself as Christian, even though there are always morning and noonday prayer options. Resisting the explicit label of Christian identity creates space for anyone who might need such programs, regardless of affiliation. In addition, some of the Circle regulars, who regard themselves as part of Sacred Family, attend other congregations of other denominations. "What in the world is Sacred Family?" is invariably a question about how the sanctuary as an explicitly marked liturgical center relates to other centers: the garden, the smoking circle, the dining hall, and the art center two miles away. It is also a question about how the sanctuary becomes a place for yoga, community meetings, or dancing.

Expanding Maps of Liturgical Practice

To map an ecclesial topography in which disability difference matters to a reading of church space requires that we investigate sacred space and who does or does not have access to that space. These maps also require us to analyze the power to name certain spaces as set apart from (or related to) others and to identify the significance of certain spaces for Christian worship. Inhabiting spaces not explicitly marked as places for prayer or praise draws attention to the fact that there is ample space for the people of God to gather and to gain access to one another.

I draw inspiration for such an expanded map from feminist and womanist liturgical scholarship that has offered methods for investigating sacred spaces through attention to the differences of worshippers. Teresa Berger, for example, has argued that attention to gender within liturgical histories invites a reworking of conceptions of time (periodization), space, and source material.[7] In the case of gender differences in liturgical history, Berger emphasizes domestic spaces and the public square as important sites for the performance of gender differences in Christian worship.[8] Through remapping the where and when of worship, many more sites come to matter in accounts of liturgical history. Thus, ecclesial topographies become richer and more varied as "the nature of gendering processes in sacred space, narrowly conceived as a church building, cannot be mapped in isolation from other spaces, which themselves can become liturgical space."[9] Attention to gender differences highlights liturgical spaces and activities that are often overlooked, which in turn draws liturgical imagination to the permeability and malleability[10] of what one considers sacred space.

Considering Christian liturgy from the perspective of womanist spirituality, liturgical theologian Khalia Jelks Williams argues that "liturgical space can be understood as the space in which the African American woman ritualizes. It is the space in which there is a gathered assembly of any size that comes together around the shared goal of experiencing community, love, and God in their midst." To engage womanist spirituality and to understand the ways that God is encountered in these spaces requires actively identifying alternative ritual spaces as well as naming the practices of leadership and authority that such spaces and practices of ritualization encourage.[11] Such engagement blurs lines between sacred and secular, an enduring practice not only of womanist thought and practice but of African American culture.[12]

While Berger and Williams urge gendered readings of liturgical space and time, Sacred Family reveals that disability differences are equally important to the ecclesial maps of a gathered community. To expand maps of sacred spaces with attention to differences both in the past and present is an act of faith that the work of "traditioning" is ongoing.[13] Through such an expansion of traditioning, Christian scholars more truthfully identify where and how the divine is and has been worshipped and the multiple places and narratives through which the Christian church comes into being.[14] If some bodies are absent or less able to participate in certain spaces, to look for the participation of these others elsewhere is an act of faith, an imperative of the liturgical practice of truthful and faithful remembering.

Mapping a Permeable Ecclesial Topography

When I first encountered Sacred Family in the fall of 2006, a priest invited me to "loiter with intent." Inheriting this phrase from a priest who came before him, Father Brian suggested an approach to learning from and belonging to Sacred Family. Such an approach often felt strange for the group of seminary interns of which I was a part, who were accustomed to more targeted and efficient practices of ministering to or serving others. Loitering with intent required us to spend time at Sacred Family in different spaces in and around the church without a clear agenda. By paying close attention to the people who came, the priest hoped we might learn to inhabit the parish in ways that honored the diversity of those who gathered.

As I was once introduced to Sacred Family through the practice of loitering, I now invite readers likewise to loiter with intent in order to inhabit a set of spaces that they might otherwise discount in their maps of Christian worship. I intentionally begin with an investigation of ecclesial space on Circle days. These two mornings a week are the heart and soul of the church for many mentally disabled congregants who not only access the space of church, but also unfold and create its meanings and possibilities. The space of the church expands through disability differences when congregants from personal care homes center the relationships, hopes, and laments of church members. Neil describes the heart of worship, work, and play as Circle time: "This community is so beautiful, and because people work nine to five, they miss the most beautiful iterations of this community—noonday prayer, Tuesdays and Thursdays."

The Smoking Circle

When I enter Sacred Family on a weekday morning, I invariably pass through multiple centers of gathering. If I walk to the church, I use the east entrance. I pass by a set of picnic tables surrounded by gravel. A popular gathering space at any time of the day, these benches mark a designated smoking area. At first, I am unsure how to negotiate this space as nonsmokers rarely occupy it. Without a cigarette, I feel like an intruder. If I sit down next to someone, she might move, wary of smoking next to me. Eventually, the smokers invite me into their circle, calling out to me as I pass to sit down and engage them in conversation. I accept their enthusiastic welcome, and I look forward to the relationships, the humor, the silence, and the news that characterize this ritual of smoking together.

One Tuesday morning in January, Margo calls out to me from the bench where she and Denny are smoking. They are discussing the seductive nature of the Family Dollar. "Whenever I get my money, the Family Dollar calls to me. It calls my name. 'Margo! Margo!' And I say, 'I got to get out of here!'" She laments the store's adverse effects on the small amount of cash she receives each month. Charles sits down near us. At this time, Charles regularly chants the Psalms at noonday prayer in his own unique song-chant style. I ask him how he learned to chant the way he does. He says, "The Holy Spirit. The Spirit's been with me my whole life, teaching me."

Across the way, Claude asks me about my New Year's celebration, and I ask about his. He shakes his head from side to side. "So-so." He hasn't been feeling well and has been falling down a lot. His family is worried about him and thinks it might be his heart since his mother and two siblings died of a heart attack. He is going to the doctor on Monday.

"Do you have hypertension?" Charles asks.

"No, high blood pressure," Claude responds.

"So, hypertension," Charles confirms; and then after some time, he gives another response, "Claude, we'll be praying for you."

On other mornings at the smoking circle, I gather initial news of happenings in the community that I have missed: memorable meals, a church outing, that someone is sick and in the hospital, that someone else is back after a long or short hospitalization. Alexander entertains the group and gets on a few nerves with his comedic monologues. He comments on something I'm wearing and teases me, asking if he can borrow it. Margo and Denny discuss a favorite TV show or a special meal. When Margo is in jail for a short time, Denny brings the group updates. Such confessions, joys, concerns, laments, and desires rarely make their way into the intercessory prayers of noonday, Wednesday, or Sunday services, but they are shared here in this center under a large oak tree.

The Parking Lot

If I drive rather than walk, I enter through the parking lot where the vans come and go at least twice a day. One or two congregants sit out on the cement blocks that frame the entrance. They wave at neighbors walking by and occasionally converse with them.

Max often sits here. One spring day, pausing to greet him, I ask him if he is going to noonday prayer. He tells me no; he has a problem with church. "I never seen Jesus in a church. He sits on rocks and stands up and preaches. He never went to the synagogue. You know how religious people are." His tone is gentle and apologetic, reluctant to give offense. I nod sympathetically. Continuing in an associative pattern of thinking, he reflects on several stories linked by the word church. His parents took him to church as a child, and he couldn't behave. They would take him out and bring him back in, and still he couldn't behave. Then he moves to a story about sleeping in a church graveyard at a time when he was homeless. He associates this experience with food—with fish and cranberry salad. I attempt to follow this thread; I wonder if the church where he slept outside also served meals.

As in many conversations at Sacred Family, I have to work to keep up with Max's train of thought; his complex patterns of association often challenge my own mind to use a different kind of intellect than I typically employ in my academic work. There are gaps in narratives, which I guess at; sometimes I test my guesses with those who are narrating, but speakers often agree with the interpretation that I offer. I come to understand that multiple interpretations are valid in linking sets of associations. My interpretations are also corrected or adjusted at times, but congregants appear less worried than I am about tracing the origins of topics. Conversation is a means of relation as much as an exchange of information, so it is less important that each part of the conversation cohere than that the parties gathered continue the thread of conversation. Max sometimes apologizes for taking up my time and abruptly ends our conversation. I take this as my cue to move on to another space and continue our conversation at another time. He is eager to talk to me and sometimes just as eager to stop talking. Standing or sitting outside near the entrance, it is possible for both of us to move in and out of a conversation with more ease than we might otherwise. This entrance, an inherently transitional space, provides a flexibility that indoor spaces may not.

Over time, Max appears more comfortable inside the sanctuary. During Tuesday morning yoga, he joins a small circle in front of the large altar, a temporary center shaped by folding chairs. Circled around a therapy dog, we stretch, breathe, laugh, and groan as we move our bodies. Some people sit in the church pews nearby and watch us. Max rarely misses an easy yoga class and apologizes when he misses one for some reason. In the second year of my research, Max attends another program and no longer comes to Sacred Family. I do not know why he has left nor do I have the means to contact him, but the church entrance is not the same for me without his regular presence as a greeter and conversation partner.

Leaving Max, I walk along the garden. Hard at work, the gardeners pull weeds, carry jugs of water from the rain barrels, dig, plant, and repot. Alongside the garden, people wander in the parking lot· looking for something to do; seeking solace or solitude; or joking as they wait for the art van. One morning, Wanita pulls a folding chair into the driveway, taking full advantage of the spring sunshine. I sit with her, crouching next to her chair. I ask how she knows so many Bible verses (she has a reputation as someone who can quote Scripture). She says that her mother would read the Bible to them all week and then make a big Sunday dinner with mac and cheese and collard greens. She lists other foods she and her siblings ate with their mother. She associates the Bible with the meals that accompanied it, as well as with the mother who read aloud and cooked. Her mother was a good woman and took good care of her, she assures me. Is she still alive, I ask, guessing that Wanita herself is in her fifties or sixties. No, she died of cancer.

"Do you like the sun," I ask.

"Oh, I love it!" We talk and then sit in silence in the pleasure of the sunshine.

THE GARDEN

Leaving Wanita, I make my way to the garden. A small group of Circle participants work in the garden and earn wages for their few hours of gardening each week. The gardeners often find the tasks difficult, a strain on tired backs and knees and medicated body-minds. They also express pleasure in the plants they grow, in the small paychecks they earn, and in the friendships they share with other gardeners, although conflicts are also common.

On this sunny spring morning, Jack is happy for my help because he has trouble bending over. "You can be my knees," he tells me. He points to each place in the earth where a plant should go, and I drop the cucumber seeds. We plant two rows. Then we rake the newspaper and straw off one of the empty beds and turn over the earth. Jack is pleased with how good this earth looks. While we garden, we discuss music and we sing. Jack gets excited over a story about the Moody Blues in one of the old newspapers. Later, in a more serious turn, he comments that his family does not want to spend time with him. He associates his feelings of loneliness with mental illness and with the way people with mental illnesses are treated by their families. He tells me that if he ever needs money and contacts his family, all he has to do is threaten to come and see them, and they send him the money right away. They would rather give him money than have any contact with him.

On another morning, Jack needs my help to retrieve a gardening tool he forgot at home. Unlike many other Circle regulars, Jack is not on the small monthly income of Social Security disability insurance. He pays rent by doing yard work in the neighborhood in spite of the fact that he struggles with intense knee pain. On the drive to a house that he shares with eight others, he tells me that the neighbors do not like him and his roommates.

Why not? I wonder aloud.

Well, we have three alcoholics living with us, and they like to sit outside and drink.

I think about Jack, who is quite open about his own difficult history with alcohol and drugs, and I wonder how it is to share space with people who invariably make this struggle more difficult, but he expresses affection for them.

It doesn't bother me, he shrugs.

When we return from our errand, Jack invites me to pray with the gardeners in the greenhouse before work. We move from the cold into the warmth of the greenhouse. Lloyd, an accomplished reader among the Circle group, picks up the prayer book and reads a psalm. Jack, Andie, and Joshua wrap their arms around each other in a prayer huddle with a hand on Wallace who also stands nearby. They murmur affirmatively to encourage him as he reads. They are far more vocal than they would be during a reading at a service. Pat stands further back from the huddle with me. I know he associates himself with another church denomination, and he appears reluctant to join them in this form of prayer. As Lloyd concludes, Joshua bursts into a long prayer, praying first for former Sacred Family members and for one of his closest friends who died several years ago and then names others who have died, praying for them in heaven. He prays for a sick van driver and for the priest and his wife. Joshua often prays silently for a long time before each meal begins, but I have never heard him pray aloud like this. Jack prays for me and for my work, and for interns who came to Sacred Family. Wallace prays for the van driver, too. After prayer, they set out to work, and I walk across the parking lot to the Circle hall, where the game players gather.

THE CIRCLE HALL

From eight to ten, a large breakfast crowd assembles. Rose, a Circle artist and soloist at noonday prayer, serves morning beverages. A group sits nearby to chat with her while she works. Rose is proud of her service here and her work at the art program. She attends another church on Sundays, an African American, nondenominational church, but she also identifies Sacred Family as her place. Belonging to multiple church identities and spaces seems natural to her, so much so that she occasionally interchanges the names of the congregations when we talk about them.

Near the coffee station, a bingo game occupies the back corner. Most players sit close together; a few sit apart, leaving empty spaces between themselves and their fellow players so that they have more solitude to play. The competition is intense, and players are called out if they try to cut corners. Ms. Mary strives to maintain the quietness necessary for everyone to hear. She admonishes anyone who gets too loud. If I join midgame, players show off their prizes or offer to share them. One morning we laugh at how much body lotion Mr. Cornelius has accrued through his winnings; his bingo helpmate Annie has chosen his prizes for him. He doesn't appear to mind the teasing.

In the back corner, church staff or nursing students take vital signs and paint nails at a table. At first, I find it strange that health checkups and bingo occupy the same space, but I come to understand the benefits in not having to leave this center of play and gossip and eating in order to talk to a health care professional. Proximity facilitates access. Besides, Sacred Family is a small church. Its limited spaces therefore take on multiple functions, requiring a necessary permeability to one another. Multiplying limited space defies certain parameters of privacy, but seems to fit with the ways that many congregants relate to the spaces of the church. They come and go from activities, enter an office unannounced, interrupt a private conversation or join it, and then leave again as suddenly as they came.

THE LIBRARY

Over time, the health and wellness station moves upstairs to the church library, allowing for more privacy. On Sundays and Wednesdays, the Bible study group gathers here, but on Tuesdays and Thursdays congregants gain access to the attention of health care professionals in the library. As the parish nurse sees it, this center functions to validate people's health concerns when "you can't access health care without standing in line, without having some kind of card, some kind of whatever . . . it's the idea that folks can get their vital signs taken, and we do some teaching, breast self-exam, that kind of thing, that they wouldn't get otherwise." Health care professionals cannot administer medications on site at Sacred Family, but they do make recommendations. They might urge a person with very high blood pressure to demand that their group home staff take them to the doctor and send a note home with them to that effect.

When it is a health center day, half of the library is dedicated to manicures and pedicures, a pleasure-filled activity that also responds to the need for adequate nail care that most Circle participants require. From my vantage point, one of the benefits that the congregants seek in the library is an opportunity to engage the nursing students, grasping an opportunity for one-on-one interaction and attention. Another health benefit that a nurse names for me is the possibility that these students, encountering these same people in a hospital space, will take from their encounters at Sacred Family a different way of relating to mental illness and poverty. Nurses have a power to listen to or ignore the stories their patients tell them about their own bodies. At a future hospital bedside, these future nurses may remember interactions in this church library.

Just before and after mealtime, the library again assumes another identity. It becomes the more private space of support groups, such as the Connections Support Group for people with diagnoses of mental illness.[15] National Alliance on Mental Illness (NAMI) facilitators are also Sacred Family Congregants, and NAMI peer-to-peer education groups also take place here. The small group attests to the support they feel in sharing their stories and struggles in this environment. Another group called Double Trouble in Recovery (DTR), facilitated by people outside of the congregation, also uses library space.[16] The DTR group supports those with dual diagnoses of mental illness and substance abuse. For a church member like Mason, attending these groups is some of the most important work he does here; the art program is equally important.

The Art Studios

One of the most beloved gatherings of this weeklong liturgy makes room for artful craft and creative expression. Sacred Family dreams, discerns, and plans for a day when the art studios will be on site, so that artists can easily access the art rooms and so that the neighborhood might also use the creative space of the church. But for the time being access to the art programs depends on a driver and a van.

A group of about twenty boards a small bus that takes it the mile and a half from Sacred Family to the art studios on the second floor of rented space in a Baptist church.[17] Mounting two long flights of stairs, some with the assistance of others, the group enters a long hallway that doubles as an art gallery, covered with the colorful paintings of Circle artists. The group disperses into rooms by the art forms they prefer. The largest room belongs to the weavers and their looms. Those who prefer to sew or crochet join them here. A room in the back is for the woodworkers and their lathes and tools. Near the front is the small glass mosaic room, and on the other side a ceramics studio. Finally, several rooms are reserved for the painters in the group. This dark and cold-in-winter wing of an old church building with its bare white walls and bright florescent lights would feel unwelcoming if it were not for the vibrant art on display and for the pleasure and collaboration of the artists. An outdated space that might otherwise stand empty and be wasted comes to life.

On the gallery walls hang several paintings of the landscape of Sacred Family Church with the small red brick building at its center. One day, Rose points out to me details in these paintings that mark the landscape as Sacred Family: the trash cans on the side of the building and a bench for sitting. These details bear evidence of a life that happens around the edges, a life that has many liturgical centers.

The Sanctuary Revisited: Noonday Prayer

After an hour, the vans transport the artists back to Sacred Family. A line for lunch forms on one side of the church building. A small group heads straight up to noonday prayer. Kayla announces as she gets off the bus one day: "I'm going to give God my time." She incants something pleasing to God in this small assembly and in the songs and prayers she offers. Noonday prayer unofficially begins with solos sung by Circle participants. Some soloists perform their pieces and hurry to lunch without waiting for the prayer to come to an end; others stay. During noonday prayer, all kinds of songs are acceptable—explicitly religious, rock and pop, folk, and patriotic. Like the prayer book liturgies, the songs are repetitious, circling round week after week. Rose sings: "I know I been changed/the angels in heaven done signed my name." Many of us come to know it so well, we sing along, which pleases her. Kayla sings, "His eye is on the sparrow, and I know he watches me." And Forest sings, "Take me to the king." Roy sings "The old rugged cross" by heart at a racing pace that no one can keep time with. Lloyd uses the hymnbook. Sometimes a soloist sings the same lines over and over until I wonder how she will ever find a way to exit the song, but another congregant seeks a small break in the melody and claps enthusiastically. Clapping, it turns out, is one of the most respectful ways to help another person, caught in a singing loop, to close out their contribution and make way for another.

After the solo performances, one of the interns will stand up and say, "Noonday prayer begins on page 103." Noonday prayer has ostensibly already begun, but the intern's words signal the text as an explicitly recognized form of prayer and the official beginning to the service. Congregants who attend noonday prayer, the shortest of the prayer book liturgies, show much greater engagement with the prayer book during these services than on Sundays. Many know its rhythms by heart. Unlike other services, they easily find the text. During the intercessions, Kayla prays the same prayer again and again. Roy anticipates the end of the short service well in advance, standing up halfway through the spoken prayer to ready himself beside the one leading. As an unofficial leader, he stands up beside the official one, ready to say a prayer over the food and move us all out the door to lunch. When Kayla or Roy is absent, I miss their voices filling out the prayer book prayers.

THE SANCTUARY REVISITED: WEDNESDAY EUCHARIST

Like noonday prayer, Wednesday evening services begin with a plurality of activities and end with a meal. Coming early for Wednesday services, the same participant might join in a discussion of the raising of Lazarus in the Gospel of John, feed the goats and pick okra at a nearby farm, do calisthenics on the lawn, or share stories over a manicure. Activities change from year to year, emerging as an experimental fit between the abilities of the nine or so seminary interns and the desires of Circle participants. Participation varies over time, as maps of gathering at Sacred Family are in flux depending on who comes and how it is they feel able to participate on any given day.

On Wednesdays, Circle congregants do not lead the service music, although some of them read the Scriptures (a very rare occurrence on Sundays). Although the Wednesday evening interns have the primary tasks of reading, chalice bearing, and preaching, a few Circle members read biblical texts, usually the same three or four people each time. Because the service is longer than noonday prayer, congregants often struggle to keep up with the prayer book order of service. Nevertheless, Wednesday sermons are short and more interactive, providing a closer fit between the embodied minds of many who gather and the shape of the homily.

One Wednesday, as we wait for Eucharist to begin, Patricia, a longtime Sacred Family congregant and volunteer, reminds us that the candles are lit, which means that we need to be quiet. Sitting quietly is a challenge for some congregants. Later Patricia will come up to Jack and Andie and lay her finger across her lips, reminding them.

Father Brian explains that we will be singing a cappella this evening and that means without piano accompaniment. He urges us to stand as our bodies allow; he reminds us that we are a resurrected people, which means "a standing up people." Many people choose to sit, implicitly defying the posture of resurrected people. We sing the spiritual "Swing Low, Sweet Chariot." On Wednesdays, we use *Lift Every Voice and Sing*, an African American hymnal. Many of the congregants, black and white, know at least some of the hymns by heart. More congregants sing on Wednesdays than on Sundays when the "white" hymnal is in use. Still, Wednesday hymns are more reserved than the longer, improvisational gospel pieces of noonday prayer solos.

Right before the sermon, Timothy, who has been looking all around him, surveying the church scene, as I do, turns around to stare at Erica behind him. Erica, laughing, asks him what he is doing and tells him to stop. Timothy and Erica speak to one another as if this were another space and time, as if they are sitting at picnic benches outside. When Father Brian comes forward to preach, he addresses them. "Timothy and Erica, would y'all quit talking to each other during the worship service? Please respect the congregation and don't distract us that way."

In contrast with Sundays when Father Brian preaches from the pulpit, on Wednesdays he stands close to the congregants. As a result, the sanctuary space feels smaller and more intimate. Closer to all of us, he draws us into the creation of his homily. The embodied arrangement of Wednesday space encourages the associative logic often used outside of the sanctuary. On this night, Father Brian preaches from a passage in the New Testament Epistle of James. "Be patient," he begins.

Immediately, Forest responds: "Yes, you're right, be patient."

Father Brian continues: "What does that mean? What does it mean to be patient? And don't just tell me 'be patient,' Forest, tell me more than that."

So Forest tries out another answer: "Faithful."

Father Brian nods. "You're on to something there. Victoria."

Victoria offers a different take: "You got to have trust in somebody."

Father Brian acknowledges her: "We're getting something here."

Another congregant speaks: "Never give up hope."

Father Brian: "Never give up hope. Y'all got it."

Roy adds: "Have faith."

Mariah continues: "Long-suffering."

Father Brian: "Long-suffering, exactly. You're reading another [version of the] Bible aren't you?" (Everyone laughs.) Father Brian calls on another "Lillian."

Lillian: "You got to wait on God . . . in his own time."

Father Brian: "Jack."

Jack has a different take: "Patience through tribulation."

Roy announces, insistently: "I have something to say."

Father Brian: "Yes, Roy."

Roy is imperative: "Have faith!"

Father Brian talks about how sometimes people say that he isn't very patient, and what they mean is that he gets irritated really easily. (Some laugh, and Forest interjects: "Have faith in God!"). Father Brian acknowledges his earlier rebuke of Erica and Timothy. "Erica, y'all saw that, didn't you? Sometimes it's warranted, and sometimes it's not. Sometimes it's just having too short a fuse." He goes on to say that here patience has a different meaning, and they all got it just right. "It is waiting and waiting and waiting and keeping on waiting. You heard that little dog out there barking, didn't you?" (Yes! we all murmur in agreement, with laughter, acknowledging the persistent dog from outside the sanctuary barking into our worship space.) "And we're often like that, aren't we? Things don't go our way and we lash out at others. . . . As we are being long-suffering, we can also get irritable. Much tribulation can foster much irritability." (Yes. Yes. Murmurs of agreement resound.) "So James says, among other things, do not grumble against one another. We get grumbly when we get tired of waiting, when our long-suffering has suffered too long . . . waiting is not easy, is it?"

"Amen!" Margaret affirms "It's not!"

"No, it's not," Wallace says. "No, it's not."

"What if waiting goes one year or two or two thousand years?" Father Brian asks.

Wallace says, "You got to pay attention."

Father Brian concludes, "But it's not easy." (Murmurs of agreement.) "That's why both Isaiah and James say pretty much the same thing because waiting, especially waiting for God, is not easy." He rereads a passage from Isaiah: "Strengthen the weak hands and say to those of fearful heart do not fear, here is your God, he will come with vengeance, with terrible recompense. He will come and save you."

This beginning leads to a very participatory, occasionally noisy service with people talking both to the preacher and to each other. I wonder if the difficulty of patience resonates with these long-suffering congregants. I also wonder if the sparseness of accompanying music results in the proliferation of sounds. The lack of musical accompaniment occasions more private conversations, breaking the communal flow, but also encourages communal response.

Father Brian suggests that the instruction to be patient might mean that the Lord is teaching us to look for his coming in all kinds of ways. He reminds us of the passage where Jesus speaks of his coming: "When I was hungry, you fed me. When I was thirsty, you gave me something to drink. When I was naked, you clothed me. When I was sick and in prison, you visited me." He suggests, "Maybe he's making us wait to open our eyes to see his coming in all kinds of small but marvelous ways, to see his coming in the face of the person sitting next to you, in the face of the person who irritated you, who tried your patience. Strengthen your hearts. Strengthen each other's hearts. Waiting is something we have to do together."

Afterward, as we take turns going forward to receive the elements of bread and wine, I hear Father Brian's voice say, "The Body of Christ, the bread of heaven." Annie looks over at me and says, "Pizza!"

"Are we having pizza for dinner?" I ask. She nods. I notice she has been checking the time on her phone, apparently finding it difficult to wait. Meals are more eagerly anticipated than almost any other thing that happens at Sacred Family, the most cherished center of gathering for many. Clergy, staff, interns, and Circle congregants wait with great anticipation to be fed.

CIRCLE HALL REVISITED: WEDNESDAY SUPPER

Walking with Victoria to the Circle hall to eat, I sit down next to her. We do not speak much but focus our energy on eating the delicious food. While Wednesday supper often consists of pizza, hot dogs, or sandwiches, meals like this are celebrated. Tonight, we enjoy a small feast of ham, mac and cheese, green beans, and homemade rolls.

Each Wednesday volunteers from another church in the metro Atlanta area come to serve dinner. There are over twenty denominationally affiliated churches involved in this act of feeding, each church coming a couple of times a year. Some send only a few volunteers, and on other nights a large group packs into the tiny kitchen. The hall is noisy as the eager and hungry congregation tries to get the attention of servers either for themselves or for another. Some near me eat very quickly, so that they can get seconds before their vans come, as well as get extras to take home for housemates. Congregants can be demanding in their desires for more food. They often try to circumvent the church rule of not taking or eating food on the vans. They also challenge the relational capacities of volunteers whose eating habits emerge from very different relationships to food and to eating. Those who come to Sacred Family from wealthier contexts sometimes appear disconcerted by the intense desire for food that some congregants express without reserve in this church hall.

On this evening congregants line up at the kitchen window for a second plate of the delicious meal. Victoria asks me to get her seconds. She says she feels afraid to go by herself, which is interesting to me since Victoria rarely exhibits fear. I wonder if she is afraid she will be turned down whereas she thinks I will have a better chance of getting her the food she wants. Seconds are usually given readily if food remains, and so I find her apprehension strange. I suggest that we walk up together. There are so many people filling the tables and aisles that it is difficult to make our way up to the kitchen. Victoria persists, clearing a path for us in a room crowded with people eating, hurrying to clean up their plates so they can go outside and smoke, asking about dessert, and making their way to the drink table.

When it becomes clear that seconds are available, I leave Victoria in line. A little while later she returns to our seats with a different kind of mac and cheese, the box kind rather than the homemade kind we had earlier. She expresses intense frustration: "She is mean. The lady serving the food is mean." When I question this assessment, she explains, "Because she didn't want to give me the smooth kind of mac and cheese we had before." I suggest that maybe the servers ran out of the first kind of food we had. Victoria disagrees. I imagine that there probably was no explanation given her for this change in the food offered for seconds. The tiny kitchen is one of the spaces in the church where Circle participants are almost never allowed, and they often negotiate for food through a small window through which meals are served. Volunteers may also come around to the tables to serve food or dessert; in this case congregants often raise their hands or call out to get the attention of a server, even if they are busy with another. Those who bring and serve the meals often eat together when they are finished; sometimes they interact with staff and very occasionally with other congregants. Whereas most spaces at Sacred Family are permeable and open to one another, there is a clear dividing line between the space of the kitchen and the parish hall where everyone meets.

The Sanctuary Revisited: Worship Live

Once a month the sanctuary turns into a worship, dance, and performance hall on a Saturday evening, an occasion eagerly anticipated. "Are you coming to Worship Live?" I am asked again and again. A worship band from another church leads the service and brings a meal. One November evening, I arrive to find the band playing a brief pre-worship concert. The assembly is singing the 1960s hit song by The Temptations: "My Girl." Once the service officially begins, the songs are a different genre: "Michael Row the Boat Ashore" and "This Little Light of Mine" and "I've Got Peace Like a River" among others. Accompanied by a band, the assembly sings with an energy rarely exhibited at any other time: The gathered people dance in the aisles, rock their bodies, and clap their hands.

During the second half of the service, soloists perform, as in noonday prayer, except that many more are present. On this particular Saturday in November, I note two unusual musical offerings. Lloyd sings "I Love to Tell the Story." Although he often contributes to noonday singing, this is his first Saturday solo. "Were you nervous singing in front of all those people?" I ask him. "No, I don't get nervous anymore," he tells me. A shy person, Lloyd often appears uneasy interacting with others, but he loves to sing in front of the Sacred Family congregation.

Then Omar goes forward to sing "The Star-Spangled Banner." Many of the solos at Sacred Family are off-key or include surprising key changes, but they are usually sung with confidence and steadiness that invites those of us assembled to trust the performer. When Omar begins to sing, his voice shakes. Then, all around me I hear other people sing with him. Soon all of us are singing the national anthem to complete Omar's solo. In spite of the fact that Omar misses phrases and switches words around, we manage to follow. Rallying to help Omar, the congregation displays great pleasure in singing together.

After a few surprise solos, we close the evening with group favorites. We sway in time to one song. Some people dance in the aisles to another, seeking out partners for the dance. Father Brian, sitting in the back tonight, urges all of us to do the motions. Unlike the encouragement to stand up during Sunday or Wednesday services, more congregants respond to this urging. They try to find some part of their body to move or shake. For many here, rocking or clapping is, apparently, easier or more pleasurable than standing still.

Making Room for Disability Difference

I offer this loitering with intent through the weeklong liturgy of Sacred Family to create a map of different interactions that become possible over time and space at Sacred Family. Following Berger's logic of attending to difference through more expansive maps of liturgical participation, I show how those unable to fully follow a Sunday service of Eucharist find and create alternative forms of participation. In this way, congregants draw attention to the significance of multiple points and centers of gathering across the landscape of Sacred Family.

Disability scholars often illumine the normal as an imagined embodiment, a metaphorical and symbolic space for human life that is too cramped to contain the actual differences of those who seek to occupy it. Normalcy, as the hypothetical middle of a bell curve, or the average on a chart of human ability, compels different kinds of lives to squeeze together into impossibly small ideals for human lives. Those who cannot pass as normal are often identified as deviants, occupying marginal spaces on the feared peripheries of centers and at the ends of a spectrum, falling outside of desirable embodiment and relationships.[18] But disability scholars also argue that the confining experiences of normal space can be transformed for all of us. With the help of those who through their differences draw desire outward, we can move from a center of normalcy to the edges where manifest difference necessarily requires more room for embodied minds.[19] A reorientation of the normalized body stretches out the imagined and inhabited spaces within which humans live and move. In this way of imagining the relationship of disability difference to embodied space, a recognition of those who occupy less conventional forms of embodiment is necessary for the amplification of spaces within which to be human.

I resonate with this description and its alternative of confinement. As a person who is often able to squeeze herself into a recognized space called normal, I persist in trying to conform to conventional expectations for how I should behave, or what I should wear, or how I should pray, or what I should be able to do to be worthy of love and respect. I condition the possibilities through which I am in relationship with others, and therefore, I have trouble loosening my mind from prescriptions for the significance of my life. Yet, when I look to those who are not accommodated in more typical embodied relations, I recognize the inadequacy of such ideals for myself. In doing so, I come to desire and trust a greater range of spaces, relations, and interactions within which to experience the divine, myself, and others.

In the space of Sacred Family, disability rearranges liturgical desire, drawing it outside the confines through which worship of God might be imagined as an able-minded activity. In my own experience as a researcher, I observe these subtle transformations within myself as I spend time in different spaces. When week after week I share a seat at the entryway to the parking lot with Max, I recognize the possibilities of his associative way of making meaning and conversation as well as the importance of connections that can take place in the flexibility of outdoor space. I recognize and value my own associative ways of making sense of the world around me. Because of this freedom, I look forward to stopping by the entryway rather than viewing it as a detour. Max and others help me relate more easily to unexpected responses that congregants offer to sermons and prayers or to questions I pose. In another example, when the community that gathers for Worship Live unabashedly encourages dancing and holding hands, I gradually lose my sense of awkwardness. At such interactions, I come to celebrate this rare, monthly form of connection at Sacred Family, even when I regard some of the song lyrics as strange or silly. My desire to be gathered with others is stronger than my feelings of awkwardness.

To rearrange such desire, the spaces of Sacred Family must be capacious enough to allow different relations to exist. Such room is made for difference by first gathering difference to itself. This difference, once gathered, cannot be contained by the more formal center of the Sunday sanctuary.

The different means by which congregants connect with one another and with God amplifies the spaces through which congregants are gathered and gain access to one another and to the church. At Sacred Family, the spaces are interconnected, and congregants move relatively easily between them. The same person may move from yoga to bingo to smoking circle to noonday prayer, completing none of these activities but participating in each to some degree. Some congregants prefer certain spaces to others, prefer their movements and choices, at least for a time, to be predictable. People try on a certain space and then find it difficult to sustain. For example, one of the artists attempts gardening for a time and then returns to art because she tells me it fits her better. She still gardens occasionally but chooses art as her primary weekday occupation.

Such a variety of spaces over the time of a week and month encourage differing forms of participation. Joshua utters a passionate prayer in the greenhouse unlike the prayers he offers inside the sanctuary. Omar and Victoria sing songs during Worship Live and noonday prayer that some would deem inappropriate during Wednesday or Sunday services. Each space encourages and inhibits certain kinds of interaction. Many spaces do not accessorize one central ritual; rather, they remain essential to the possibility of gathering difference. The space at Sacred Family unfolds in relation to that difference.

Crip/tography and the Theological Task of Unfolding Space

In the context of Sacred Family, loitering with intent involves a practice of critical engagement that crip philosopher and theologian Sharon Betcher has described as "crip/tography": the work of mapping the interdependence of shared spaces by tracking the presence and absence of disability, as it intersects with race and class, in public spaces.[20] Crip, an intentionally provocative reclamation of the stigmatizing word cripple, is a term widely used by disability activists and artists. Feminist, queer, crip scholar Alison Kafer celebrates the overtly political thrust of a term intended "to jolt people out of their everyday understandings of bodies and minds, of normalcy and deviance."[21] Alongside crip theorists Carrie Sandahl and Robert McRuer, Kafer embraces and emphasizes the "contestatory" orientation of crip theory, as compared with disability studies: crip theory queries the possibly exclusionary practices of disability identity politics, desiring more expansive crip coalitions, while also embracing the important work that disability identity played in the disability rights movement. As with the term queer, crip theorists emphasize the fluidity and paradox of identities, identities shaped by imagined and yet-to-be imagined futures toward which crip coalitions forge alliances, contesting the dreams and desires of able-bodiedness and able-mindedness.[22]

Cripping the imagined (and yet-to-be imagined) futures of urban spaces, Betcher invites her readers to trace the movements of those whose presences and coalitions contest their own erasures from city maps and urban planning. Crip/tographers reveal the "physical and psychological space" that the choreographies of city life entail and create. They also trace the "lines of force and avenues of resistance" by which aesthetics and expectations of inhabiting the city together are revealed.[23] Disability difference attunes the crip/tographer to enforced expectations for beautiful spaces through the implicit or explicit division of certain individuals from others.[24] It also locates sites of empathy and shared pain.[25] Betcher assumes that mapping is a process of unveiling the complex relations that unfold between and among various spaces as well as the aversions that divide some spaces from others. To map a space is to track the different relations possible across a set of interconnected locations.

One way to interpret the interconnected dots on a map of Sacred Family is to understand them as separate but equal. On the one hand, different spaces allow for different kinds of relations, aesthetics, and activities. Each person can enter the church by finding a mode of participation in one of the spaces that they are unable to achieve in another; no one person is equally at home in each of them. Such a map encourages a fit between different human persons with different modes of engaging one another and the divine. On the other hand, such alternatives may encourage practices of segregationist charity, by which diverse people are welcomed without being invited to transform the primary symbols, ostensibly marked around the sanctuary—God, Christ, Spirit, Trinity, holy, meal, church, unity. Thus, Joshua prays a prayer in the greenhouse on a Tuesday that would not be welcome in the same way on Sunday morning. Wednesday volunteers can serve dinner from behind a small window in the kitchen without deeply engaging parishioners. They can return to their home parishes with their conventional and impoverished images of the poor and the mentally ill. They can leave without any real desire to change the political and social structures as a result of which these people of God with mental illness—many of whom are poor and black—are dependent on Sacred Family for nutritious meals. A Sunday congregant might never attend weekday liturgies or Worship Live and never gain access to the kinds of prayer and friendship that emerge from the weeklong liturgy. Divided spaces can encourage a long-suffering of poor people with mental illness within a liturgy that nevertheless remains resistant to those differences. Divided spaces can also become sources of miscommunication or frustration, as when Victoria assumes that a woman in the kitchen does not like her because the woman gives her what Victoria considers to be inferior food without any explanation of the change in menu.

Divided spaces also become evident when behaviors that are acceptable in one place are discouraged or openly rebuked in others. Thus, the sitting together that shapes many relationships outside the sanctuary is allowed but discouraged at a number of points within the sanctuary. "Will everyone please stand (as you are able)?" the priests say again and again although they know that many will not stand. While sitting is tolerated, the congregation is occasionally reminded of the importance of standing as a theological symbol, as Father Brian does when he speaks of standing as a symbol of resurrection without suggesting that remaining seated might also be theologically right and fitting. Other behaviors such as whispering, or wandering, or walking in and out at certain times during the liturgy are sometimes tolerated and are at other times restrained by a leader in the community when they are viewed as too disruptive or irritating. Sometimes these behaviors are modified through a verbal request to stop talking, or through a lay leader trying to calm or remove someone from a space.

Yet the promise of human difference manifests and unfolds multiple access points for those who are willing to recognize and, with help, navigate them. At times space clearly divides persons at Sacred Family; but it also unfolds differences, revealing relationships that frequently surprise me in relation to other contexts. For example, Lloyd is often shy when engaged in one-on-one conversations outside the sanctuary, but with great confidence he sings before us all during Worship Live or noonday prayer, proud of the sound of his voice.

In mapping the aversions and erasures as well the possibilities of sacred space, Betcher recalls the Christian naming of Holy Spirit as "*pli*," as a vision of the divine energy that unfolds shared spaces in relation to one another. Theology's work is the naming and loosing of "a *pli*—a pleat, a fold, a manifest—of Spirit over cosmopolis."[26] The *pli* or fold of Spirit invokes a multiplicity that does not place plurality in opposition to unity; rather, it teases out the possibility of unfolded spaces rather than divided territory.[27] As she articulates it, this "fold of multi*pli*city does not so much then signal plurality in opposition to unity, as it looks to the actualization of plural space, of the many-enfolded—thus, of the active and energetic manifold."[28] The Spirit unfolds spacious places that shelter all forms of human life without dividing some from others.

Joining the Spirit's work of unfolding spaces is a religious practice,[29] one that is able to create anew "social flesh." Through this flesh, people assume responsibility for one another in ways that are not divisive or condescending but that deepen understandings of mutual reliance and the need to share limited resources.[30] Such "social flesh" requires actual physical locations within the city to acknowledge together what Betcher (and before her, Judith Butler) calls the "precarity" of flesh, the "existential fragility" we inherit at birth, and to nourish "corporeal generosity and forbearance" with others as a practice of nonviolence.[31] Thus, the spiritual work of those who occupy the city is to reveal the spaces where social flesh becomes apparent and to nurture these possibilities. Requiring particular locations of gathering and encounter, this spiritual work deepens one's awareness of the patterns through which one way of life affects or is affected by another.

Betcher is interested in city space rather than church space, and in the religious vocation of seculars rather than the liturgical vocation of churchgoers. Nevertheless, her invocation of Spirit as *pli*, the One who unfolds a possibility of gathering through difference, invites us to look again at Sacred Family.[32] One notices how those who occupy the church also unfold the spaces around and within the church that would otherwise be spaces merely to pass through or by (entrance, parking lot, garden, smoking benches).

Despite the limitations of square footage and other resources at Sacred Family, its decentered liturgy maps one approach to sheltering and making space for those with different mental abilities. Almost every inch of space is made available and is entrusted to those who gather (except for times when the sanctuary and church offices are locked). Those who unfold church space likewise multiply its meanings. The church library becomes a health clinic and a beauty salon simultaneously. Both weekday and Sunday congregants often refer to the significance of church space as safe space or refuge. At Sacred Family, if a space is to feel safe, it usually unfolds as multiple spaces over time. Entrustment, generosity, and forbearance require room for people to be together and alone, in conversation and on the move, bringing the polyphony of their faith and life backgrounds into the church as well as their different mental abilities. Christian liturgy emerges as a relation across spaces that manifest the differences of those who gather and the divine energies that make space for those differences; it emerges through relationships that help to map the community's pleasures and struggles to be together.

These spaces are sacred refuges not because they are divisively set apart, but because they remain porous to the people who gather within them. If we take seriously Berger's and Williams's attention to permeable ecclesial topographies, or Betcher's desire for in-Spirited and response-able crip/tographies, then the question remains: To what degree do these different spaces at Sacred Family touch each other, inviting recognition of the differences that each space manifests? At Sacred Family, the pleats of a church can unfold, in-Spirited outward, making room for different ways of sitting, standing, singing, praying, proclaiming, lamenting, and giving thanks together. But, how does such unfolding of difference hold together within a common liturgy, rather than multiply it in order to divide the work and importance of some persons from others? How does Max come to be recognized as the greeter that he is if the entrance to the church parking lot is not considered part of the space that counts as liturgical? How is the greenhouse also imagined as a house of prayer? How does the Saturday sanctuary, envisioned as a dance hall, also carry the weight of sacred space, as it does when there is a Sunday service of Holy Eucharist? (And there are members of the Sunday service who do not see Worship Live as real liturgy.) How is Wanita's folding chair in the parking lot recognized as an important place for recalling a holy meal her mother fed her as well as the Scripture that continues to sustain her? Liturgical power lines often highlight the activities of some, recognize them, and obscure the participation of others. For example, when a staff member or intern opens the prayer book for noonday prayer, only then does prayer officially begin.

Rogation Sunday: Liturgy on the Move

I imagine an unfolding rather than dividing liturgy as a process by which a tightly clasped hand relaxes and opens, fingers unfurling, pointing in all directions, and then folds again, fingers touching back to the palm. Berger uses another metaphor, imagining public ecclesial space, as "the hinge" that opens out to other spaces,[33] an invitation to liturgy on the move. As I reflect on this unfolding and unfurling of church space, an example from Sacred Family's own liturgy comes to mind. I offer it here as a form of recognition and interconnection that highlights the possibilities of Christian liturgies to name, honor, and nurture a variety of human and other life forms within interconnected spaces.

One Saturday in June, I receive an email about a special service:

> This Sunday, May 25, we will mark the 'rogation days' which precede Ascension Day next week. Traditionally, rogation days are times of prayer and fasting when a community asks for God's protection of its land and natural resources. Because we have a magnificent garden and a special garden ministry, we will mark this day by a procession around the grounds and a blessing of the garden and gardeners. We will gather by the large tree near the side entrance (by [the Avenue]) and process around to the greenhouse. Please join us to give thanks for our garden ministry and ask for God's protection. Holy Eucharist will follow in the sanctuary.

On Sunday morning we assemble near the smoking benches under the oak tree. Mother Daria describes the plans for our travel together around the space of the church: the gardeners will lead us, carrying watering cans, and there will be birdseed to scatter along the sidewalk. Mother Daria will sprinkle water on us from a pail she carries, dipping a tree branch in the water. Then, without the usual hymnbooks in front of us, she will teach us a short song we can sing as we move.

We set off walking along the sidewalk that marks Sacred Family's land, so that Belinda in her wheelchair can move with us. We quickly get separated from one another. I am in the middle group, separated from my spouse, who has accompanied me this day. I keep walking and try to sing even though I can hear that the group behind us is on a different syllable of the same song, creating a polyphony in the sound of our movement. We arrive near the garden and wait for the third and largest group (led by Belinda in her wheelchair) to arrive. On this sweltering day, we sweat profusely; it feels like hard work, but it is also an occasion when we watch out for one another in ways that we rarely do inside the sanctuary. When everyone arrives, the deacon reads the gospel, and Mother Daria prays over the garden. She invites the gardeners to stand in the center of our gathering and the rest of us to lay hands on them as they center us. She prays for them by name, recalling even those who are absent today.

During this procession, my mind wanders as the bodies of some congregants often do. I ponder the risks of trying out a new path for liturgy and what it takes for this group of people to move together around the entire space of the church. What I find most significant about this movement is that it gathers and incorporates into itself a number of the sacred spaces that are part of Sacred Family's weeklong liturgy, spaces made sacred by the people who entrust themselves to one another across the weeklong liturgy.

During the typical Sunday liturgy, the gardeners bring vegetables to the altar as part of the people's offering. After the service, congregants can choose a few vegetables to take to their homes. I am always moved by the beautiful basket of fresh produce, a small representation of the gardeners' work and friendship. In comparison with the Sunday offering, Rogation Sunday unfolds space differently, for the service moves us out to the garden to bless and touch the work of some congregants who are less often recognized as leaders of the community. Liturgy on the move, such as this one, does not make differences in abilities easier to navigate. In fact, it is more difficult for some to traverse the uneven sidewalks than to sit in the cool of the sanctuary. It does, however, reveal our differing paces and our mutual reliance on one another for moving a communal liturgy through time and space. In this way, it is a liturgy that generates a sense of social flesh, a sense of trust and obligation that does not assume each person has the same abilities as another. It reminds me of the reason Tanya gives for the importance of recreational outings beyond the landscape of Sacred Family: "It gets us out and about and makes us more mindful about people who need help getting off and on the train during [a field trip], or who need help walking or stuff like that, and it gives us different scenery. There are people who are a little bit slower, and you don't have to focus on them as much when you're here doing your own thing." She qualifies this, "You do, kind of, but it's more obvious when you're boarding a train, or (pauses), I don't know. It's hard to explain . . . It's good to help people try to stay together."

Tanya refers to what happens when Sacred Family moves outside of this small plot of land and into the space of the city. Still, her reflections are helpful for interpreting the work of an unconventional celebration like Rogation Day. When the liturgy loiters with intent on what may be considered the peripheries of Sacred Family, it traces complex lines of folding and unfolding difference within common prayer. Drawing on an old tradition, it marks a new path, encircling the church. When people with and without disabilities gather to be church together, they invite others to perceive new maps of what counts as liturgy, disturbing any isolation of a central sanctuary from other sanctuaries created by relationships around the church grounds. At the same time, Sunday and Wednesday services are more attuned to the relationships that inform the services when they acknowledge the spaces of the weeklong liturgy. In this way, the word sanctuary itself is decentered, marking the beauty of safe spaces in which those who gather feel free to share their lives with one another in prayer, jokes, songs, and games.

Liturgy assumes the possibility of some relation between those who gather to worship God together as the church. Such connections require ample space(s) for trust to emerge and for the beauty and pain of those who gather to be revealed, for the physical proximity of the gathered community does not assure consensual relationships among those who gather for worship. These relationships therefore require the artistries of those who negotiate differences and draw attention to the assumed peripheries of communal life. To the work of these social artistries I now turn.

In the art room where Circle members weave together, a congregant's painting of a loom hangs over a table laden with yarn. (Photo credit: Cindy M. Brown)

CHAPTER 2

Weaving: Aesthetics of Interdependence

One February morning in the art studios, I stand beside Mr. Edgar, a faithful Circle participant. Weaving at his loom, he shows me how the shuttle fits through the open spaces he calls "the warp." He ponders aloud the multiple meanings of "warp." It's a funny word, he says. Warp can also mean stubborn. And the sun warps things. He takes pleasure in following a strange thread of divergent meanings. (Later he will do the same with the word shuttle, creating laughter in the room with a joke about Henry Kissinger and his shuttle diplomacy.)

Mr. Edgar's musings have triggered my reflection on the multiple meanings of warp. When I get home, I search the web. An online dictionary tells me that "a full definition of warp" means:

1 a: a series of yarns extended lengthwise in a loom and crossed by the weft
    b: foundation, base <the warp of the economic structure is agriculture—American Guide Series: North Carolina>
2 a rope for warping or mooring a ship or boat

3 [²warp]
   a: a twist or curve that has developed in something originally flat or
   straight <a warp in a door panel>
   b: a mental aberration.[1]

   The warp appears as structure and anchor as well as deviation or abnor-
mality. Using these three definitions, and following the thread of Mr.
Edgar's free associations, I reflect on how the warp of perceived mental
aberration affects the warp of the liturgical structure. Once gathered into
Christian liturgy, disability must twist and curve the standards of participation and nonparticipation of individuals. The challenge is to identify liturgical forms for mooring a community to one another and to God that are
also warped or idiosyncratic in their departure from the formal expectations of communal gathering.

An Art Form for Liturgical Difference

What might such flexible and adaptive liturgical forms look like? In the case
of Sacred Family, I observe that liturgical forms require those performative
artistries of social interaction, improvised by congregants that tether to one
another those gathered for common prayer. For art is more than texts and
objects; it includes performances by individuals or groups that assume the
possibility of a relation or connection with an audience—much as theater
and dance do. Thus, we might say that liturgical forms make possible the
art of communication with and through God as well as with and through
the worshipping assembly.

   The novelist and literary critic Ali Smith explores the concept of form,
making sense of the work it does for art. Smith imagines the hostility that
might occur between different forms or between form and formlessness,
until there is a word, in the beginning, that traces a relationship, a new
form:

> Until, that is, God, or some such artist, starts throwing weight
> around. Form, from the Latin *forma*, meaning shape. Shape, a mold;
> something that holds or shapes; a species or kind; a pattern or type; a
> way of being; order, regularity, system. It once meant beauty but now
> that particular meaning's obsolete. It means style and arrangement,
> structural unity in music, literature, painting etc.; ceremony; behavior;
> condition of fitness or efficiency. It means the inherent nature of an
> object, that in which the essence of a thing consists. It means a long
> seat, or a bench, or a school class, and also the shape a hare makes in

the grass with its body for a bed. It's versatile. It holds us, it molds us, it identifies us, it shows us how to be, it gives us a blueprint in life and art, it's about essentiality, and several of us can sit on it at once.[2]

Shared forms of communication and the work of deviation from common forms are both vital for good art and good liturgy. Forms are pleasing to us because we can share them, and we desire different forms to work our minds differently and to offer different means of identification. Thus, the forms we rely on to mold us, that offer a shared benchmark for identification, also require deviation.[3] While form is a matter of rules and expectations, it also frequently bends those rules, and emerges through dialogue and "crossover between forms": "Through such dialogue and argument, form, the shaper and molder, acts like the other thing called mold, endlessly breeds forms from forms."[4] Bending the rules makes the viewer reconsider how they see and understand the art in which they participate. Moving creatively through deviation, forms have an inherent affinity to the apparent edges to which they respond. Art forms often take shape in response to sharp edges of difference that can wound us but can also form border spaces where the magical resides.[5] The warp that both anchors and is an aberration is necessary for good art to engage our minds.

We can apply this understanding of art to the liturgy of Sacred Family; when the Spirit of God moves around the edges of community, giving fleshly form to the worship of a local assembly, there must be forms for different embodied minds to communicate with one another. Love, refusing any coercive uniform pattern, weaves the perceived periphery into the warp of community through forms of their own co-creation. Not always recognized as liturgical forms, these unconventional shapes take their cues from the edges of those shaping the gathering, weaving into the fabric of community those at the perceived margins.

In this chapter, I identify relational art forms that weave those who gather into a community across difference. Conventionally, common prayer assumes certain common forms, and those forms typically assume particular bodies and abilities. How then to figure those who are unable to participate in the same way in common prayer? How to think of their presence, their belonging, their connectedness or disconnectedness from the other worshippers? During my time as a researcher, the metaphor and image of "weaving" became central to my understanding of how a community of difference is held together across persistent hierarchies and divisions—without ignoring the differing abilities, statuses, and resources of members. Using the metaphor of weaving, I evoke liturgical art forms by which congregants create more flexible and adaptive relational patterns of belonging that are not premised on conformity to one liturgical practice or norm.

Weave Us Together in Unity and Love

There is a beloved song sung once a month at Worship Live. Its high point, a moment of emotional release in the vocal sounds and faces of those who sing, is the chorus: "Weave, weave, weave us together, weave us together in unity and love."[6] One of the gardeners, Joshua, first sings this song to me at a plant sale. We are talking about the upcoming Worship Live when, faltering, a tentative smile on his face, he tries to sing this song alone. I later recognize the melody at Worship Live when some people dance in the aisles, and the rest of us hold hands and sway back and forth in rhythmic time. Congregants move their bodies to this chorus with a force of participation rarely found at other moments of communal gathering. During the after-service dinner, another community member, Alexander, tells me how much he enjoys this service. He was disappointed last week when he didn't get to weave. "My roommate just doesn't understand that I can't weave alone in my apartment," he jokes.

In a Circle newsletter, a staff person, Eve, employs the concept of "weaving" publicly to honor the memory of a relationship between two Circle artists. The story, entitled "Woven Together," recounts an unconventional kind of love story:

> Grace Jones, long red curls wild like in a fairy tale, suffering from schizophrenia, the effects of homelessness and medical neglect, the champion of 83-year-old artist, Mr. Cornelius. He, quiet and undemanding, smiling, his eyes cast down, could easily have been disengaged but Grace took him under her wing, encouraging, praising, and cajoling, seeing that he was noticed and provided for in and out of the studio, his seat belt fastened, his meat cut up. Her New York accent resounding across the Parish Hall: "Mr. Cornelius needs more bread," "Get Mr. Cornelius some tea,"—and woe betide a driver ready to load up a van before Mr. Cornelius was finished eating.
>
> Grace died last August. We miss her dearly. Mr. Cornelius is still painting and weaving. One of his works stands in the sanctuary, part of Sacred Family's banner, a weaving by several of the Circle artists. We are all woven together—unintentionally, but here we all are, together. Some sent to the Circle by our personal care homes, some sent by a less discernible hand, all woven together in unexpected mutuality.

Weaving, the author observes, is often unintentional or unexpected when it takes a concrete form: something happens between Grace and Mr. Cornelius that makes more space for both within the church's liturgy.

Sacred Family is a place that makes space for differences by multiplying the spaces of its weeklong liturgy. At the same time, the dangers of divided spaces, arranged in a hierarchy of value, can segregate congregants one from another rather than unfold in relationship to one another. Across these power lines, community members, with very different backgrounds and resources, claim and perform a belonging to Sacred Family as community. They improvise forms through which they weave themselves and others into the fabric of community. The weaving is both active and passive as the stories at the beginning of the chapter reflect. Alexander comes to the church in order to weave because he is not able to weave alone. Joshua holds hands with others and beseeches God, "Weave us together in love," implying that the church is unable to weave without a divine accomplice. Eve describes the weaving as something that inevitably happens to those who gather as they spend time together. Weaving entails and assumes both ability and inability, both agency and passivity, confusing these categories without dissolving them.

If weaving is an embodied art of holding community, one of the rules of this form is clear: weaving happens with and through particular others, not so much in the shape of a gift, one to or for another, but in the complex pattern of artful relationships. I could argue that Grace helped Mr. Cornelius, or that Mr. Cornelius allowed Grace to be his advocate, but I read their story as one in which she participated in Sacred Family through a desire to watch out for him; in turn, his engagement was altered by her presence. His desires and needs drew attention in a different way than if she were not around. Their presences interpolated one another. Now Grace is gone, and Mr. Cornelius continues to be woven into the community with and through others. He was not dependent on Grace; rather, while she lived, they created something together for the community. Weaving depends on who is beside whom and what this accompaniment creates for good or for ill.

Disability organizations like L'Arche, an international network of communities with intellectually disabled persons as core members, emphasize accompaniment as necessity for communities of difference. Jean Vanier, Catholic theologian and founder of L'Arche, describes the power of accompaniment for each one of us. To find one's way along a path to freedom and to grow in one's vocation requires another's proximity: "One of the most important factors for inner liberation is how we are accompanied. We must ask ourselves: Who is walking with me?"[7] Vanier writes of accompaniment as an intentional relationship and a mutual exchange: the accompanied and the accompanier give and receive from one another as they journey together, growing one another into the truth of the sacredness of human life, which is always both verity and unfathomable mystery. The person who accompanies us is one who "can stand beside us on the road to freedom, who loves us and understands our life." Vanier names those who often fulfill this role—a parent, a therapist, a teacher, a friend, a minister—again evoking intentional relationships over time as necessary for the freedom to love ourselves and others.[8] While Vanier emphasizes the profound importance of intentional accompaniment as mutual gift, accompaniment at Sacred Family also takes shape through another form: fluctuating, elusive, emerging for a time only to disappear again, and less a gift than a shared creation that arises from occupying a particular space and time together.

At Sacred Family, some congregants benefit from intentional accompaniment as part of their everyday lives, but mentoring and advocacy are also privileges that not everyone's circumstances allow for in the same ways. Within the liturgy of Sacred Family, less organized and stable forms of accompaniment are equally important and more readily available. Improvised forms of belonging shift among different persons. They often involve more than two. Two or three people happen to share a bench; together they shape the meaning of a moment or gathering for those who are beside them. Their sitting together may be intentional or unintentional.

I become aware of this pattern when I intentionally choose to occupy different spaces in the sanctuary. I experience the same liturgical forms, such as scripture reading, prayer, and communion, differently depending on the people with whom I navigate participation. The same prayer prayed next to a person who is exhausted, bored, or in pain sounds and signifies differently than if I pray alongside an excited or attentive person, or if I happen to sit beside a person intent on filling the small space between us with commentary, regardless of the authorial voice of the one presiding over the liturgy. My co-participants and I shape the liturgy through our divergent responses to each other and to the forms at hand; together we improvise access to the standard liturgical forms through our interaction. In this way, even a conventional liturgical form is constantly morphing through relationship to those who sit or stand nearby.

For example, when I sit next to Annie on the left side of the sanctuary, she is more likely to sing some of the hymns because I am near. I help her navigate them, my finger running across the page, so that she can follow words she struggles to read at the pace of Sacred Family's liturgical time. Annie almost never stands, and so if I am to hear her voice, and she is to hear mine, I must sit to experience the service with her even if many around us are standing according to the expectations of the liturgical form. Annie sings with me for a time and then turns away from the hymn and back to her portfolio of poems and drawings. Turning, she invites me into her devotional form, and so I spend part of the service reading the rhythmic prayers she writes in the notebooks she carries. Our communal worship involves helping her spell the words of her prayers. While singing, I acknowledge the portfolio of human and animal faces that also accompany her.[9] Through singing, lining hymns, whispering, drawing, and spelling, we shape one another's experiences of the liturgy. We both distract and focus one another. We mold Christian worship through our encounters with one another. I cannot get to God by another way.

Such encounters rely on the premise of incarnation, the possibility of bodily encounter within the assembly. This significance of relationships liturgical theologians Andrea Bieler and Luise Schottroff emphasize in their descriptions of Christian sacramentality: "sacraments are not things we possess; rather, they are relational events and personal encounters among people and God. These encounters are always embodied."[10] If, as theologian and sociologist Nancy Eiesland observes, "a body, perhaps especially a disabled body, is not a space one occupies alone," the challenge is to account for how bodies encounter one another, incorporating others into their own sense of flesh, without losing their particularity.[11] "This alternative understanding of embodiment," Eiesland suggests, "is a social accomplishment, achieved through attentiveness to the needs, limits, and bounty of the body in relation to others."[12] Confusing clear categories of autonomy or dependence, relational encounters illumine the art form of one beside another.

For example, Roy shows up for yoga every Tuesday but initially chooses not to participate directly in the movement and breathing that joins the encircled group together. Rather, he occupies a pew near the yoga circle and frequently distracts the group with stories from his childhood that seem irrelevant to the postures the group is assuming. Aware of Roy on the periphery, the yoga teacher, Laura, weaves him into the circle as she engages his stories and often brings them to a conclusion. As she weaves him into our common yoga practice, she taps into his vivid imagination. Laura suggests that we imagine stirring custard, as we move our arms in a great circular motion in front of us. Roy joins in by changing the imagined custard to applesauce. Roy brings up sawing wood, and Laura uses that image to guide our stretching motions. She explains that these concrete images help our brains communicate with our bodies so that we understand what we are supposed to do. While Roy's presence often interrupts us, distracting us for a time, he inevitably morphs the form of yoga for us; through Roy and Laura's co-creation we move and breathe yoga into a form that fits this community.

On a morning that Roy misses yoga, we worry about him and are grateful when he rushes in, breathlessly, halfway through the session. Apologizing for his lateness, he sits faithfully beside the circle, both participant and nonparticipant, as important to the group as any of us who sit within it. After many months on the periphery, Roy explicitly joins the circle, sitting inside it although he still participates intermittently in poses and breathing practices.

Artistries in the yoga circle also include Marvin, a blind participant, who often worries aloud that he is not able to follow the verbal commands because he cannot see the motions we all make together. He asks Laura to repeat phrases, which she finds difficult because she wants to create silent pauses for the circle to meditate within. One day, Marvin occupies a chair next to Laura to make way for a person joining the group halfway through the session. He discovers that sitting beside her, closer to her voice and her body movements, alters his own participation and, therefore, hers, enabling her to instruct less than when he sits further away from her. Rearranging the relationships in the circle rearranges the shape that easy yoga takes at Sacred Family. Marvin beside Laura, and Laura near Roy artfully make space for a different form of chair yoga, just as sitting beside Annie changes my prayer and Annie's poetry.

The literary critic and queer theorist Eve Kosofsky Sedgwick reminds us of the importance of prepositions and stresses the possibilities of the preposition beside, conjuring what work this word can do for our perception, in place of the behind or before of most interpretation:

> *Beside* is an interesting preposition also because there's nothing very dualistic about it; a number of elements may lie alongside one another, though not an infinity of them. *Beside* permits a spacious agnosticism about several of the linear logics that enforce dualistic thinking: noncontradiction or the law of the excluded middle, cause versus effect, subject versus object. Its interest does not, however, depend on a fantasy of metonymically egalitarian or pacific relations, as any child knows who's shared a bed with siblings. *Beside* comprises a wide range of desiring, identifying, representing, repelling,

paralleling, differentiating, rivaling, leaning, twisting, mimicking, withdrawing, attracting, aggressing, warping, and other relations.[13]

While we may be tempted to interpret relationships in terms of what came before (what makes these two similar or different? why does one respond in a certain way?), or what is behind such relationships (who does what to or for whom?), *beside* instead focuses attention on an expansive range of possibilities and interactions that emerge when one, several, or many reside near others.

Sacred Family's art forms evoke the liturgical possibilities of *beside* and *with* and *through*. They involve individual abilities but are not premised on a similar capacity in each individual. The proclaimed, capitalized We of the liturgical participation assumes a unity that is impossible for Sacred Family or any church community to achieve. In different ways, the I of Grace or Mr. Cornelius is able and unable to be part of the We. Between this We and I occurs the small we of Grace and Cornelius or the we of Laura and Roy and Marvin, or the we of Annie and me. This small artful motif warps the community at a certain point in time as the we of each constellation of social interactions weaves itself into the Circle liturgy. This we becomes an art form because of its functions in the community, the individualism and communalism it disables as well as the individual differences it recognizes and the community it enables.

The we that shapes liturgical form is difficult to recognize because We tend to speak of the diverse gifts of community as distributed across individuals: Grace has certain gifts and Mr. Cornelius has others. As gifted givers, they each offer something to God and to each other. Truthful from a certain vantage point, such language does not render how Grace's activities are elicited, contained, and recognized within the responses, resonances, smiles, and silences of Mr. Cornelius. He is implicated in what she can and cannot do. When she dies, his presence and participation are rearranged and reinterpreted through the others who now participate in Sacred Family through him. There is no one-to-one correlation with such gift giving, where some are able to give and others not, but a pattern of cocreation. Through a theological lens, I might identify God as the One beside us, who makes room for the smaller configurations of persons that improvise the access that good liturgy requires.

Christian theology often interprets good human interactions in terms of charitable dualisms. Givers and receivers are divided, even if the givers also discover something in return. "I came to give but I received so much" is the sentiment I hear from newcomers to Sacred Family. Such a way of dividing human participation resides within Sacred Family's own liturgy: congregants are often encouraged to give thanks for those who give to the community. Such thanksgiving explicitly recognizes the gifts of those who are financially and physically able to sustain the liturgy through liturgical leadership, making food, financial support, and volunteer work. Givers also have mental capacities that enable their giving. The ability to give is highlighted in liturgical forms that name God as the one who has given so much for us that we want to offer something in return (even if what we return to God is already God's). Such descriptions of human interaction inevitably divide some from others. Recognized forms of participation judge the merits of different contributions to liturgical form.

The Work of Art and Theological Imagination

The arts, religious scholar Anthony Pinn argues, are valuable to religion and to theology in part because some forms of artistic expression evade the modes of judgment and discipline with which we divide some forms of embodied life from others. Pinn highlights particular visual art forms, such as abstract expressionism, outsider art, and pop art, as "an important way of viewing and exploring intersections between experience and representation, including exchanges between the body (material and discursive) and the social body." Such art possesses the possibility to interrogate existing social structures while not abstracting the human body from modes of participation in the art that is created, "uncovering and bringing into question modalities of interaction and relationship" through which we derive the meanings of embodied life.[14]

Occurring at the intersection of embodied experience and the representation of the body, such artistic expression can help theology to question the fundamental structures of reality and to communicate new meanings and possibilities.[15] Pinn argues that certain art forms "require of viewers a surrender of the safety of visual comprehension" because they cannot be understood through the eye alone, which "allows distance and disconnection."[16] Such art forms make no sense without observers altering their relationships to what is communicated; correlatively, they compel the observer to seek an alternate sense for what is not easily understood within shared discourse.[17] They are both interrogative and connective, creatively disregarding the boundaries we put around human bodies and possibilities.

In my reading of Pinn, such art forms do what liturgy often fails to do because they invite and create more flexibility and fluidity for complex experiences of embodiment, tracing them without forcing them into one mold.[18] Theological discourse regarding the human body tends to sharpen the edges (the structures and frameworks) that divide or reduce the complex experiences of embodied life.[19] Such edges are unavoidable because of religious desires to norm those who participate within religious traditions, even if we interpret these forms as divinely intended toward human goodness and freedom. We elevate certain humans as being more worthy of participation than others: some as able to give or receive as others cannot; some as dependent on the autonomy of others. For Pinn, art elicits theological imagination because it can help theologians ask questions and envision alternative arrangements of bodies in time and space insofar as an "artist seeks to give new dimension to reality as encounter by the observer" and at the same time "also pushes the boundaries of what is real about reality, and what is the nature and meaning of relationship between humans and the world."[20]

Eschatological Imagination and the Art of Liturgy

While Pinn thinks theologically through popular art forms, Don Saliers writes of good Christian liturgy itself as holding the possibility of such an interrogative art form, the art of receiving God's future for the world in an "otherwise way." According to Saliers, "Liturgy is a common art of the people of God in which the community brings the depth of emotion of our lives to the ethos of God. In these acts we discover who we are, but also and primarily, we discover who God is in this art."[21] This is possible, he argues, in part because of the depth and breadth of liturgical forms that assume and require a spectrum of emotional affect, all of the varied postures of a real human life in discovery of the "mixed texture of the world."[22] An adequate liturgy provides a form for the complexity of human experience to take shape as enacted prayer, as we remember the whole of ourselves and the whole of our world to God, both the beauty and the terror.[23] Liturgical forms require complex embodiment through multiple forms of prayer: praising, thanking, blessing, invoking, beseeching, lamenting, confessing, and interceding.[24] This diversity of liturgical forms "*wait[s]* for us" to bring the breadth and depth of what we experience, sharpening and bridging the edges of human pathos and divine ethos. Liturgy as prayer is an art form through which we "receive [our] own mystery back."[25]

In this way, Saliers argues that liturgy itself has the potential to counter the dominant perception of the world and its content, raising questions about the adequacy of the language we have for describing our own lives and the divine. The art of the assembly is revelatory when it animates the full "emotional range" of human life, from "ecstatic praise to the depths of lamentation" to "daily struggle to be human" without dividing some possibilities from others.[26] Therefore, it requires both discipline and time "to become an artful symbol of the church in communion and dialogue with God."[27] The art of liturgy also occurs through limit. It creates the possibilities that we know and experience more than we can sing, say, know, lament, and confess on our own. At the limits of our individual abilities, the art of the (communal) liturgy takes shape.[28]

With Pinn and Saliers then, we might ask whether and how the art of Sacred Family's liturgy resists dividing some from others and represents the full range of what it means to be human. To do so, it must represent the real limits and inabilities of all who gather as well as the real possibilities of connection and interdependence. Rather than new gifts and abilities, a new ableism within the liturgy, I look for a different frame to describe ecclesial relationships and to reconfigure the ideals of liturgical ableism. Such art forms embody an alternative liturgical imagination about what forms of participation and nonparticipation in community mean.

Artistries of Social Interaction and the Weaving of Community

These interdependent art forms do not dispel the normative habits through which Sacred Family orchestrates community life. Instead, they keep visible, audible, and palpable the differences within community while at the same time transforming the possibilities for participation and exclusion. Watching two people walk together, leaning on one another, or playing bingo through the other's presence suggests an alternate response to assumed liturgical capacity. It reforms a church that often assumes capacities either on the level of individuals or on the level of the community as a whole. To mark this as an art form, rather than as a reciprocal gift between two people, or as the intentional relationship between a dependent person and an independent one, is to emphasize what is created through relationships in the community. Such new creations become possible within particular, shifting configurations of people, threads of lives coming together and then apart. Such patterns would be difficult to prescribe ahead of time. They emerge from this community's life together as congregants improvise forms that weave each life into another's. Such art forms have theological significance for a community where God's presence and transforming love are often claimed through sermon, song, and in conversation.

I think, for example, of Timothy, whom I perceive as a difficult individual and with whom a number of community members struggle from time to time. I could describe him as unresponsive and unaware of those around him, contrarian, and frequently oblivious to the flow of communal activity. I could venture that he does not give much to this community—a nonparticipant in the liturgical life of Sacred Family except that he is always present. During my time at Sacred Family, I find him one of the most difficult people to interpret or understand, opaque in his intentions and forms of interaction, but I cannot discount him in this narrative of Sacred Family because several other people in the community alter my sense of him. Through them, I come to recognize his presence in the ongoing creation of Sacred Family. Timothy often shuffles around with headphones over his ears, isolating himself from others through sound. On a particular day, I find him sitting next to Victoria. He has placed his headphones over her ears. She is moving her body to his music, so she can't hear me when I greet her.

What is she listening to? I ask Timothy, since she can't hear me and because I am taken by her absorption within the music.

She doesn't know, he tells me, and he laughs with pleasure at the musical mystery he has created for her. She begins to move, dancing to the sounds I cannot hear, and in order to communicate with her, I dance, too, following her gestures to music I also cannot hear.

Now I got you both dancing, he says smiling, ostensibly pleased by his work of moving us together.

Timothy does not become an easier person for me to grasp, but somehow through Victoria, I have access to Timothy, or Victoria beside Timothy is no longer able to hear me and I must speak through him to find her, or together Timothy creates the occasion for dancing through which Victoria and I communicate. It seems inconsequential, I know. Such a moment in a parking lot waiting for a van, the form is so brief it can hardly be captured. Still, it alters my perception of Timothy, and my understanding of his relationship through Victoria to Sacred Family.

At another moment, I find Timothy with Kayla. She has enlisted his help in making her art project, so that he hovers nearby to prepare the materials she is using. He comes when she calls out to him.

'I need you to cut the brown,' she tells him, pointing to the color of tile she needs.

'What do you need me to cut?' he asks, shuffling over to her.

'Make it look like this.' She holds up another piece as an example for him.

'I'm going to try to do that,' he tells her, willing to work with her.

I offer him my seat so he can sit next to her and assist her in the creation of her art. I am surprised by his sudden attentiveness, his willingness to do a menial task for Kayla, a task she is able to do but has no desire to complete on her own.

What makes Timothy behave this way? we might ask. Are Victoria and Kayla the cause of Timothy's participation? Do they give him something to do and enable his flourishing at these moments? This interpretation is possible. But it also simplifies the complexity of the arrangement. Sedgwick reminds us that the great difficulty in acknowledging the influences of one beside another is that we desire to determine the world through cause and effect.[29] Rather than getting behind Timothy's action, we can reformulate the question: What happens through Timothy when certain people are beside him? Timothy next to Victoria or near Kayla at these particular times and places alters the colors and textures of Sacred Family, weaving Timothy into the fabric of community at some moments, but also allowing him to isolate himself among the community at others. Timothy does not become an easier, more generous person, but he nonetheless co-creates the fleshly forms of access that are essential to Sacred Family.

Identifying Liturgical Art Forms

The art program at Sacred Family has rooms designating different kinds of art forms: woodworking, weaving, painting, glass mosaic, drawing, and ceramics. Similarly, different artistries of interpersonal connection that I witness at Sacred Family draw attention to different styles and genres of communication. Varieties of each kind depend on the configurations of people through whom and among whom they are created. Each form bridges the edges of a difference in a liturgy that anticipates gifts, abilities, and desires that congregants often fail to exhibit. The forms do not reconcile or unify those differences. They do not erase edges, but foster relational encounters through the deviations that occur. At the same time the deviations take form, creating a warp, a tether, albeit fragile, that invites the incorporation of persons for whom more traditional forms fail or unfold into other forms.

All three of the art forms I describe in this chapter respond to the edges of verbal communication, to the ways disability warps more standard forms of liturgical communication including text, sermon, dialogue, prayer, and confession. Each of these traditional verbal and aural forms contains aesthetic assumptions about fitting modes of participation. While these forms suit some embodied minds, the responses of people at Sacred Family frequently test their assumptions. For example, during a sermon, listeners may not grasp or show any interest in the content. They grow bored and fidgety, or want to speak into the sermon, adding their own voices or stories to a form which finds those voices off topic, a distraction from the function of the form. Or, in a dialogue between congregants, a form which assumes the possibility of sharing and mutuality, balance and/or reciprocity may be difficult to achieve: a congregant might overwhelm the conversation with his inability to stop talking, or alternately appear unable in her silence to propel the conversation forward, exhibiting little or no response to questions asked. As gaps occur between anticipated forms and embodied minds, artistries of interpersonal connection arise.

ARTS OF TOUCH AND GESTURE

On Sunday mornings, those who read hymns, prayers, and creeds and participate fully in the explicit liturgy of the community and those who ostensibly cannot read are set apart from each other. Every Sunday I watch congregants refuse to engage the two to three books we use to worship. I watch others begin with the texts and then close them, apparently giving up or growing disinterested. Still others keep the books open without singing or reading. Often one or several people shout out, "What page? What page?" as they try to keep up.

At the same time, other gestures and movements are unique to this liturgy. In moments where written and spoken communication sometimes fail to connect congregants, people often reach out to touch each other, massaging a back or touching an arm or the top of a head, or reaching out to hold another congregant's hand for a brief period of time. One Sunday, early on in my research, worshipping next to Victoria, here is the way I describe my participation in the liturgy:

> As we sing the first hymn "Jesus lives! Thy terrors now" both people on either side of me bow their heads and cradle their heads in their hands, seemingly tuning out everything around them. Then a man sitting behind us reaches over and touches Victoria on the hand, stroking her hand. She looks up and reaches back her hand and takes his hand in hers, holding it for a minute. Then she offers her hand to the other two men sitting beside him, holding each person's hand for a brief while. Pete, sitting at the end [of the pew] catches my eye, watching Victoria, and smiles at me, waving his hand. I wave back. He waves at me several more times during the service, a big smile on his face. . . . Victoria will also perform her hand ritual with several others. At one

point, without any particular prompting that I can see, she will reach over to Shane on the other side of me, as he is huddled over, and grab his hand and shake it. On her way down the aisle, taking the offering, she will touch the shoulder of another man bowed over, and touch this same man again on the way up to take communion, causing him to stand up suddenly and get in line for communion (out of turn).

As she is touched by and touches particular people she knows in the congregation, I observe Victoria weaving them into the liturgy at moments when they seemed least engaged. The people she touches respond to her with warmth and energy. Her hands touching their hands and shoulders creates an alternate form of connection than the unison of voices reading the creed and the prayers.

Waving is another form of weaving. Parishioners frequently, persistently, wave to others during the service and on their way up to take communion or for prayers of healing, waving and then waiting for a reciprocal gesture of acknowledgement. If there is no response, they may wave again. Forest often sits sideways in his pew so he can keep one eye on the front of the sanctuary and one eye on the back of the church, keeping watch as congregants enter the sanctuary. While he greets almost everyone by name, certain people inspire him to traverse the length of the church to wave them into the service or to grasp their hand or touch fist to fist or elbow to elbow. Forest does not prefer sustained conversation, does not look anyone in the eye for long, and often chooses some physical distance from those around him; yet, he also uses gesture and touch to engage those around him. Forest routinely waves and calls out to congregants who seem unresponsive to anyone else around them until they acknowledge him, even when his persistence irritates them. One day, as I sit next to Albie, another person whom I often find it difficult to engage, I am grateful for Forest, as he rushes back down the aisle to claim Albie's importance to this space and to claim me as well. Forest gestures each of us into this space by saying our names and by filling the silent spaces between Albie and me with gestures.

On another evening, during Worship Live, Jack and Andie place their friend, Travis, between them in the pew. Travis has been struggling with his medications and with severe anxiety ever since I began my fieldwork at the church. He often requires the close physical presence of people with whom he works in the garden, if he is to participate in services or other community activities. Jack and Andie put their arms around Travis and pat his back from time to time. Andie shares her hymnbook with him and makes sure he can follow what is happening in the service. With Travis between them, Jack and Andie's own postures change within liturgical space; rather than facing toward the altar and pulpit the whole time, they often center their worship on Travis, watching his face and movements for signs of engagement or discomfort. Through their gestures and postures, Jack, Andie, and Travis create an alternate vision of family in a church where many members do not attend with their families and may have little to no contact with their blood relatives. I recall Andie's description of coming to church as coming "from a dark place to where I wake up in the morning, and there are things I want to do and people I want to see." Over time, Jack and Andie will both slip out from the regular pattern of interaction that is Sacred Family due to illness, intense physical pain, hospitalization, and their ongoing struggles with addiction. They will require other congregants who weave them back into this community. Yet, for almost a year of my time at Sacred Family, they significantly affect the fragile yet resilient warp within which Travis and others participate within community.

Though they shape the configuration of community, not everyone present embraces the arts of touch and gesture in the same way. Some congregants maintain a physical distance from others and move away if someone gets too close or tries to touch them. Such refusal of touch is also acceptable and does not seem to reflect negatively on the person who desires not to participate through this form. Such responses may also vary from day to day. I learn this early on when a woman named Miriam, one of the gentlest people at Sacred Family, eagerly gestures for me to sit down next to her one morning and engages me in conversation. The next day when I seek to replicate this gesture, she moves one seat away to create distance between us. At first I wonder if I did something to upset her, but I come to understand that she is not upset with me, but this morning requires a different mode of interaction than the previous. I gradually follow such subtle movements toward and away from others, finding assurance in their honest arrangements.

Conflict and irritability are also patterns within Sacred Family's daily life, as people get in each other's space in ways that feel disturbing or threatening. A man walks around shouting "You bitch!" to someone we cannot see, and a path opens around, giving him space to move; yet, the community also accepts his need to act out even when they maintain a wide berth from his anger. The subtle navigation of shared space, through touch, often widens the circle so that there is more space for those who sometimes need to remain at some distance from others.

At times, explicit liturgical forms acknowledge and incorporate this art form of touch and gesture, enunciating its importance within the community. On a Sunday morning or Wednesday evening, the passing of the peace takes place after confession and forgiveness of sins, which many do not read or say. Yet, the nonreaders or the ones who could not find the page in time, the silent ones during confession, enthusiastically take time to stand and walk, or to sit and wait for those who seek them in order to shake a hand or bump an elbow. Where the spoken confession fails to establish the relatedness of the community, the physical gestures and movements of the peace do.

The bumping of elbows, too, becomes an art form of interpersonal communication. One evening Father Brian announces that because many people are sick, we will not shake hands so as not to spread germs among us and suggests that we bump elbows. He offers this gesture as a temporary solution to the perils of flu season, but some congregants take to it with great enthusiasm, so that a year later, some still offer me their elbows, forcing me to bend my arms akimbo as we awkwardly touch bodies in a way that often makes us smile. A form of touch to prevent the spreading of flu morphs, takes on another shape within the liturgy, and becomes an acceptable means of offering peace to another and of spreading laughter midservice. Over time the elbow bump is replaced occasionally by the fist bump, which also becomes an acceptable gesture through which peace is spread. Thus, the elbow bump crosses forms and occasionally morphs from an art of touch and gesture to an art of jokes and laughter, another creative form of weaving within Sacred Family's liturgy.

Arts of Jokes and Laughter

Jokes I don't quite get force me to think about the role of laughter in the liturgy of Sacred Family and how this form weaves people into community. Laughter punctuates Sunday morning services with sounds disproportionate to the verbal forms that occasion it. While congregants mention to me how much they enjoy the sermons, I notice that many become restless during this portion of the service, getting up to leave the sanctuary for a time. I also observe that certain congregants seek out opportunities to laugh during a sermon, joining its challenging form to their embodied participation in it. The preacher tells a joke, or makes a comment that isn't quite a joke, and some parishioners burst out laughing. If two or three laugh together, their laughter is contagious. Even if my mind cannot grasp the joke, I find myself joining in the congregational laughter, feeling the reverberations of human sound around the sanctuary. The jovial vibrations make the room resonate with the breath of people all around me. Such moments feel life-giving and energizing to me, and I observe a similar reaction in those around me. We wake up together! In such moments, I reconnect with those from whom I often feel separated due to differing abilities: whereas my mind easily grasps and fits within some traditional liturgical forms, with their cognitive assumptions, others cannot. When I speak or pray through a particular form, others are silent. Yet laughter defies this liturgical boundary. Such laughter usually begins when one or two people seize the opportunity for participation in the sermon, and their responses spread to the rest of us. Even those who do not laugh smile at those who enjoy participation in a sermon. One's laughter is an invitation to another.

The joke is an erotic form, one that desires another to accept and find pleasure in what is offered. The joke can go badly and fail to achieve the desire and pleasure it intends, but it is a hopeful genre, desiring connection with another as it intends mutual pleasure.[30] The disability activist and comedian Alan Shain emphasizes this invitational quality of comedy. "Using the arts to effect equality," disability comedy woos a listener to cross bridges of stigma. Meanwhile, the comedian rearranges the meaning of disability, inviting listeners to reconsider their ableist assumptions.[31] At Sacred Family, the power and intimacy of a joke are often shaped as much by listeners as the one who intends a witty provocation. These listeners rearrange meaning in order to connect bodily with others, claiming what is spoken as a joke (or sometimes ignoring what is spoken, if it fails to connect), transforming its auditory possibilities within common prayer.

After I notice the effects of laughter in the service, I start noticing jokes in other places. Some congregants use humor, especially when other forms of small talk or communication become tenuous. Wallace and Joshua, for example, encourage each other's laughter, and they laugh especially heartily when Jack, their fellow gardener in the church gardening program, teases them. Something Jack says might cause these friends to burst forth in laughter that (from my vantage point) far exceeds the occasion that generated it. Such laughter, like much comedy, makes use of disproportion. It becomes something they share as their bodies shake together, an exuberant sound echoing over the church grounds. I do not find Jack's jokes as funny as they do, but I watch their faces stretch and open with laughter and cannot help but laugh too at the pleasure of watching them enjoy themselves so much. Their laughing bodies become a connective tissue that Jack and I share, even if we do not laugh as they do. While they are laughing, I try to think of other funny things to say. I want to be a part of their pleasure and connection.

Improvised forms of laughter also create connections as part of easy yoga where the powers of formal and informal laughter merge together, bridging differences in physical and mental ability among us and rousing tired, medicated bodies and minds together. Laura often invites us to fake our laughter as we breathe out all of our stress and anxiety emphatically together: Ha! Ha! Ha! Ha! The fake laughter invariably leads to real laughter—we sound ridiculous to ourselves and to each other—and to a sense of cohesion as a group. Rather than looking down at our laps or at our own limbs as we stretch, we smile at one another as we listen to the strange sounds lingering among us.

This artistry of connective laughter parallels another form of witty pleasure that frames Wallace and Joshua's experiences of church together, and my participation in liturgy through them. Wallace and Joshua comment to one another with huge smiles after the sermon, "That was deep!" "Yeah, that was deep!" One time I probe, "What was deep?" trying to get behind the commentary, but they refuse my inquiry into the particularities of the homily. "The sermon," Wallace responds, in a tone that suggests how self-evident his answer is: What is wrong with your mind? He circles around a question he cannot or will not answer to show me what makes my inquiry irrelevant. I am not catching the function of the form, trying to elicit facts and information instead of recognizing the art of relatedness where communion is at stake. Later, returning from receiving communion from the priest, Wallace and Joshua again share the pleasure of the experience with one another, "That was tasty!" "Yeah, that was real tasty!" Just as their laughter with Jack near the garden shifts the contours of my morning at the Circle, their enthusiastic commentary on the Holy Eucharist occasions a different sense of worship through and with them that day. They create a new connection for me to the dry wafer I just consumed, to the words "The Body of Christ, the Bread of Heaven." Likewise, responses to the sermon, exhorting the significance of testimony, shift as they share their impression and thus enjoyment of its profundity with me.

Arts of Silence and Imagination

In the first chapter, I introduced loitering with intent as a form of interaction that characterizes Sacred Family and involves an intentional being with others, rather than doing for them. I suggest how difficult a form it is for many interns or volunteers within the Sacred Family community, who are accustomed to more active and goal-oriented forms of community building. Loitering with intent is awkward and strangely unproductive to those who desire to help and serve others in quantifiable ways or to receive something measurable in return. Even after years of loitering at Sacred Family, I still find that shared silences, during which congregants rarely acknowledge one another, often make me uncomfortable even though I can see that many others take them as a matter of course. While these silences are customary to many congregants, those who sit silently also invariably seek an entry point into dialogue and relationships yet find this entry difficult if not impossible to sustain. There is a struggle for forms of communication that bridge difference through interaction and that also respect side-by-side silence as its own form of legitimate communication.

I talk to one of the seminary students, Cassie, a couple of months into her year-long internship at Sacred Family. Like other interns, she initially finds it difficult to loiter among Sacred Family members rather than assuming a particular role or task. She finds the church community overwhelming, in part because she misses the welcoming banter she associates with many churches' forms of affirmation and belonging. Finding the silences difficult, she worries about being intrusive as she learns to know other congregants. Over time, the visits to Sacred Family that initially feel difficult and disingenuous become a high point of her week. In part, she attributes this change to the discovery of a form that allows her to communicate and to respect those who welcome her in unconventional ways. She starts giving manicures, using touch to create pleasure for people, and then also, simultaneously, finds verbal forms easier while engaging through touch. She becomes more comfortable with silence and with engaging experiences of reality that are not her own. She comes to appreciate the modes through which people at Sacred Family communicate with each other and develop strategies of communication across differing, and daily fluctuating, mental abilities.

When I ask about building bridges across the differences of congregants' lives, a priest's wife, Hannah, a quiet, beloved figure in this community, tells me a story that helps to illustrate these arts of connection across perceived barriers of communication:

> One day I sat down and two guys were talking, and they were just having the best time, and I just sat down with them. I realized their conversation, what they were saying . . . one would talk and then give pause for the other to talk, and what was said by one person had nothing to do with what was said [by the other]. It wasn't a conversation,

but they were just talking and laughing and giving each other time to speak, and like, one would say, 'I just sometimes hide things and I can't remember where they are.' And the other person would say, 'That meal over there . . . I just love the spaghetti.' They were just talking but not connecting at all. So I found myself just enjoying being there because it was so pleasant and we were laughing and talking. Like it would not be if one or the other of them weren't there, and you were just sitting there by yourself. It was community but it wasn't connecting. And I just sort of chimed in by saying, "Well, that's sort of like squirrels. I wonder if they ever find . . ." and they just went on to other topics that had nothing to do with the sentence before.

For Hannah, this form of conversation has stayed with her as a particular image of what it means to be a church community across and through mental difference at Sacred Family. People at Sacred Family often talk about their lives in more typical ways as well, Hannah is quick to point out, but there is often a need for other forms of communication and connection to create bridges across the differences of mental ability and logic.

In another example of the arts of silence and conversation, Donna, a woman from the neighborhood, only attends Sacred Family on Wednesday evenings in order to sit outside at a picnic bench with another woman, Martha, who can no longer participate in an entire Wednesday evening service. At one time, Martha would become increasingly agitated within church services and would disrupt the community by shouting; she would insist that the priest stop preaching or would make other derogatory comments. While many forms of disruption are tolerated, if not always welcomed, this one tested the patience and abilities of both the leadership and the community. Now Martha is only able to come if Donna is also present, and Donna only attends church if Martha is there too.

Donna first met Martha at Sacred Family, and she describes to me what she and Martha do outside the church while the rest of us are inside the sanctuary, singing and praying. There are always four topics of conversation—cigarettes, food, family, and schizophrenia. "So do you still think of it as worship when you're outside?" I ask Donna, knowing that she considers Sacred Family her church. "Oh sure, sure, sure," she responds. "You know, we're just doing our thing, and it's . . . God knows where we are." Donna often brings Martha into the sanctuary just to receive communion and then takes her out again, aware that the voices in Martha's head might make it hard for her to sit still and listen to a sermon or participate in the service even if she wants to be in or near the church. (Donna offers an explanation for why Martha has trouble participating as others do: "Nothing keeps the voices quiet, you know, we just try to keep the voices laughing. But the way she [Martha] quiets the voices if she speaks out, and says "I'm hungry, Father Brian. Hurry up!") When Donna and Martha walk to the front of the church to receive communion, holding hands as they go, they create for this church some other vision of what it means to receive and to become the body of Christ. Together they are a reminder of another part of the church's liturgy, taking place outside the sanctuary at the picnic benches.

One of the deacons tells me another story about an encounter between Albie, who has a reputation for silence and for sitting alone, and an intern, Ben. She recalls a chess game Albie improvises with Ben, when Ben finally catches on to the art of a game on Albie's own terms. The deacon describes it this way:

> Albie was playing with a chess board, and Ben wanted to play with him, so he [Ben] said, "Can I set up the board, the normal way?" and Ben made his opening move, and Albie made his opening move, and it came into being that Albie would just kind of move [a chess piece] in a way that didn't have anything to do with the rules of chess. Ben was going along with it, trying to figure out what he [Albie] was trying to do, so he finally ended up . . . [with] Albie [taking] almost all of Ben's pieces off the board, and the change that Ben described [as] from "we're going to have a game" to "oh I'm gonna try to figure out what's going on with him, what does he want with this [game]?"

In the deacon's interpretation, the form of the game morphs from a way to pass time together to a form of communication between them. In the end, a third person helps to configure the meaning of the game: "So somebody came up to say 'oh you're playing chess, who won?' and Albie smiled (and gestured to himself)."

Perhaps the whole point of the game is that Albie wants to win a game of chess on his own terms, but Albie also initiates a repartee by which the two can play and in which the intern, the newcomer to the community, does not control the game in a normal way. Ben is not the teacher of a game Albie cannot play. Rather than either of them telling the other how to play, Albie moves pieces around a board, allowing a nonverbal dialogue on the board to unfold between them.

As in the game between Ben and Albie, improvising artistries of communication often involves different senses of reality and normality. For example, the artist Kayla often experiences her possibilities in the world in a way that differs from those around her. Driving back in the art van to church one day, she announces that she is going to Paris over the weekend. Most of us know that Kayla has no means to travel to France for a weekend getaway. Rather than contradicting her, the van driver and others help her to imagine what her weekend in Paris might be like. What will she eat? What will she drink? What will she do there? Kayla's desire to visit Paris becomes an occasion for communal interaction.

While many times different senses of reality are negotiated in uncontentious ways, one person's truth can be very upsetting to another person's equilibrium, a snag or a tear in the fabric of community. Sometimes this happens when one is speaking angrily with a voice or voices in his head in a way that unravels other interactions in the community. At other times, tensions occur on the level of trust and belief, and test the good faith between friends. One morning Kayla announces to a group of us at morning coffee that she and one of her husbands own two houses, a mall in LA, and a movie theater. A conflict ensues. Rose, who often accompanies Kayla in song and art, shakes her head in disbelief. She stops Kayla; she has never heard any of this before! Kayla shrugs and retorts: Rose doesn't know that much about her. Rose keeps shaking her head in disbelief while a small group of us listen in to this conflict unfolding between them. I feel anxious about this rift since Rose and Kayla weave one another into community, and I enjoy their friendship. I ponder an intervention but decide against it. Kayla invites Rose out to LA to see the mall she owns; Rose shakes her head, refusing to accept Kayla's claims. Neither of them wants to relinquish their position. Finally, as the tension thickens, Kayla says with both urgency and flippancy: "Well, what would you do if you had a hundred dollars?! Would you stick with it?" This question about money, the apparent heart of both the initial story and the ensuing argument, is now put to all of us bluntly as a rhetorical question. It makes everyone else at the table begin to laugh. Annie, Miss Carla, Rose, and Kayla laugh and laugh together. I too join in the laughter through their enjoyment, although I am not sure why we are laughing. I then ponder the artwork of the joke as a resolution to the rising tension and as an imaginative bridge in the arts of conversation.

As I perceive it, Kayla has used this joke to turn something that was becoming confrontational (contesting truths about familial wealth) to return the friendly banter to a place where she and Rose and the rest of us can imagine a common vantage point: the indisputable fact that we all need money and would welcome an opportunity to travel or to own a piece of property or to better our material lives if we could. Kayla's story about her

family's wealth, the mall, and the movie theater in LA align with an opportunity grasped, one that in her sense of reality, at that moment, she had to
stick with and could not walk away from; none of us would have if we were
in her shoes, her comment implies. We may not agree with her sense of
reality, but she jokes us into the sense of her stories and reestablishes communication with Rose. Rose, in turn, brings Kayla back into a more typical
conversation with us, leaving the LA property behind. At least, this interpretation is my fragile attempt to get behind the interaction and to analyze my
own participation in it. (It is not a Sacred Family form of interaction to offer
such interpretations.) What I know with certainty is that Rose and Kayla
allow this joke to soften the anxious spaces between them and all of us.

Sometimes contested interpretations of reality are not so easily resolved;
they can linger and disrupt artistries of social interaction at Sacred Family.
I think, for example, of a rift between Wallace and Joshua that persists for
several months and alters profoundly their participation in life at Sacred
Family. Such conflicts affect not only their participation but also the weaving into community of people like me, who have come to experience their
art forms as essential to my own worship at Sacred Family. I continue to
interact with them individually but miss what is possible when they improvise access to community together.

Occasionally, a form of social interaction becomes abusive to one of
those participating in it, and a congregant is then asked to stay away from
Sacred Family for a time. Roy, for example, remembers a harmful relationship with another congregant, Jason, who deceptively extracted money
from him. When staff at Sacred Family discovered what was happening,
Jason was asked not to return to Sacred Family. While his departure made
Sacred Family a safer space for Roy, Jason was also missed by others at
Sacred Family whose participation was altered by his absence. Often, when
someone is asked to leave for a time, there are conditions given and possibilities for a return to community. Jason did return during my research but
only attended for a short time before leaving again.

Weaving as a Form of Participation

By illustrating the arts of touch and gesture, of jokes and laughter, and of
silence and imagination at Sacred Family, I have described some art forms
through which those who gather weave one another into community and,
therefore, belong to a church with and through one another. It is common
to speak of belonging to a community as a linear sequence of events; you
weren't a part of the community and then you are taken into it. You were

once excluded but now you are included; or, you were part of the church and then are no longer welcome. You came to give something to the community but found you needed help instead. You were an active member and then something happens in your life to change your desire to participate.

Sacred Family troubles this linear logic of belonging by its practices of weaving, through which inviting and being a part of one's own and another's belonging is an ongoing art that happens over time, again and again, in different ways. It is a continuous work of incorporation that also entails intermittent departures or distances from the community. Weaving assumes that death and loss, illness and difference, stigma and oblivious-ness, medications and relationships, continuously affect forms of participation; the forms of communal participation must, therefore, persistently respond to the possibility of change and loss, a topic I will discuss further in Chapter 4 when I describe the art form of naming. Weaving through art forms allows different kinds of participation and nonparticipation to exist alongside one another. The art forms do not displace the sermon, the hymn, the celebration of Holy Eucharist, or the conventional expectations that visitors bring to their relationships with Sacred Family members. Rather, they come alongside able-minded tradition, revealing the belong-ing of those who might otherwise be relegated to the edges without a bridge into the heart of community. Through these arts, community mem-bers consent to share time and space with one another even when interac-tions are difficult or confusing.

Mason, a Circle participant, describes these emerging relationships of difference at Sacred Family as a gradual shift in perception:

> Slowly, slowly, slowly, I'm learning to respect everybody, you know, you can't say my condition, my mental health is better or worse than anyone else's. I don't want to do that or look down or look up at any-one. I look at these people; they've been medicated, they're being medicated heavily, been on medication a long time, 'cause some of these long-term medications cause people to have certain involuntary movements and embodiment, and some of them never had much edu-cation, any skills, or any real profession as far as working, but I want to encourage them and encourage myself to continue to live and to have hope for the future. You never know when things may change, when things may get better than I am right now, and I never want to give up hope. I want to encourage people like me never to give up hope; one person no better than another, we're all human beings, we're people, we're persons, whatever, and we may have limitation, but we're not

incapable of doing anything because we have a mental health condition.

Weaving, following Mason's logic, is slow and persistently hopeful; no one is incapable and no one is worth more than another. This truth, often hidden, must take creative shape within the community's liturgy. Thus, art forms of touch and gesture, jokes and laughter, silence and imagination carve out the possibility for two or more to sit on a bench together. They weave a loosely held web of relationships with respect for difference together. Each relies on relationships of one beside another so that when we speak of Sacred Family as the church, each pew or section of a sanctuary matters, each table in a fellowship hall has its resonance and web of relationships.

Interpreted as an art, Sacred Family's liturgy offers an alternative imaginary as it represents, assumes, and questions current social and political arrangements of human relationships by anticipating an arrangement of the world as God desires it. Liturgy as a common art requires communal art forms: the creative activities of small groups within a liturgy who embody such imagination and worship but do so perhaps not in the same way as each other or as other congregations. As they participate in art forms that hold a community of difference together, congregants implicitly raise questions about what social arrangements define Christian liturgy, they anticipate alternate forms of communal belonging, and they interrogate any liturgy premised on ableist assumptions about what counts as participation in the work of a church that gathers to meet God together.

Liturgy as Workshop in the Creative City

Saliers evokes liturgy as an eschatological art through the expansive nature of prayer forms—all of the gestures and postures and emotions required to remember the world to God and God to each of us. Liturgy is "the ongoing prayer and word of Jesus Christ," enlivened by the Spirit through all of us together in the world.[32] We not only pray as God prays in and through us, but we become a prayer as we enact our hope in divine love for the entirety of creation. We can take up Saliers's invocation of liturgy as embodied and performed prayer to imagine laughter and the touch of a hand to a head, or the bump of an elbow, or two or three bodies sitting near one another in silence, or sharing an imagined reality with another, as forms through which Sacred Family remembers all of human life as sacred before God.

Alongside liturgy as embodied prayer, I offer two other metaphors that help us imagine the holy work of these art forms: the church as workshop and the liturgy as holy play. Both metaphors help to name the arts of Sacred Family as essential to its liturgy rather than a distraction from or supplement to those actions recognized as Christian worship. These metaphors remind us that worship is not right words about God, nor a set of actions we accomplish for God, but a set of relationships through which humans might encounter together both the beauty and the creativity, as well as the strangeness, of divine love.

In *On Liturgical Theology*, liturgical scholar Aidan Kavanagh describes church as a "workshop" for city, in which city serves as an icon for world in its modes of diversity and creativity. Kavanagh argues that God gives liturgy in order for humans to make something new for the city through an altered relationship to discourse.[33] Because sacraments and rites are primary language through which the church gathers, those who assemble come to engage divine presence and activity in the world in a different medium than in their everyday lives: "In the case of City and Church, the need to image in order to know gives rise to special sorts of discourse which are more necessary than optional. The discourse thickens meaning found in reality and then increments that meaning with style."[34] Because it relies on symbol and sense as much as verbal articulation, liturgy occasions different modes of relating and apprehending than the discourse of City readily occasions.

Because the assembly gathers not for information about God, as an object of human mental capacity, the liturgy invites encounter with God in a style that troubles discursive tendencies to imagine Christian liturgy as informational or educational rather than through relationship or encounter. While Kavanagh posits a traditional canon that shapes Christian liturgy, he also insists that liturgy is never first words about God; rather, it is the occasion for a communal entity to move and discover itself as a body. The church, like a human body, grows into a sense of its own self, as a small child might initially regard some of her own body parts as strangers and gradually grow into their sensation as she moves and discovers herself: "Analogously, a corporate entity such as a church might perhaps be said to grow itself into a sort of envelope of sensation which then forms its own peculiar self-image, its own real awareness of corporate identity which is its own fundamental principle of operation."[35]

Such embodied encounters with the divine regularly bring a community to the edge of "chaos" and force that communal entity to make adjustments.[36] Through such continual theological adjustments to the

possibilities of chaos, a liturgical assembly gradually grows into an understanding of itself and its own norms of life and faith. Liturgy, Kavanagh
argues, should offer a new sense of normality, but it does this in a way that
is more akin to the flow of music than to a classroom lesson: "Therefore
Christians do not worship because they believe. They believe because the
One in whose gift faith lies is regularly met in the act of communal worship—not because the assembly conjures up God, but because the initiative lies with the God who has promised to be there always."[37]

Ironically, Sacred Family often seems to be the kind of congregation
that Kavanagh dismisses as inadequate to a true vision of Christian liturgy:
"a commune of friends whose main purpose is to get along with each other,
a moral uplift society, a group dedicated to aesthetics or therapy, a sheep-
fold of the unsure, a home for the dull."[38] Yet Sacred Family gives a concrete shape to Kavanagh's strange and sometime confusing descriptions of
liturgy. At Sacred Family, worship of God requires a community to
encounter the brink of chaos, and make continual adjustments to its creativity in light of these "ecclesial transaction[s] with reality."[39] Liturgy at
Sacred Family works through bodily connections, which grow into new
sensations—gestures, jokes, silences, strange games and dialogues, different senses of reality—sensations that expand liturgical media in accord
with the mental differences and diverse movements of the bodies who
gather. The jokes, gestures, and silences may not be "about God" in any
traditional sense, but they shape the possibility of relations and encounters
within liturgy. Such relations and encounters with others are not optional
to a liturgical gathering but fundamental to a community who gathers to
encounter God together. Different senses of reality that feel chaotic to
some force an adjustment, whether or not this adjustment is explicitly
acknowledged. A church community whose liturgical tradition assumes the
participation of abled individuals transacts with a reality that worships
otherwise.

Such artfulness, as Pinn reminds us, is interrogative, "a creative disregard."[40] Might praise through the laughter occasioned by a bad joke offer
as much to God as beautiful prayers read aloud from the book? As Sedgwick reminds us, to put the question like this is to frame our relationships
with the divine in the world in terms of cause and effect and in competitive
terms rather than the collaborative logic of what might happen when one
is beside another. Creative disregard can also be a form of creative regard
rather than a competition. We can put these interrelated forms another
way. Alongside the prayer book prayers, the raucous laughter also rises so
that a beautiful prayer for unity finds its resonance and disruption in the

lure of a witty illustration, which weaves together those who laugh their prayers with God.

Liturgy as Holy Play for a Sensible Community

The priest and liturgist Romano Guardini, who himself lived with mental illness in the form of depression most of his life,[41] provides us another metaphor for liturgy alongside that of prayer or creative work. The liturgy, he argues, can be seen as holy play because it refuses the logic of purpose, something we set out to achieve for God and for ourselves. Like Kavanagh, Guardini argues that liturgy is not primarily didactic. Good liturgy is purposeless, which is not to say it is unplanned or unstructured or that it is ineffectual. Rather, good Christian liturgy is purposeless because, according to Guardini, it cannot prescribe particular cures for certain ailments. It reveals human beauty when it does not press humans into a particular shape or toward a foreknown action or end but, rather, allows those who pray to be their beloved selves for God.[42] The one who prays "with the aid of grace, is given the opportunity of realizing [her] fundamental essence, of really becoming according to [her] divine destiny" what she "should be and longs to be, a child of God."[43] Guardini imagines the liturgical posture as a wandering through nature. Rather than a pursuit of the shortest route to a proposed destination, the spirit of good liturgy creates space for what may seem to us an idle or circuitous route.[44] Its humble gestures make room and give time for that which cannot be known or quantified ahead of time: how a community will make its own way through the songs, gestures, prayers, scriptures of the day, and what it may find along its way. When a liturgical assembly exhibits restraint by allowing the beauty of each person to emerge, it serves as both a form of communal hospitality and a way of humility.

Guardini is concerned with how we become beautiful to one another without instrumentality or objectification, because the beauty of others and the created order often remain hidden from us.[45] Guardini imagines that if we take time to play, God will reveal this beauty to us, but he makes a qualification. For someone or something to be true to what or who they are, liturgical language must restrain its desires to improve us. In its restraint, it performs respect for that which it cannot know about the trajectory of any one human life.

The challenge of holy play at Sacred Family is that one person's form of access, a wave across the sanctuary in the middle of the Eucharistic prayer, affects another's sense of reverence. The creativity of Sacred Family's liturgical art forms creates not only connection but also real tension as different forms of prayer and play collide, and as traditional forms interface with improvised forms of access. When Wallace and Joshua or others access liturgical forms through their commentary, their voices might also obstruct another's access to the priest's voice. In this potential dissonance, Guardini's understanding of the interrelationship between holy play and restraint comes to bear. His invocation of restraint echoes a comment Father Brian makes when he reflects on how his own participation as priest at Sacred Family has changed over the years. Even when he struggles to keep this premise in mind, he finds that any authoritarian rebuke of a perceived disruption is always more disruptive than the original activity; unkindness is the greatest disruption to a communal liturgy that seeks to remember God together as unconditional love. Thus, Sacred Family's holy play also manifests the mark of kindness as a liturgical posture of restraint so that the most creative of liturgical art forms might flourish.

Weaving Traditional and Improvised Art Forms as Common Prayer

Both Kavanagh and Guardini write about liturgy as "workshop" and "holy play"; yet both emphasize canons and structures passed down to the Church. The sacred and necessary givenness of the church's traditional forms hold diverse persons together in patterns across time and space. (Guardini describes Christian liturgy as "reminiscent of the stars, of their eternally fixed and even course, of their inflexible order, of their profound silence, and of the infinite space in which they are poised."[46]) Neither imagines that improvised forms such as the jokes or the waving at Sacred Family become essential to any liturgical media. Yet Sacred Family creatively embodies and expands the sense of their metaphors of workshop and holy play: its creative art forms illumine the necessity of a liturgical language; its communal performance requires interdependent persons rather than a recitation or reception of facts about God by a unified communal entity of autonomous beings.

In its practice of liturgical art forms, Sacred Family is both unique and just like any other congregation. Individuals gather, and the abilities to pray, play, and work together are always interpolated by the idiosyncratic presences of those who shape artful possibilities of connection and restraint. As one of the Sacred Family gardeners laments to me one morning, in a tone of exasperation, when I ask him how he is doing, "I am doing fine. It's everybody else. . . ." He intimates that despite his best intentions to have a good day, the struggles of those beside him create and condition the possibilities of how fine he is able to be. His participation in community is inextricably intertwined with theirs. The gardener's experiences might be more intense at Sacred Family, where moods can shift more quickly and the experiences of daily life through poverty and mental illness are more challenging than in many places; yet, his sentiments apply to any communal struggle.

Sacred Family helps us to notice that liturgical forms fundamentally require artistries of connection and communication among those who gather. They are a necessary craft for any expansive prayer, or creative work, or holy play. The challenges of difference draw as much attention to the forms of communal interaction as to the explicit theologies of liturgical language. When Victoria, as an usher, jokes with a row of us who have no contributions for the offering plate—"Y'all ain't got any money?"—how does one understand the theological meaning of offering? Do those who dig through their pockets to give a dime to the congregation assume a theological arrangement in which the poorest members must give some monetary contribution in order to belong to a church, or do those who give money raise questions about the meaning of such an act, as they insist on their rights to participation even if what they give has almost no monetary value for the church?

If liturgy is not about gathering to memorize or articulate a set of ideas about God but is about how those who encounter God become beautiful in their relationships with God and one another, then such artistries that improvise the belonging of one to another are not peripheral but essential to any liturgical gathering. The question remains: if such artistries are essential, to what extent can the traditional forms that hold communities across time and space weave the improvisations and creativity of art forms into their own formal senses of prayer, work, and holy play? Can those who assemble acknowledge God's presence in improvised forms of access to communal gathering, in the artistries of interpersonal connection, and in the differences of mental disabilities?

As I contemplate these complex questions, I allow my imagination to wander, assuming other possible realities at Sacred Family, other arrangements of bodies in time and space that help those who gather to pay attention to the realities of human interdependence. I imagine a priest inviting us not to look to our bulletins as our guide for "everything we need," but to look and listen to those beside us who will guide us through the service and to rearrange ourselves if need be so that we have who we need by our side. I imagine one of Annie's devotional prayers or pictures as a liturgical prompt alongside a prayer book. I imagine the words spoken and read from a book always accompanied by a gesture or touch, or by objects and artworks from the Sacred Family gardens and studios. Such concrete images, like the stirring of the imagined custard and applesauce during easy yoga, hold the possibilities of traditional forms moving toward and creating with and through the body-minds of those who enact them. I imagine that those in the front of any space or meeting at Sacred Family continually weave disabled voices into the formal sounds of those spaces, understanding the work that those voices do even if they trouble the perceived conceptual coherence of a gathering.

This is one possible alternate reality that emerges as my mind follows the thread of Sacred Family's art forms. Such explicit weaving of traditional and improvised forms requires practice. Such weaving may entail difficult work and challenging play for many of our mental capacities. Alternate understandings of time would be required for peripheral artistries to inform liturgical language, a sense of time that does not perceive a liturgical gathering as an efficient set of accomplishments or obligations. Such a sense of time requires an exploration of implicit and explicit theologies of liturgy as work and as pleasure. To the subject of time, I turn in the next chapter.

One Sacred Family congregant uses a pitcher to pour water over another's feet during the Holy Week ritual of foot washing. (Photo credit: Cindy M. Brown)

CHAPTER 3

Disrupting: Aesthetics of Time and Work

> The hill of Zion yields
> a thousand sacred sweets
> before we reach the heavenly fields,
> before we reach the heavenly fields,
> or walk the golden streets,
> or walk the golden streets.
> —Hymn sung by Sacred Family congregants[1]

On Marcus's last day at Sacred Family as a full-time intern, we reflect together on a year of service and vocational discernment.[2] A conversation about the experience of time at Sacred Family begins with a memory of light: "I remember my early thoughts of this place was the amount of light that I saw—so much light—a great space of light, a thin place in the Celtic tradition. Light being a place of immense growth, a great source of life, a place where we say 'surely the presence [of the Lord is in this place]' in the song that everybody sings in Worship Live . . . a close place between where God can be readily felt and is very present and all of these other things, but it doesn't necessarily have to take on a spiritual vibe, it's just sort of a very highly positively energized place."

"Have you felt that during your year here? Would you say that your experience of the presence of God has changed here, during your year here?"

Marcus goes on to describe the varied textures of time at Sacred Family: "Well, I think presence can be a continuous thing depending on how much we are willing to be present. . . . But like any relationship, in any course in time, we change. And so I think that voice, that feeling, that presence has taken on different tempos, different levels of energy, different colors, and flavors, and textures over time. Like the amount of myself that I'm putting in this place, it changes. Sometimes that's really wonderful, and sometimes that's less wonderful, and sometimes it's scary, and sometimes it's remarkably joyful."

"It depends on a given week?"

"Yeah, on given circumstances, it's like watching baseball. I don't like baseball, but it's like periods of intense excitement, followed by long periods of nothing happening, and then suddenly something will pop up. That's the thing about this place, it's very unpredictable."

Later in the conversation, I encourage Marcus's description of time at Sacred Family by reflecting on my own experience: "I often think of Sacred Family, as moving at its own . . . there's a different sense of time in being here."

"Yeah, it's funny how much of a vacuum time holds. In the early months [of my year] here with so much time ahead, it was like this slow-moving time, where you had the space. Time is like this space that you have, and so I had this long amount of space for a long time to figure things out and to be present and to lean back into the moment that I was in, and to be here. And in a way, that is very exhausting, just, I guess, the sense that time is such a long thing. This whole year has been enormously exhausting, I think, but I've also been kept very busy outside of here."

"I often think about life at personal care homes, these spaces of time where there is only the television . . . and I wonder about that sense of time that is part of the personal care home experience."

"Yeah, I wonder about that too. When I think about Roy [a longtime congregant who lives in a group home] and his years and how he, how Roy remembers these pinpricks of time . . . it seems an odd thing. It seems meals are a good indicator of that, time being centered around meals, here and in the personal care home, and I wonder if that is part of why there is such enthusiasm around them, I guess, to be there and eating."

"That it marks time in a certain way? Meals as points of time in a day?"

"Yes. And for people who don't participate in the programs, I often feel like time is a sad thing with them, and I don't know how to engage that. Like Sharice will sit there and tell me she is doing nothing, and she doesn't want to do nothing and that she has no interest in just coming here and leaving, coming here and leaving, and I just don't know theologically or personally what that is or what that means, but it is challenging."

Texture and the Feel of Liturgical Time

The challenge of Sacred Family, from Marcus's vantage point, comes from a time filled with light and energy, the possibility of growth, and through a time that is slow moving, a long space to be traversed, exhausting, and for some a difficult experience of doing nothing. Sacred Family is both luminous with divine presence and monotonous with an emptiness that the community struggles to fill for one another. There is a mixed texture to time that feels strange to Marcus and to me.

During its weekly liturgy, Sacred Family draws attention to aesthetic dimensions of liturgical gathering that are often overlooked in more formal theological proclamations, mission statements, fundraising goals, and in the sermons and prayers of the community. Using a frame of difference attends to liturgical space as it unfolds or divides here, and to liturgical art forms that incorporate disability into traditional structures within the community. Such a liturgical frame requires analysis of the textures of time, varied experiences of repetition and disruption that affect this congregation's common prayer. How does liturgical time feel here, and why does this feeling matter? How does this congregation navigate liturgical time, and how does it disrupt it?

Constant disruptions punctuate life at Sacred Family. They interrupt the anticipated and intended movements of services, events, tasks, and interactions. Someone who is supposed to collect the offering disappears, and community members search for him right before the offering is to be taken up. A woman is telling me a story, and I must stop her to acknowledge another who urgently demands my attention. A congregant wanders around the altar as the priest preaches, and another parishioner leads her back to a seat. A gardener pulls up all the onions, mistaking them for weeds, and the morning is spent replanting.

Yet the disruptions of individual responses and behaviors, while affecting the smooth flow of communal interaction and movement, are less disruptive to liturgical choreographies than other subtler sensibilities about what can and should happen during Christian liturgy. Such textures brush up against assumptions about the intended results of liturgical time, as well as assumptions about the charitable work of the church. Thus, a challenge to the consent to be a community of difference comes when employed and unemployed, wealthy and poor, abled and disabled negotiate time together as a part of a weeklong liturgy.

How does it feel for a person like Marcus to share time with people who do not work, in any conventional sense of that word? By the same token, how does it feel for Sacred Family's unemployed members with disabilities to gather with people whose jobs take up most of their time? What textures of time inform the aesthetics of Sacred Family's liturgy? Literary critic and queer theorist Eve Kosofsky Sedgwick defines texture as "an array of perceptual data that includes repetition, but whose degree of organization hovers just below the level of shape or structure."[3] At such a level of perceptual data, passivity and agency blur, as textures wait for us even as we create them: "to touch is always already to reach out, to fondle, to heft, to tap, or to enfold, and always also to understand other people or natural forces as having effectually done so before oneself, if only in the making of the textured object."[4] While many of us associate texture with the sense of touch, Sedgwick emphasizes its intersensory quality.[5] For example, I see the smoothness of the hymnbook I touch or hear the brush of my leg against a pew, and not only feel but also hear and taste the crunch of a communion wafer on a tongue. Such textures are never neutral but coexist intimately with the feelings that arise through them: "[T]he same double meaning, tactile plus emotional, is already there in the single word 'touching'; equally it's internal to the word 'feeling.'"[6] Sedgwick draws our attention to spaces, objects, and texts as textured; they make us feel certain ways as we feel our way through them. And we make them feel the way they do through our relations with them.

While Sedgwick emphasizes the spatial dimensions of texture, texture is also an important dimension of liturgical time and its disruption at Sacred Family. For example, while I mark progress through a service by checking off items on my bulletin, anticipating how long each one might take, I can also sense the conclusion of the service in the taste of wafer and wine, which for many congregants prompts a feeling of anticipation about another meal to follow the service. Likewise, a liturgical season such as Lent or Advent corresponds to a calendar year but is also known through the feelings that each anticipates and evokes. The season of Advent anticipates a longing for Christ's coming. At Sacred Family, such time is primarily experienced through the joy and confusion associated with the many church parties and outings that take place during the month of December.

The significance of textured time at Sacred Family also emerges during Lent when discourses of confession, sacrifice, and suffering brush up against other sensibilities that inform Sacred Family's gathering. During Lent and Holy Week, in particular, communal senses of pleasure, time, and work, as interrelated phenomena, emerge as disruptive textures to the anticipated liturgical feel of this season. Two examples from the Lenten life of Sacred Family help to demonstrate this disruption. The first example draws on the imaginative world of an artist with mental illness from outside Sacred Family, whose work a priest at Sacred Family uses to elicit Lenten reflection during the weekly Sunday education hour.

THE STATIONS OF THE CROSS OF MENTAL ILLNESS

At Sacred Family, the liturgical time of Lent begins with an Ash Wednesday penitential service in which the community participates in a lengthy confession of sins as well as the marking of each participant's forehead with black ash. A priest or a deacon touches each forehead with a reminder of mortality: "Remember that you are dust, and to dust you shall return." We can see the touch of ash on each other's foreheads. The mark of ash begins a season that in many Christian churches involves spiritual disciplines: acts such as fasting or prayer as Christians remember Christ's journey to the cross. Sacred Family observes the season of Lent not only in the songs and prayers of its services but during its weekly Sunday education hour in the library.

During one Lent, congregants use artwork by an artist and theologian from another congregation to participate in a devotional practice: the stations of the cross invite congregants to follow Jesus imaginatively and prayerfully from his time of sentencing to the cross upon which he was executed. This artist and theologian, Mary Button, employs a traditional liturgical form, stations of the cross, to reflect on the social and ecclesial stigma of mental illness. While she draws Jesus in each of the traditional poses assumed as part of a stations of the cross (such as falling for the first time, meeting his mother, being stripped of his garments), Button also expands each station with a plethora of images, which she draws from stories of beauty and suffering that characterize first-person narratives of mental illness. Alongside Jesus with his cross, Button layers biblical images with images from the writings of individuals with psychiatric disabilities. By this transposition of images, disability testimony and Jesus's journey are juxtaposed and intertwined.

As an artist with mental illness herself, Button illustrates experiences such as mania, depression, suicide, and post-traumatic stress disorder as well as medicating practices that are violent to those who experience them. She honors particular individuals with mental illness by writing their words on the cross and illustrating images from their writings. In doing so, Button hopes to engage the reluctance or refusal of many churches to acknowledge the experiences of those with mental illness in

their midst, a refusal that contributes to the suffering of those with psychiatric disabilities.

During a half hour before each Sacred Family Sunday Eucharist in
Lent, a small group of congregants pass Button's artwork around the
table. The priest invites all who gather in the library to imagine the story
as it unfolds. "What do you think he is feeling at the moment?" she asks
one morning, late into the Lenten season, as we all stare at the ninth
station: "Jesus Falls for the Third Time." Jesus lies alone next to a large
wooden cross with his eyes closed. Behind the cross we contemplate
images from the testimony of a man with mental illness who participated
in torture practices during the Iraq war. Wallace points out the demons
hovering around Jesus, small colorful figures along the edges. I notice the
soldiers.

"I'm sure he's very exhausted," Tanya empathizes with Jesus.

"He's probably taking a nap," Scott follows her train of thought.

"I'd take a nap," Rufus agrees.

"He's not sure he can handle to go anymore because he's so tired,"
Tanya continues. She suggests he might be feeling insecure or not sure if
he's going to make it.

"He's getting ready! Yeah, he's getting ready." Wallace is sure about this
answer.

"He's trying to regroup to get energy," Tanya concurs.

Offering a suggested Scripture passage and the story of moral injury
from the Iraq war, the priest wonders whether Jesus is apprehensive about
his crucifixion and is wrestling with the evil that is to come. Hearing about
moral injury makes Roy think of a time his mother smashed one of his toys.
He wonders aloud why she smashed the toy.

"He didn't want to deal with it," says Wallace bringing us back to Jesus,
"There's no way he wanted to deal with it. He's had a hard week."

"Do you think he was trying to avoid for just a second what he was about
to do? Do we ever try to avoid stuff that's hard?" asks the priest, admitting
that she avoids things all the time.

"I do!" Wallace laughs, resonating with the priest's confession.[7] Wallace's laughter reminds me of all the times in the past year that he has given
up on activities that were once life-giving to him: his work in the garden; a
class at the church; and more recently the art forms that he and his friend
Joshua create together through their laughter and commentary. He drops
out of his obligations and commitments at Sacred Family due to fluctuations in his physical and mental health and due to abrupt changes in his
desires and perceptions of his own abilities. In this, he is similar to many

Sacred Family congregants, who appear unable to fulfill communal roles with a conventional consistency.

As Wallace, Tanya, and others bear witness to Jesus's journey, they have mercy on Jesus. They give him more time to carry his burden and to arrive at his destination. He might not be avoiding responsibility. He could be resting, gathering his thoughts, or getting ready for what comes next.

But Jesus and the story of his journey are only one aspect of Button's stations of the cross. Alongside each cross are layers of images also drawn from the words of those with mental illness, a proliferation of detail that eludes our narrative control. The stations take place on a background that teems with vibrant patterns from the natural and human-made world. Kingfishers fly and mackerel swim behind a cross in the third station. Snowflakes crystallize around the fourth. "Look at the light bulbs!" Wallace notices the patterns in the eighth. While Jesus moves through a sequential narrative of suffering, forward toward death and resurrection, another meaning accrues to the stories he symbolizes through an intensity of detail behind him. In the most tragic of stories, the patterns grow darker and more abstract. On the first Sunday of Lent, the Sacred Family group wonders about such strange designs: the brilliant fruit and the butterflies behind Jesus as Pilate condemns him to death. In a later Lenten gathering, it takes longer to notice the wings like black lace behind the cross.

In her description of her artwork, Button explains how the patterns and colors of her art relate to her experiences of mental illness:

> The 2015 Stations are deeply personal. After years of misdiagnoses, medication, side effects worse than the symptoms they were meant to treat, and the patronizing disdain of health care providers, I was diagnosed with bipolar disorder. It has been five years since my diagnosis, and most days I'm overwhelmed by the sheer force of color in my life. Friends often comment on the bold colors present in my work, even in seemingly gloomy subject material. Because at the age of 25, with the help of talk therapy and mood stabilizers, it was like the color was switched back on. I began to experience the world in a profoundly new way. . . .
>
> The artwork in this series begins in an attempt to express some of the experiential quality of mania. As the colors darken, I hope to illuminate the darkness of depression as well as some of the implications for social justice presented by American society's mistreatment of those with mental illnesses. The narrative shape of the series comes from Kay Redfield Jamison's magisterial book *Touched with Fire: Manic Depressive Illness and the Artistic Temperament*. It's this book that

shepherded me through the first year after my diagnosis. It helped me to understand the central point of this new series of work: people with mental illness experience the world in ways that illuminate great truths about the very nature of the human experience.[8]

One of the themes Button highlights in her stations is that of the complicated feelings of invisibility that can be part of mental illness. "Do you think that Jesus feels invisible? Do you ever feel invisible?" asks the priest as we consider Jesus on the ground. Rufus claims that he just ignores those for whom he is invisible; he walks away from them. But Rufus loves to tell stories, and it is difficult to imagine him ignoring anyone for very long. The topic of invisibility sprouts an idea in Rufus's mind. "Look, Roy, I'm invisible!" He pretends to hide under the table, while the rest of us laugh at his joke. Roy plays along, "Come on up!" By Rufus's third attempt to make the same joke, we ignore him, lest he draw the group off topic, as he frequently does. The priest focuses our contemplation back on Jesus's suffering and our own. Rufus's silly game feels disruptive to the sorrow and reverence that liturgical time intends for us, and we subdue his strange pleasure into the background of our conversation.

The Duties and Pleasures of Washing Feet

During Holy Week, the congregation follows Jesus's movements in another way as congregants wash one another's feet. This Maundy Thursday, a friend and I arrive early for foot washing because I have missed instructions about an irregular time for this annual service. I apologize for making my friend leave work early, although many congregants are already gathered. Inside the sanctuary, Annie and Kirby page through his sketchbook. Roy talks to a visitor about the Lone Ranger.

Gradually, the sanctuary fills. Before we wash feet, scripture and sermon frame this ritual act. Mother Daria begins her homily with a confession. After telling us that we will take part in a ritual that makes people uncomfortable, she admits to the challenge of writing a sermon for this community.

> You see, I had a sermon written for this evening that would have worked fine at most churches, but of course, Sacred Family is not like most churches. My sermon was about how God invites us into vulnerability through this activity of foot washing. My sermon was all about how Jesus himself becomes vulnerable as he takes on his humble role in front of his friends and how Simon Peter risks the greatest vulnerability allowing the Son of God to wash his feet. So I had this sermon

all figured out, and then I remembered the obvious. Sacred Family has
a foot clinic, and so each week, Sacred Family engages in this very
activity that most of the world finds so uncomfortable. So Maundy
Thursday doesn't come once a year to Sacred Family but once a week.

Acknowledging that the weekday liturgy alters the foot washing ritual, she
continues:

But before I let you off the hook and shorten this sermon too much,
there is something that even this beloved community can take away
from this gospel text, and it lies in that moment when Simon Peter
questions Jesus. Simon Peter says, "Lord are you going to wash my
feet?" How do you think Simon Peter feels when Jesus kneels to wash
his feet? Anyone?

She looks to the congregation for answers.
"Embarrassed," says Roy.
"Jesus told Simon Peter that he will understand things later," Kirby offers.
"Finding grace with God," Ritchie suggests.
"Wash . . . disciples' feet. Jesus's feet!" Forest says, eagerly raising his
hand and then pausing to come up with an answer that weaves him into the
moment.
Mother Daria acknowledges each one by calling their names and lends
her own interpretation: "I think Simon Peter was surprised. Does anyone
else here think he might have felt a little bit surprised?" Murmurs of agreement follow, and small ripples of dissent. She continues:

He was surprised that God was calling him to an activity that didn't
seem fitting for God. It didn't seem like a holy activity at all. . . . The
lesson is that God surprises us even if we are as close to God as Simon
Peter is to Jesus, even if we think we know God as well as we know our
best friend. God still surprises us. God does this by inviting us to step
into uncomfortable regions and for many, many, many Americans—
American Christians—learning to be vulnerable in a society, where
power and privilege and money are supremely valued, may be the main
task at hand. But for folks here, who in many, many ways are comfortable with vulnerability, it may be something different.

She describes how we shape circles around ourselves, thickening the
boundaries of the ways we imagine that God is present with us. One of our
holy tasks is to keep those boundaries open and porous:

So I want to invite you into a mental exercise for a moment. Imagine
you are standing inside a circle, and in this circle is where you feel
comfortable and where you imagine God residing with you. But then

God surprises you and calls to you from the other side of the circle, from outside the boundary, and she invites you into a life that you didn't consider, that you didn't imagine was holy. As we stand on the eve of Christ's crucifixion, we have all of Jesus's teachings before us, and this is an opportunity to be surprised . . . and it may be different for each one of us [according to] the ways we need to grow.

She concludes by inviting us to imagine ourselves as characters in the gospel text and to remember how each person is invited to step outside the circles of comfort they imagine as holy. As with most sermons at Sacred Family, some congregants listen intently, some drift in and out of attention, and others give no sign of engagement.

After the sermon, Father Brian prepares us for foot washing; he tells us to hold each foot over the basin with the help of the person washing our feet. He is adamant: "Don't put your feet down in the basin; because there will be a lot of people's dirty feet water in that basin by the time we get through, and we don't want to share whatever we've got." Then he jests with some seriousness: "There are some things we don't want to share."

Two sets of three chairs, facing one another, frame the altar. A small group goes forward. Lay leader Jill and Deacon Elizabeth bend over Mr. Cornelius's slender frame and wash his feet side by side. Jack and Andie, husband and wife, wash each other's feet, return to their seats, and then from time to time eagerly rush to the front to wash the feet of another. Albie shuffles down the aisle, a brightly colored necktie above the collar of an old dress shirt; he returns with a rare smile on his face. Jill invites Wallace and Joshua to join her; they decline her invitation. Quite a few congregants participate as onlookers. Debbie jumps up and goes forward. On the way back, she hugs Jack and embraces Erica. I, too, am eager to participate in this beloved ritual. One of the deacons washes my feet. Next to me, Walter, a gardener, washes my friend's feet. Back at my pew, I enjoy gestures of pleasure and affection spreading through the room. I wait for my friend to return.

After we leave the service, my friend tells me why it took him so long to return to his seat. Walter, disregarding the priest's instructions, plunges my friend's feet into the basin and scrubs them vigorously. When it comes time to wash Walter's feet, my friend does not feel right dribbling water in return and washes Walter's feet in like manner. In the car, we laugh over the surprise of having one's feet so thoroughly washed during a ritual, the symbolic gesture taking a literal form. We laugh at my friend's discomfort with disregarding the priest's clear instructions.

About a week later, a church intern and I visit Walter's group home. Seventeen men live in this group home in a set of apartments, and six of them come to Sacred Family on a regular basis. We try to make small talk across very different kinds of lives. It is an awkward but pleasant conversation, as many social exchanges at Sacred Family are, punctuated by silences. Then I remember foot washing, and so I bring it up, searching out a common memory for us to share. Walter nods, recalling it with a smile: "Yeah, I enjoyed that!" he stretches out the syllables of the word enjoy so that the word lasts longer.

Disability Aesthetics and the Enjoyment of Church

Disability scholar Tobin Siebers offers one definition of aesthetics as "track[ing] the sensations that some bodies feel in the presence of other bodies."[9] As I track the sensations of this Maundy Thursday, Walter's declaration of pleasure surprises me, stretching out the circles of my assumptions about what the ritual of foot washing means. Walter's experience of enjoyment in a ritual of touching one another's feet is, on the face of it, in dissonance with the context of the darkest week of the Christian liturgical year and with the difficult circumstances of Walter's own life. Yet, I find that his response resonates with many interactions at Sacred Family that might occur at any point in liturgical time.

A short time into my ethnographic research, I become aware of my own embodiment as a source of interest for the people I worship with and the pleasures of shared embodiment as a way to pass time. In a pew, a woman praises the colors of my manicure and invites me to admire her own. Another comments on the color of a dress I am wearing, stroking it, and expresses curiosity over my choice of shoes. When I discuss haircuts with another gentleman, he examines my hair, looking carefully for split ends. I begin to dress with Sacred Family folks in mind, not necessarily with an eye to contemporary fashion but with a feel for what colors or patterns might evoke good conversation. I enjoy the creativity with which some congregants adorn themselves: hats, beads, ties, wigs, vests, aprons, bows, jewels, and elaborate hairstyles. Loitering with intent, I find that congregants rarely desire to go in depth about their day or week; instead, we admire together new items from the clothes closet, or sniff the bottle of lotion won at bingo. I run my hand along the inside of an artist's carved wooden bowl, praising its smooth surface. I admire a photograph. I read aloud or listen to a poem someone has written. We discuss the color of the sky, the cold air, or the plants in the church garden. We recall the tastes of items eaten for breakfast or discuss the menu for lunch. We remember or anticipate an outing—viewing the Christmas lights, riding the horses. On the van ride to a group home, passengers move to the rhythms of a favorite pop song. On the radio, the hip-hop artist Tupac sings, "I wonder if heaven got a ghetto," and from the back of the van Wallace shouts, "Turn it up!" and reticent Elena, who often sits alone, seconds his request with a rare smile.

Sometimes sensory pleasures are evident, and sometimes they are imagined. One Wednesday evening in Ordinary Time, I arrive early. Victoria beckons to me. She shows me a bee sting on her leg. We talk about the church Thanksgiving dinner the following Wednesday evening. She tells me she intends to cook a meal and then changes her mind. I think about group homes and the fact that few Wednesday congregants will participate in preparing a meal or in hosting guests in their home spaces. A few will join family or friends, but many will eat food provided by their house managers.

Sitting in the sanctuary before the official start of the communion service, Victoria imagines an elaborate dinner that we will cook together for Thanksgiving. She names each dish and with it her place as an African American in this Southern city: mac and cheese, mashed potatoes, sweet potatoes, ham, turkey, chitlins, shrimp, and oxtails. With each new dish, she laughs with pleasure. It becomes a game. I protest at the excess, and she adds more ingredients to our dinner. Gradually, we quiet down. Victoria, tucking her head inside her winter coat collar, falls into a deep sleep. She sleeps through most of the service, unaware of all the singing and movement around her. She isn't awake for the reading of scripture. She doesn't go forward to take communion. Whether her sleep results from a tiring day, boredom with the service, or the effects of medications, I do not know. No one wakes her.[10] At the end of the service, as the deacon gives a benediction and prays over our meal, Victoria lays her head on my shoulder, propping her body against me. Such intimate moments between acquaintances would feel strange to me in other settings, but at Sacred Family it feels natural to me and seemingly to Victoria to share space in such proximity.

Sensory pleasures, such as the ones I experience in Victoria's presence, occur around the peripheries of the sanctuary, accumulating as we pass time, waiting for events to begin or end. They occur inside the sanctuary, during the time of a service, along the peripheries of the official liturgy: the prayers of the prayer book, the reading of scripture, the sermon, the creeds, the confession, the offering, and the eucharistic prayer. Such textures often distract from the centers of instruction or proclamation. They also appear inconsequential in light of the suffering some congregants bear. What difference can any textures of pleasure make when those who gather have been asked to carry so much and when their difficult journeys are not yet finished? As Aisha explains to me, she worries all the time. Even when she feels happy, she worries that she will be sad again. Even when she feels good about her life, she worries that, one day, she will try to take her own life again. Sacred Family is by no means a happy ending to the problems that many community members face. It is a place where some take a break from the daily routines of personal care homes and rest for a time, but it does not resolve the burdens of past and future time.

When I ask Sacred Family congregants to reflect on what makes this a church, they often talk about the prayer book services. They mention morning and noonday prayer and the Sunday and Wednesday Eucharist. They talk about singing, sermons, and communion. Like Marcus, some sense God's presence here. They speak about a place of acceptance and non-judgment, a safe space where you can always ask for help. People who are not from a group home may reflect on how Sacred Family is a real place and not a superficial one: you can come as you are without worrying about what you are wearing, without needing to impress others, without hiding your sufferings, and without pretending to comply with conventional norms of dress or interaction. While such marks help to identify Sacred Family as a church, other textures, which are not directly associated with ecclesial or Christian identity, also define this gathering. Such surfaces, interfaces, and vibrations involve the pleasures of eating, tasting, touching, smelling, and hearing that feel like Sacred Family. So how, we might ask, do these pleasures affect an understanding of liturgical time? How do they disrupt expectations for a time of worship and how do they transform it? What might the struggles of the people of God to share time reveal about the sensations required for a community of difference to flourish?

Discomfort and the Consent to Pleasure

A service of foot washing ends with a testimony to pleasure: *I enjoyed that!* A memory of a ritual creates a point of connection in a conversation. Its pleasure is juxtaposed with the story about Jesus's act of foot washing that is often interpreted through a feeling of discomfort as fleshly feet are exposed and touched by friends and strangers. In many churches, the ritual act assumes uneasiness, as the priest does at first when she writes a sermon on discomfort and vulnerability. Sacred Family already disrupts the assumptions she brings to the ritual by making the vulnerability of exposed feet, the exposure of bodies, a weekly activity.

The exposure of bodies is an ordinary rather than occasional part of human interaction at Sacred Family. By refusing to hide the realities of embodied experience, community members frequently voice or manifest their discomfort or distress. When I ask the question, "How are you?" my respondent might discuss vomiting, heartburn, fatigue, desire for food, frustration with a difficult roommate, or feelings of boredom or anger. Father Brian remarks on how such honesty makes being a priest at Sacred Family different from many other churches: "Vulnerability is just lying there on the surface. It is there in all other places, but [here] it isn't covered over by nice cars, nice clothes, the masks of affluence. There is very little to be had to mask the vulnerability. Not to say we just throw our arms open and willingly expose vulnerabilities, but there's little choice, no resources for masking."

The priest's comments echo a theme in many disability theologies, which emphasize that people with disabilities call Christians to an openness to human and divine vulnerability.[11] Yet regularizing vulnerability at Sacred Family does not remove discomfort from the fabric of community. To congregants' surprise, they are often less comfortable than they thought with the bodily differences of others (a discomfort that is shared in different ways by congregants across differences in ability, race, gender, and wealth). Some are uncomfortable with others' eating habits. They eat too much or too quickly. Some are uncomfortable when others move restlessly or stare at them or laugh during a time that feels especially reverent to others. Discomfort also comes when a communal intimacy elicits unexpected feelings. Andie describes the difficult process of coming from loneliness to the feeling of being desired by others in community: "It's not easy being in touch with all these feelings; they rub me, they rub me." The unfamiliar chafes; discomfort reveals the contours and textures of a circle of comfort.

Mother Daria, like the gospel writer she quotes in her sermon, assumes that it is God who works, probing and softening a circle of social consent on the level of bodily comfort, altering the textures and feelings of church life. Indeed, Sacred Family illustrates that individual and shared circles of comfort can be stretched out to include those we would not choose otherwise. Yet although discomfort powerfully reveals the bodily and religious assumptions that stigmatize some people, dividing them from others, it is often the feeling of pleasure that makes porous certain boundaries of discomfort that some feel in the presence of others. Pleasure softens the edges of dividing lines, by which one might shut out another. It disrupts assumptions about difference from within a shared circle of comfort as congregants navigate time with one another.

After all, Walter is not alone in his expression of enjoyment; many of us come to the service of foot washing anticipating pleasure. More generally, congregants from group homes come to Sacred Family seeking to fill their time with a few small pleasures. The pleasure of good meals and laughter and brightly colored fingernails and new-to-them clothes from the clothes closet and a cigarette or two before and after church and crossing social boundaries that exist outside the parish. Congregants exhibit pleasure at hearing their own voices sounding in the sanctuary: singing, offering commentary, queries, and prayers. Through these pleasures, the community chooses to share time with one another.

Christian theologians often speak of joy as a deeper relation to God, to others, and to oneself than the surface textures of pleasure. If pleasure is the immediate, superficial feeling promised by a consumer culture, joy connects the human person to a deeper stream of divine love, to the deep emotions and affections that help a person bear the suffering of any human cross. Yet at Sacred Family pleasure often appears far more attainable than joy, as pleasure affirms and roots a person, even for a brief time, to the goodness of one's own body and thus the possibility of embodied relationships with others. At Sacred Family, many congregants share their joy easily and freely with others, but others frequently appear anxious and lonely. Yet, even when joy eludes, a pleasure in the taste of food and in other sensory experiences serves as a vital texture within which a community gathers and seeks respite together.

Through many congregants who speak of loss—the loss of families, of homes, of respect, of a name other than mental illness, or of the familiar workings of their own minds—such expectations for pleasure can disrupt liturgical discourse that names pleasure as selfish, and sacrifice or selfless obligation to another as a virtuous way to give one's time to God. At Sacred Family, pleasure, rather than sacrifice, often softens the circles of social consent so that one finds a way to live with one's discomfort through another, to come again and again, back to the smell, the sound, and the taste that disturb for the pleasure of spending time with another. How this sense of pleasure accompanies discomfort, disrupting the aversion that differences also bring, is a strange reality of Sacred Family's assembly before God and with one another.

I am surprised, therefore, when a non-disabled member, a lay leader who works enthusiastically on behalf of this community, and professes her love for this congregation, confesses to me: "You know I'm doing this for me! I am selfish and self-centered; this isn't about me getting gold stars. It's about what I'm getting." She wants to be clear about the murkiness of her motivations. In her confession, I read an assumption that a sense of sacrificial obligation would be a better reason for being part of Sacred Family than her pleasure in participating in the community. When I press her, she admits she doesn't think anyone who comes here is sacrificing themselves, although many of the volunteers work very hard. Instead, she suggests, everyone comes because there is something pleasing to them about being a part of this gathering. Similarly, another Circle congregant Mariah declares to me when I describe writing for those outside the congregation: "Tell people we're good people. We love the Lord, and we eat all the time. Three times a day!"

Most congregants go forward during communion, a few bringing the wafer, the body of Christ, back to crunch on it in the pew. But the most eagerly anticipated meal happens after the service is over and the doors of the church open to fried chicken, lasagna, peanut butter and jelly sand-wiches, or hot dogs. Some congregants rush toward the priest at the open door as if this were a football game and the priest or deacon a quarterback. During the last hymn, some change seats to get into a better position near the doors; the benediction before the meal serves as a countdown for the meal to be had after the service. A priest or other staff sometimes show dismay at such blatant lack of restraint. The impropriety of such desire, the rush for the pleasure of the meal, brushes up against anticipations of those of us who associate liturgical texture with a measured reverence and care-fully moderated responses.

This emphasis on pleasure may periodically disrupt those who lead the congregation with great efficiency, keenly aware of the passing of chrono-logical time, as some congregants slow down a service to enjoy it more. Such theological textures become palpable and audible as some take their time to find a page, whispering to one another as they go, and as they take pleasure in their participation, slowing down the movement of a prayer or sermon toward its conclusion. Such textures are felt during the offering, as ushers with disabilities pause as long as it takes if anyone exhibits a desire to give. The ushers wait even if that person searches for what feels like a long time, trying in one pocket and then another for a few coins. The ushers appear unruffled even when the change clatters to the floor, scatters, and must be scooped up again, without evident shame or embarrassment.

Across differences, shared pleasures, expected and surprising, stretch the circles of comfort and discomfort: the pleasure of dropping change in the offering plate; the pleasure of dancing next to another person who is moving as awkwardly as you are; the pleasure of nurturing a plant in the garden; or the pleasure of making art side by side with another; the plea-sure of knowing all the words to the Lord's Prayer or of guessing the words a priest will say before she says them; or the odd pleasure of watching someone else enjoy their body, rapping the large ring on their finger against the chair in front of them all the way through the sermon, or humming throughout a Sunday School discussion. Many people allow their pleasures to center them rather than assuming that God expects a sacrificial relationship to those around them.[12] At times, such differences raise hard questions about how a community spends its time. To understand such tensions in the experience of time, I turn again to an analysis of the Maundy Thursday foot washing.

Different Senses of Liturgical Time

My friend and I arrive at the church early on Maundy Thursday and account for thirty unanticipated minutes. Ahead of time, we calculate the amount of time we need to spend at a service, anticipating a further point in time when we will rest from our ecclesial obligations. Once the service begins, the priest's elaborate instructions assume that if we are able to remember what we are supposed to do (a challenge for many in the congregation), we can perform this ritual capably and efficiently, without a risk of harm to ourselves and without slipping or sharing diseases in the dirty water.

Walter, with his own plan for washing feet, seems unaware of the potential risks of washing feet, or a future point in time when this ritual must be finished. He is not anxious about the other people waiting for their feet to be washed, nor about those who are waiting for communion. He does not appear concerned that there is a long half service before we all go home, and that this is Holy Week, which means there is another service on Friday and one on Saturday as well. Walter, like many Circle participants, assumes a sense of time that is both part of the texture of Sacred Family and that disrupts it.

Taking such time is assumed in the very way the community is assembled and the amount of time it takes to gather this group from the city. It begins on the way to the church as the vans pick up groups from different homes. This time of sitting next to other people, body next to body, in the back seat of a van is prelude and postlude for parish gatherings. There is much pleasure in these rides, but the time of waiting can be exhausting.

I recall a church time whose duration I could not bear. On the way back from a special weekend art event that we all enjoyed immensely, the art director drove around Atlanta for five hours, dropping off participants at their homes all over the city. Unaccustomed to this ritual, at the end of a full weekend, I found my own way home after two hours; I gave up on this extended postlude to a weekend of wonderful camaraderie. It felt impossible not to begrudge the slow feel of a time in the van I did not anticipate, and I had access to another ride. Others were also tired but had no choice than to wait their turn.

Relative newcomers to Sacred Family describe to me the challenges of unstructured time, the waiting time before and after services, the time without goals or agendas or tasks. Circle participants sometimes describe this time to me as "same ol', same ol'," highlighting the difficult repetition of days inside and outside Sacred Family. They want something new to happen, something to surprise them. But paradoxically, the surprises that come at Sacred Family involve slow time and repetition, the "same ol' same ol'" of waiting and sitting together that constitutes as much time as the actual service, as the meal, as the outing, or as the program activity.

The intersections of time with pleasure and discomfort hinge on the intersections of disability with poverty and unemployment. In order for loitering with intent[13] to be an ecclesial option, there must be congregants whose time is not scarce. There must be people who have time before a service to flip through a sketchbook with a friend or tell the tales of the Lone Ranger. Those who arrive by cars (sometime called "the ABCs") experience less of this time since they are able to arrive just as a service or event is beginning and to depart as soon as it is over, as long as they do not have church work to do. The resources and demands on their time make holy loitering difficult and, therefore, constrict their sense of church as a source of communal pleasure. Their time, like mine, is carefully measured out to make time for the many obligations and pleasures of busy lives.

But the feel of time at Sacred Family not only disrupts the ABCs, it also disrupts the day-to-day personal care home routines: the walk to the store for snacks and the hours of watching television. When I ask many of the Circle members why they come to the church, they talk about "something to do." The irony to newcomers from outside of the personal care system is that some of those who come to do something apparently do nothing. Circle participants sit side by side with other silent community members. They listen to others sing, watch others play bingo, and wait eagerly for meals to be given and for vans to come again and take them home. They work with time in a different way than those of us who live by points in time as a series of accomplishments. Both of these ways of feeling and passing time have their frustrations and pleasures, but one sense of time can feel disruptive to another.

For example, one morning I walk out of my home to go for a quick jog and then get a jump on the tasks of the day when through the early darkness, I make out a familiar shape and movement. It's Roy! He is knocking on my neighbor's door, to no avail. Roy often tells a story about being given a ticket for urinating in public, and I worry that he is in need again. I call to him. He crosses the street; he has been walking around the city this morning and needs a cup of coffee. He declines breakfast but sits for coffee with my husband and me. He looks at a travel guide we have on our coffee table. He tells us a funny story from the first time he visited Sacred Family. He tells us some very disturbing stories from his childhood. (Roy lived part of his life in an asylum, which he freely describes as a "living hell.") Roy doesn't worry that he might be making us late for work or interrupting the schedule for the day. He will not be offended if we have to go, but he assumes that we are happy to be there too. At the end of a cup of coffee, he asks for a ride to McDonald's, four blocks away, because he is tired from walking. My husband is late now for his bus, so we all get into the car. Roy has trouble climbing into our small car, and without any evident embarrassment, he asks my husband to help him get his feet in.

The assumptions Roy makes about time could be interpreted as a mark of social obliviousness on his part, but the practice of loitering with intent also requires that other people assume you have time for them. This encounter becomes an important memory that Roy and I share. He enjoys reminding me again and again of this pinprick in time, a measure of our knowledge of one another. Across the aisle in church, he calls my name, "Rebecca, remember that time I came to your house for coffee?" And I do, with pleasure.

One of the best illustrations of the way this assumption of time affects the community's liturgy takes place at noonday prayer. The shortest of prayer book services can feel too long for first-time visitors who become anxious that the Circle singers have lost their sense of time. I frequently observe a new intern's furrowed brow and anxious glances around the room as soloists sing on and on with no hymnbook to measure the verses. Accustomed to Sacred Family time, I am amused by their concern and want to assure them that such fear is unnecessary; no one at noonday prayer would jeopardize participation in the pleasure of the meal to follow.

One noonday, Rose and Kayla sing a duet. Standing in front of the altar, they invite Charles, to join them. "Come on up!" they gesture to him, insisting he belongs with them in the front because he is singing with such enthusiasm from his pew. As he rises to their call from the back of the sanctuary, it becomes apparent that he is using a walker and moves very, very slowly. There is a pause as we all look at him, and I wonder about the wisdom of the invitation. Then Rose improvises the liturgical time he needs, by changing up their song; she chooses another favorite song about walking, and they sing Charles up to the altar. After the original song is performed, Rose anticipates that Charles needs time to get to the back of the church before the prayer book prayer begins. Rose asks if he would like to walk back accompanied by the sequence hymn, which on Sundays accompanies the deacon's procession down the aisle to read the gospel. The small choir chooses another walking song, a spiritual, "I want Jesus to walk with me," as the man processes very slowly back to his seat. Creatively, Rose and Kayla work with the time that disability assumes. Drawing on repertoires of song learned in other church spaces, these two black women also draw on other liturgical sensibilities and styles that disrupt the white church time that is often given preference at Sacred Family. In the meantime, they live into the texture of pleasure, reveling in their chance to sing three songs rather than one during noonday prayer. Their act of making time for another is in no way sacrificial because it allows them to sing two more favorite numbers; nonetheless, it is generous in the grace with which they disregard any felt desires to hurry or postpone Charles' role.

This sense of time disrupts, in part, because it finds itself in tension with other textures of time also present. The longer Wednesday and Sunday services move quickly when employed congregants take the lead. These employed members have a different aesthetic of time that corresponds to the scarcity of time and to a more able-minded efficiency. Such an approach to time is one with which I usually approach the work of going to church or planning liturgy. While Circle participants are not more virtuous and patient than others, their approaches to time, shaped in part by different relationships to work and to church, alter the feel of a communal gathering. Such different senses of time raise the questions: What does it mean to do the work of the church together? What counts as work in God's time?

Responsibility and a Sense of Work

My friend Jude comes from a full day of compensated work to our service of foot washing. He comes from a job that doesn't dirty his feet. By contrast, Walter comes to the service from a life where he does not have financially compensated work to an event that he has likely been anticipating all day. He comes from a world where feet are often in need of care. In the weekly foot clinic, nursing students volunteer to do the work of cutting nails, applying lotion to feet, and painting the nails with bright colors. Here, during this special service, Walter scrubs with vigor as if he were giving a pedicure.

When I ask Circle members, "What did you do today?" they will often say to me, "Oh, I went to Sacred Family" or "I went to school" (by which they mean another day program). Although no attendance is taken and no penalty given for missing a day or a week or a month (except perhaps losing a space on the van for a period of time if another wants the spot), the director tells me that some Circle participants will call to tell him they will miss a day. Some, like Kayla, lament this fact. Why does she have to get sick on a day when she is expected to be at Sacred Family? She describes her activities at the art program as a vocation: "I think I am cut out for art . . . I tried other jobs but none of them worked out . . . God speaks to me through art." By showing up for the weeklong liturgy of services and programs, Kayla and others work at the task of occupying the church, filling it with the pleasures and discomforts of noise and friendship and silence and art, even if not many are doing anything anyone would call "work."

Such unconventional work reveals that conventional forms of employment both sustain and disrupt the shared time of a community of difference. Many Sunday-only congregants work at daily jobs and help to keep the church doors open by supplying much needed financial resources. The church would not survive without this paid work, and church leaders desire more employed members to sustain the church's budget. Sunday congregants also perform the more conventional work of serving on committees, supplying food for potlucks and other meals, and organizing special events. This hard work is not always pleasurable, although congregants generally approach these responsibilities with good cheer. Occasionally, abled Sunday members feel tired of the fact that they have to do all of the work of the church because other congregants are able to do so little. One lay leader thinks maybe she and others who perform most of the tasks of the church should be "asking people to do more [not only] in the service but serving meals and also picking up and cleaning up. Why aren't people held more responsible? I sometimes think that we're enabling, and we're not expecting much."

Circle participants could be entrusted with more work of the church, both liturgical leadership and also more logistical tasks. But sharing responsibility for such work would slow time at Sacred Family in ways that also disrupt efficient patterns of church gathering. Some congregants enjoy helping with the tasks of church life, but this takes more of everyone's time: some of us move and think more slowly than others; some aren't as consistent as others. A committee meeting might take longer if someone who uses a different logic weighs in on church decisions. Sharing responsibility is also affected by the van schedule since those who ride the vans are not in charge of their own time. Entrusting responsibility makes more work for a small congregation. As one who carefully measures out time and covets each hour, I empathize with a fear that sharing the responsibilities of work increases church work, even as I agree with congregants that such changes are desperately needed. Many staff articulate a desire for more representation and shared responsibility in the tasks of community life, and I observe an increase in shared responsibility and lay leadership over my research time; but such changes happen slowly. Questions of representation in leadership remain a theological challenge to Sacred Family's life together as it claims the dignity of every human person as God's claim upon the church. Like many churches, this parish struggles to imagine and to honor that dignity through the kind of time, and thus the amount of work, required for shared leadership, particularly in a church with limited financial resources.

At the same time, Sunday-only members rarely spend time at the Circle because of their jobs. Many of them do not attend Wednesday services, which begin right after a long day of work and in the midst of rush hour traffic. Thus, the liturgical work of the week falls to staff and to Circle participants. Ostensibly, Circle participants come for programs, food, and clothes from the clothing closet. They benefit from services they did not plan in a space provided for them. As such, they are recipients of charity. And yet, without the presence of people who have time to gather during the week without getting paid for it, the liturgy of Sacred Family could not take the theological shape it does. The people who receive the most from the work of others also perform the work without which this congregation could not worship God the way it does. Such a sense of work, of those who come to the church to take time for pleasure, disrupts an understanding of the church's mission as accomplishing charitable work for the mentally ill and of liturgical time as accomplishing something important for God.

For example, on a tour with a potential donor, I note this visitor's discomfort upon catching sight of a group of Circle smokers enjoying cigarettes during program hours. This wealthy woman from another congregation interrogates the tour guide, a lay leader in the church. What is this group of people doing? The Sacred Family guide assures her that these folks are just participating in the smoking social circle now, but that they also participate in other programs. You can't ride the vans without doing something. The guide quickly assesses that this woman, whose money is needed for the work of the church, desires solid evidence that the church is working to help people with mental illness, a fact not evident to the visitor in a group of idle smokers.

Yet, one of the nurses at the church offers a different view: "The most wonderful unique thing is that people don't have to have a goal; they can just come. That would be my story: you don't have to produce a product, you just come." She contrasts the work of a church from other kinds of programs for those with mental illness: "It validates that people are people, that they have rights and that they are loved because they're human beings, and that they're not being evaluated all the time. Yes, in society we do it [evaluate], but if you live with mental illness, people are objectively doing it all the time, so this [is] the least judgmental place I've been." For the nurse, this possibility exists because it is a church:

The whole God thing is what makes it special. People come here, and they say everybody is made by God, and everybody is loved by God, no more no less, and if that's my premise, then my definition of friendship isn't as narrow. I do think it's a faith thing. I do. I do think you see God in everybody and that's where I come from and that is what I try to teach students. . . . I think that it has changed the way they take care of people, wherever they work; it doesn't necessarily change that they are going to come here and volunteer. (That's my big goal. They're all new in their careers and paying back debts.) That's my premise. We're all more human than otherwise.

The nurse worries about what might be lost if this sense of the church's work ever changed: if Circle participants were expected to produce measurable outcomes from their time at Sacred Family, or if a priest stopped understanding conservation of and participation in joy as the heart of ecclesial work. She wishes that the staff were able to stop worrying about running out of money for this work. She wishes the broader church would believe in this work and freely give.

The director of the Circle hopes that one day some unemployed congregants may no longer be able to do the work of Sacred Family because they will have paid work. He wants them to recover so that Sacred Family is no longer at the center of their daily activities and so that they can have meaningful lives outside the congregation and Circle. But the reality is that many congregants cannot obtain paid work. They struggle even within the church to validate a life of poverty without regular employment. At the same time, by virtue of not working at conventional jobs, congregants with psychiatric disabilities gather and share the pleasures at the heart of Sacred Family's liturgical life and holy work.

A former member, now serving in another parish, writes about the strange shape of Sacred Family's life before God, recalling how it hearkens back to the work of monastic communities, albeit in a different way:

The communion of the saints at the Church of the [Sacred Family] consists of all those people who have, by twists of fate or acts of providence, been thrown together into the eccentric church-house on [this] Avenue, and who are gradually discovering, through the sustained practice of praying, working, and eating together, the presence of Christ in their midst. It is not a communion of personal preferences or liturgical tastes, theological like-mindedness or invisible cohesion; it is rather a communion of those who have been offered and who have accepted in the midst of their winding pilgrimages a real place of respite to eat and pray with fellow travelers.

And in this way, the Church of the [Sacred Family] seems, somewhat ironically, like a parish lingering contentedly on the fringes of Christendom. Its members come because it is close and because it is there—simply because it leaves its doors unlocked and provides structure to the passage of time. They come without much autonomy and without great expectations. And by doing so they have formed a community whose dedication to the mundane movements of grace is both obsolete and visionary.

The challenge of such an "obsolete and visionary" mode of church draws attention to a different sense of work, work that disrupts certain anticipations of liturgical time as a sacrifice for God. It accounts for the pleasures of a group that gathers, assuming the time to do so even though many of them will only be at Sacred Family for a short time.

The Work of the Church and the Distribution of Resources

A struggle to value the work of those who do not have jobs nor accomplish objective goals for the congregation reveals how the texture of pleasure disrupts Christian liturgical time in which feelings of work and pleasure are often divided. How then to acknowledge the work of pleasure without disregarding the real divisions and power differentials that exist, when some have compensated work and some live in poverty on meager disability incomes? How to value such idle work without making invisible the power structures and real inequalities that arise from the fact that some congregants will never have paying jobs and that some take on more responsibility for others, particularly as these dividing lines often fall along power lines of disability, wealth, and race?

These tensions are highlighted one day when I run into Margo in the hallway. She stands in front of the bulletin board and points to a large poster of smiling children with the words, "Outreach Ministry Supporting Orphans in Kenya." I recognize these children as ones that Sacred Family prays for every Sunday. "Those are my friends," she explains. I ask why they are her friends. "I love kids no matter where they are in the world. Kids have helped me out." And after a pause, "I ain't got no kids. I look up to the Lord. You know why I look up to him? He knows how to handle things. That's why the Lord knows. He puts people in your way." She repeats that she doesn't have kids, but that God has a plan. God knows.

Margo moves quickly from talking about God's plans for her to talking about the current priest's plans to leave the congregation and how that might affect her life. The priest before this one would give out money. Now this priest doesn't give money. Maybe the next priest will be a nice man. "He'll be a good man, but I know people are going to ask him for money." She seems upset that the current priest, a beloved figure in the congregation, doesn't give out money for cigarettes, but she also feels conflicted about her own desire for help. She wants to know if I agree that people should not come here begging for money. "You're supposed to take care of that yourself!" she says, playing out the logic of why not to beg at church. "What would you do?"

"I don't know," I try to imagine her position. "I don't know what I would do if I didn't have money. I would probably ask for help." I also don't know what I would do if I were the priest; it's hard to imagine giving out money for more cigarettes to everyone who asks.

"He [the priest] pretty much puts his foot down," she concludes. "Cigarettes and money are problems!" She tries to figure out where I stand on these questions of church and the distribution of money for cigarettes or other goods. "You don't agree with it?"

As we stand there, negotiating the power to give and withhold money within the church, contemplating the vast wealth disparities that make such an inherently troubled negotiation necessary, we stare at the posters on the bulletin board of the smiling orphans in Kenya. Margo moves to the subject of the upcoming presidential election, now wrestling with another set of authority figures. She is still concerned with the persistent problem of money and the conditions for trust: "If the Democrats get elected, they are going to cut Social Security, Medicare, Medicaid. They think everyone should work, but some of us can't work. We have mental illness, and we can't work. I'm gonna vote for Hillary Clinton. She'll take care of us." I ask her if she means Republicans instead of Democrats since Hillary Clinton is a Democrat. Margo agrees, but she seems far less concerned about a clear distinction between political parties than that there be a politician with the power to affect change who understands her inability to hold a paying job.

Margo can do the work of prayer and holy play if praying entails standing before the poster of the children of the church's charitable intentions, in order to regard their faces and greet them as friends. At least during this period in her life, she is able to show up and do this brief task, taking a break from the anger she also describes feeling toward people and situations in her life. But the shape of her current devotion sometimes makes her feel that she is at the mercy of those who decide her fate in big and small ways: the God who may or may not give her children, the priest who might turn away her request for cigarettes, and the political authorities who might think she could work when she cannot. Margo's struggles reveal the way that wealth disparities affect the very heart of the church's work and its struggle to be a place where congregants are able to trust one another. The value of compensated work outside the church deeply affects the church's own textures of time, pleasure, and holy work.

When Father Brian describes what makes it hard to be a priest at Sacred Family, he identifies socioeconomic differences as the biggest challenge to becoming a church and refers to his own wealth: "I have found it hard to be a priest here living with my own affluence in the presence of all the poverty, trying to sort that out, and I'm still trying to sort all that out because I haven't abandoned my affluence." Likewise, Lloyd describes the importance of worshipping God with other "people who don't have much money like I do; my mental illness is not very, very severe but as far as being poor, I'm poor. Sometimes it's hard to go to wealthy churches, see what they have, but then having a lot of money had never been important for me, but I'd like to have enough to live off." The challenge of valuing the work of the unemployed is that this work is not valued more broadly and often fails to resonate in ways that are essential for a community seeking relationships of mutuality rather than ones built, theologically and communally, on patriarchy, paternalism, or ableism. If one's time is not marketable, can God be trusted to provide for the future? Can the church and its leaders? Can the government? These questions are intertwined in Margo's mind as strands that affect her feelings of hope, trust, frustration, and shame as part of this community.

The subtle repetitions of Sacred Family that emerge through slow time create alternate senses of work. Such textures divide and unfold liturgical spaces and make possible the art forms through which a community of difference assembles. At the same time, these forms of liturgical time feel strange and disorienting within larger social and ecclesial contexts. The productivity of paid workers, as well as the charitable sacrifices of individual Christians with the means to give money, create rival senses of work. If Sacred Family is a way to rehabilitate or occupy the time of those judged "not feasible, unemployable, with a questionable quality of life,"[14] such holy work is easier to sell to donors. Whose work and what kinds of relationships to time ensure the survival of a church for whom time is also the currency needed to provide the basic pleasures the church offers?

Making Time for Communal Pleasure
as the Work of the People

Christian liturgy invites our participation in symbolic time.[15] Liturgy is sometimes evoked as the work of/for the people, hearkening back to a set of meanings contained in the word's origin, *leitourgía*.[16] If liturgy is the public service of people who consent to share space, form, and time together with and through God, such work involves entering an abnormal relationship to a linear sense of time. Again and again in liturgical time, Jesus is born, teaches and performs miracles, is betrayed and executed, rises, ascends, and sends the Spirit to comfort and advocate for a church trying to find its way through Ordinary Time.[17] And then the church waits for Jesus's coming again: both as a child and as the one who comes in judgment at the end of time. Saliers describes this strange circle of sacred time when he writes, "Christians mark the beginning of liturgical time by recalling the end of time. But beginning by remembering means that something has gone before: a witness, an intersection of images, a promise."[18] Such circling of liturgical time, like the layered collages of Mary Button's stations of the cross, produces liturgical textures as a way to feel the church's time together (the anticipation of Advent, the jubilance of Easter triumph). The liturgy is designed to feel, touch, taste, and sound differently at various points in the service or liturgical year, but it also anticipates a feeling that will come later or earlier in another liturgical season.

Such textures may invite resonance between an individual life and liturgical time, as happens when Wallace sees a Jesus who gets tired, takes a break, gives up, and gets ready to go again. At the same time, liturgical time is often at odds with the way that mental illness or any human experience disrupts a liturgical season. Button writes of this when she describes the difficulty of attending church when she is depressed:

> For me, the most horrifying aspect of my depression is the feeling of separation from Christ that it leaves in its wake. When I feel this way, going to church only makes the feeling of separation that much more painful. I worry that my depression is an offense to God, that my inability to pull myself out of my pity means that God hates me. I open my mouth to sing hymns of praise and the words turn to ash in my mouth. This isn't to say that churches should never sing praise hymns, that caring for those of us who live with chronic mental illness means to dwell in the darkness. Rather, we should live out the Scriptural understanding that there is time enough under heaven to tear and to mend.[19]

The textures of her individual experience are often at odds with what liturgical time invites her to feel. Yet, they also manifest her hope for enough time for people with mental illness within Christian practices of keeping time.

At Sacred Family, the disruption of disability often comes from the texture of a communal life pressing against liturgical time, as when the routine pleasures of Sacred Family's life together feel at odds with the penitential or sorrowful feel of Lent and Holy Week, or when the exhausted bodies of worshippers challenge the claims of Easter triumph. Such varied moments of aesthetic disruption create a gap for theological reflection: Is God requiring continued sacrifice and the dismantling of pride from people who live in situations of deprivation and stigma? Has Easter triumph come to those who live in poverty? In such cases, the experiences of some at Sacred Family disrupt liturgical language that feels inadequate to the lives of many who gather. For example, during another foot washing service a year later, a different priest speaks about Simon Peter and God's desire for us to give up our pride. "Are you okay?" Wallace whispers to me, apparently noticing the way I shift nervously in my seat. I am visibly disturbed by a sermon that asks this particular congregation to give up their pride and ask for help. In contrast, Wallace affirms the sermon with a refrain he reserves for a compelling delivery: "That's deep!" I can feel his enjoyment over the resounding conviction with which the preacher sounds her message. He does not look ashamed or remorseful. The sermon is "deep," but he does not feel compelled to wash feet as an antidote to pride. He appears to feel the sermon in a different way than I do, not as a set of ideas about God's demands but about the emphatic tone of a sermon as a point of connection between himself and the preacher, who preaches in a manner he relishes. The sermon is an aural experience as much as a set of assertions to be affirmed or denied.

Liturgy, Eschatology, and Crip Time

Christian liturgical time, circular in its movements, often anticipates an inbreaking of future time: "The realized eschatology embedded in the liturgical action of the community at prayer in Jesus' name is not simply a recall of the 'fact' of a resurrection in the past. Rather it bespeaks and enacts the impossible possibility of the future becoming present."[20] Disability scholars remind us that such impossible possibility is often evoked in Christian churches through the symbols of disabled bodies. Even in Sacred Family's liturgy, the blind, the lame, and the chronically ill appear in texts as those whose bodily transformation marks a future time when sorrows will cease, a time that is impossible to imagine fully. One of the Circle participants, Kayla, frequently evokes this eschatological time during noonday prayer when she fervently prays that God would "find a cure for all diseases."

The circular pattern of liturgical time, which waits for and assumes eschatological time, often coincides with what feminist, queer, crip scholar Alison Kafer identifies as "curative time," a time that cannot imagine hope other than through intervention. In "a curative imaginary," disability stands in the way of a linear narrative of human progress, a symbolic obstacle to what the human race might one day become.[21] The "ideology of cure," as disability poet, essayist, and activist Eli Clare describes it, rests on a number of tenets. First, cure identifies harm with an individual body-mind and seeks restoration within the individual rather than within relational/political ecosystems. Second, cure assumes an origin that is better than the present. And third, cure assumes that an individual can return to that origin. If for many people an "original nondisabled state" does not exist, cure marks the body that should be or could have been, devaluing the person that is now.[22]

Kafer identifies a set of questions that reduce a person's experience of time to a "curative temporality": "Were you born that way? How much longer do you have to live this way? How long before they invent a cure? How long will a cure take? How soon before you recover?"[23] In Kafer's view, the harm is not that Kayla prays for a cure for all diseases, but that future hope, as essentially curative, reduces the possibilities of the present time.

Kafer contrasts "curative time" with "crip time" as she queries an assumption that there is time to find a cure but no time for disability accommodation and improvisation:

> Crip time is flex time not just expanded but exploded; it requires reimagining our notions of what can and should happen in time, or recognizing how expectations of "how long things take" are based on very particular minds and bodies. We can then understand the flexibility of crip time as being not only an accommodation to those who need "more" time but also, and perhaps especially, a challenge to normative and normalizing expectations of pace and scheduling. Rather than bend disabled bodies and minds to meet the clock, crip time bends the clock to meet disabled bodies and minds.[24]

She imagines crip time as bending time toward the textures of human life to create more time for disability so that all of us imagine more generous ways of inhabiting time.

Kafer's description of crip time reveals how assumptions about clock time affect the ways many of us construe good work. If work involves a measure of efficiency by which we know how much can be accomplished in a given amount of time, then crip time at Sacred Family also serves as a disruption to the clear boundaries between work time and leisure time as well as a disruption to the feelings that paid work continually presses upon the worker with all that needs to be done.

A close examination of the texture of time at Sacred Family reveals that if there is a felt sense of the in-breaking or bending of time, where minutes and days are not captive to a feeling of either scarcity or anxiety, it comes from turning back to the immediacy of the material pleasures of taste and touch and sound, the rocking of one's body back and forth in the pew, whatever feeling soothes or quiets a troubled or busy mind and enables one's being there with others in the first place. Time at Sacred Family is frequently exhausting and also precious; this is evident whenever I witness the ways that congregants celebrate and insist on bodily pleasures. Such insistence turns the symbols of the hungry and the poor and the destitute of liturgical discourse back to the experiences of the bodies who have known hunger, illness, racism, and poverty, sometimes disrupting a focus on the symbols themselves (the wafer, the splash of water) by pointing them to the sacred feelings of eating and scrubbing.[25] Even the foot of the cross becomes a place where Wallace and others imagine lying down and taking a nap, a symbolic space and narrative imagined in literal terms as time enough for respite on a long, hard journey.

The demand for pleasure at Sacred Family through the liturgical lens of Lent could be interpreted as a childish narcissism facilitated by a lack of discipline or mental illness. But communal pleasures at Sacred Family, while particular to each person, are not usually a turn away from a neighbor; for when congregants consent to enjoy the material world with others at Sacred Family, they do not turn away from another but root their bodies into a shared space with others. In this context, turning to one's own pleasures is also a turn to life with others.

The invitational mercy of this kind of work is harder for those of us who tend to divide work from pleasure and who feel church time as an obligation eased by finding church people with similar financial resources to share private pleasures. To understand the church not only as a place of service for others or of growth within oneself, but also as a site of shared communal pleasure requires a different sense of time and work and a different imagination of past and future deprivation. Bieler and Schottroff remind us that: "Practicing eschatological hope is an act of imagination . . .

a sensual embodied activity and a sociopolitical practice. Imagination makes accessible to our minds an idea, a concept, an image, or a symbol as well as body knowledge, and a felt sense of something that would otherwise not be available to us."[26] Such imagination is an "artful practice of disruptive perception" which is "grounded in a practice of anamnestic empathy."[27] To imagine the hungry as present symbolically at an imagined eschatological meal, and to celebrate with those who know hunger and turn eagerly toward a non-symbolic meal are different feelings of God's presence and absence in the world. One of the greatest challenges of Sacred Family is to imagine the in-breaking of ample time to share both the responsibility for work and the time for pleasure that such a community of difference requires. In order for this to be possible, Sacred Family imagines that more employed people desire to stop and share communal pleasures with those who are unemployed, thus multiplying the time there is to bend and share among the faithful.

If liturgical time is not measured through an ability to grasp a set of ideas about God, or to accomplish a set of liturgical practices, but is grounded in the possibility and gift of human lives woven together through God, then liturgy requires ample time for those who gather to trust one another creatively with their time. The artistries of social interaction assume time for this creativity to emerge. The possibility of such relationships might require those who gather before God to inhabit time differently together. By claiming crip time as eschatological time—a sense of divine time that holds and disrupts carefully or anxiously measured time—congregants might sense the pleasures of the kinds of time required for human difference and community. Crip time reminds a community of their memory of a future not defined by the profits of paid work. Such "end times" are held and given by the One who turns back human time to the feelings of promise and pleasure. Thus, a weeklong liturgy anticipates enough time to love and know ourselves and others and to name the God with whom we share the beauty of the world.

A gardener and a volunteer wash seed starter pots. (Photo credit: Cindy M. Brown)

CHAPTER 4

Naming: Aesthetics of Healing and Claiming

Give me the names for things, just give me their real names,
Not what we call them, but what
They call themselves when no one's listening—
At midnight, the moon-plated hemlocks like unstruck bells,
God wandering aimlessly elsewhere.
Their names, their secret names.
— Charles Wright, "The Writing Life"[1]

How do we know ourselves without knowing God? How can we love God without knowing God? But then how can we know what we do not love? Names for God propel a desire to know more about the one who is named and yet also reveal the inadequacy of human language for God. The act of naming both signifies the limits of knowledge and arouses desire for relationship with the divine. Christian theologians puzzle over this conundrum of the relationship between love and knowledge at the center of human/ divine relationships.

In prior chapters, I have explored the relationships to liturgical space, form, and time that create vital conditions for a diverse group of people to gather and consent to a weeklong liturgy together. In this chapter, I investigate another aspect of a communal liturgy that honors human difference: the arts of naming human and divine relationships, particularly as these relate to the needs and desires that congregants share with one another. I begin with an exploration of names for human lives manifest at Sacred Family rather than with the naming of God. I describe how arts of naming both fail and flourish within rituals of healing, health care, and friendship as each of these parts of Sacred Family's liturgy elicit visions of a good human life. Each set of rituals reveals not only the limits of different kinds of language used at Sacred Family but also the desire for better names. The dissonance or resonance of names with persons who are known and loved through them are key to a theological aesthetics of a community of difference: the way it feels to share and create relationships across mental differences and power asymmetries. I conclude by arguing that the struggle to name another adequately at Sacred Family is essential to Sacred Family's love and knowledge of God.

Identifying Persons, Defining Mental Illness

I have been describing an unusual church whose congregants live with and without diagnoses of mental illness, but I have not defined these illnesses. This omission is intentional; it represents the actual experience of Sacred Family, a community where people are not known by their particular diagnoses and who seldom represent their lives as unusual. Mental illness thus marks this nonconventional community, but it does not define it. It is ever-present and yet elusive as community members live with psychiatric disability, each person manifesting that experience differently.

As I attend to manifestations of mental health and mental illness at Sacred Family, I have used a disability studies approach to neurodiversity. Assuming the theoretical and activist premise that "minds are best understood in terms of variety and difference rather than deviations from an imagined norm"[2] productively complicates the work of naming mental illness. Disability scholar Margaret Price enumerates this challenge by listing terms used to describe mental disability:

> Who am I talking about? So far I've used a variety of terms to denote impairments of the mind, and I haven't yet exhausted the list. Contemporary language available includes *psychiatric disability, mental illness, cognitive disability, intellectual disability, mental health service user (or consumer), neurodiversity, neuroatypical, psychiatric system survivor, crazy,* and *mad.*[3]

In response to this avalanche of terms, Price advocates for an ethic of identification that negotiates the need for solidarity and diversity: "Although I use *mental disability* as my own term of choice, I continue to use others as needed, and my overall argument is for deployment of language in a way that operates as inclusively as possible, inviting coalition, while also attending to the specific texture of individual experiences."[4] While my own terms of choice differ from that of Price, for reasons I lay out in my introduction,

Price helpfully articulates the work of good names, ones that facilitate coalition and community without reducing individual experiences.

Price reminds us that naming, as a culturally dynamic process, is always value laden. Claiming an identity can allow persons to build coalitions across remarkably diverse human experiences, but in the case of mental disability, as Price notes, common terms "have explicitly foreclosed our status *as* persons."[5] Most names that designate categories of people have a preferred corollary. Mental illness, for example, "introduces a discourse of wellness/unwellness into the notion of madness; its complement is *mental health*, the term of choice for the medical community as well as insurance companies and social support services."[6] Such terms, even when helpful to individuals and those caring for them, affect the lived texture of individual experience and the resources available or denied as social supports. To invoke one's status as a person while also claiming the resources one needs for survival can be a struggle.[7] The patterns of identification we use for ourselves and others evoke and require a response; names establish relationships. They frame our needs and desires. Using one framework, one name, might establish access to vital medical and social supports and, on the other hand, obscure important aspects of neurodiversity, mental disability, and humanity.

Psychological anthropologist Tanya Luhrmann also writes of the power of a name when she describes the two different approaches, biomedical and psychodynamic, that are often used to interpret and respond to mental illness in North American cultures.[8] As she analyzes different "moral instincts" that each approach fosters, she posits that "psychiatry is inevitably entangled with our deepest moral concerns: what makes a person human, what it means to suffer, what it means to be a good and caring person."[9] Such moral concerns affect not only those who receive diagnoses but also those involved in diagnosing illness and administering treatment:

> One of the oldest ideas in human thought is that when you name something mysterious and out of control, you gain mastery over it. In magic and religion in cultures throughout history, to know the name for a tree or a person or a malicious spirit was to grasp its essence and so control it (unless you were too weak or impure, in which case uttering the sacred name might kill you). In medicine, of course, diagnosis gives a doctor control because it tells him how he might be able to help a patient. But something of the old magical echoes linger. To produce a name makes you feel that you have begun to master the reality of the problem and that there is, in fact, something there to master.[10]

Luhrmann argues for the reality of madness and for taking seriously the suffering it causes many people[11] but also suggests that no name, medical or otherwise, is finally adequate to the complex reality it seeks to reflect. She reminds us that mental illnesses are not isolatable phenomena in a body-mind but a cluster of diverse symptoms, feelings, and behaviors that are given common names.[12]

The naming of psychiatric disability involves an individual person's embodied experiences; it also figures a set of relationships that are foreclosed or become possible through the patterns of identification brought to bear. Thus, in a community like Sacred Family, I encounter congregants who insist on the importance of using "people first" language—people with disabilities or people with mental illness—so that the person might not disappear under the mantel of an illness or disability negatively associated with them. Distancing their person from their illness gestures toward the multifaceted nature of their being, one that is never fully captured by their diagnosis. A divergent approach, one equally concerned with human dignity, emphasizes the explicit claiming of language such as disabled or mad. This occupation recreates meanings associated with disability and madness, in turn creating activist coalitions. Such an approach is wary of the dualisms that imagine people apart from vital aspects of the body-mind with which they inhabit the world and express their needs and desires. Rather than distancing oneself from a disability, one claims its centrality in experiencing the world and relationships, even when such experiences depart from certain ideals of health and well-being.

Sacred Family, like other churches and communities, struggles for good names and body practices that attend to congregants' losses, desires, and dignity without also erasing particular aspects of mental disability. How to name disability difference, attending to the coalition it creates and the ableism with which it must contend while also fostering desires for solidarity implicit in a community of difference? How to respond to individual textures of loss and suffering that congregants experience without regarding another congregant as a pitiable thing, as one whose life I am fortunate that I do not have? For inherent in a name is a relationship. Who are you to me? Who am I with you? How am I to call you? How are we to speak about some of us?

Such forms of address are always multiple. There are proper names, such as birth names or surnames or nicknames. Miriam. Mr. Cornelius. Brian. These names become aligned with a second form of naming as roles and attributions accumulate. Brian is the vicar, so he becomes Father Brian. And Father Brian is a good preacher. Miriam is a kitchen helper and a Scripture reader. Moving out from the individual to identifying groups of people, names serve to distinguish some groups of people from others. Miriam helps in the kitchen without being called a volunteer because she is also a Circle participant. Kirby is not only an artist. He is an artist with mental illness and a group home resident. Neil is a staff person with mental illness, an ABC (arrives by car), is married, and is a homeowner.

Finally, there is also a naming that arises when one congregant asks another for help or names their struggles or desires before God and community. To intercede for ourselves or others requires a set of names adequate to those described in our petitions. In asking for another's help, Sacred Family congregants rarely represent their lives as tragic, but the reality of loss lingers and leaves a motif of grief that alters the tone of community and elicits a desire for communal response to the needs of those who gather.

If Sacred Family's art forms hold and weave community together, they must also address the beauty of each congregant's life as well as the losses and the sorrows that congregants name. The desire to name one's own life or experiences adequately, to offer those to another, is part of the work of the people at Sacred Family. At the same time, receiving care requires certain conditions and forms of address, adequate names that facilitate trust rather than objectify members of the community. Such a complex task incorporates and assumes these various forms of naming and misnaming as well as the limits of any one name. The struggle to find precise yet expansive names that resonate with those whom they identify demonstrates a liturgical imperative: the quest for better names.

Between Life and Death: The Struggle to Name an Experience of Mental Illness

I begin with an elusive conversation that illustrates one woman's struggle to name her own experience and identify the meanings of both her intense suffering and her love for her life. On an April morning in the Easter season during my second year at Sacred Family, Miriam and I sit together on a picnic bench. Everywhere the churchyard is in bloom. The gardeners are weeding and watering. Miriam tells me she was a mess when she first came to the church. She wasn't sure what she was living for. She feels that she is being cared for here. She gestures to the left side of her body. I imitate the gesture, as an inquiry, wondering if she means it to specify something. She repeats the gesture, touching her side this time, to show me.

"I don't feel a lot, but I feel it right here along the side. It didn't take a lot. I thought it would, but it didn't. I don't know what it took, but it happened. I hope I don't lose it. It's special but not that special."

"What makes you feel taken care of?"

"The people on the job; they talk to you, and they don't just throw you away."

"It's a way of being talked to?"

She nods, "Then I look for my death. I keep seeing Rev. Jess bury me in the cemetery." She has tears in her eyes.

"Did you tell her that?" I am concerned and want her to share her burden with the priest.

"I'm afraid it would be too heavy for her." She goes on to explain, "It worries me: not to die—death doesn't worry me—it's like a nagging toothache, death and life, death and life."

"It's like feeling between them?" I am trying to understand.

"Yeah, it's taking me one way or another. I can't get any more emotions in. I hope I can get it together."

I observe her as a peaceful presence at Sacred Family and am always impressed with what she brings to the community through her kindness. She looks surprised when I tell her this, but then she nods. She makes a comment about giving back. I assume she is talking about giving back to a community that cares for her, but actually she has another meaning in mind.

"Give back to the Lord and let the Lord do what he wants to do. Sometimes it don't turn out the way you think it should. I don't know why [the Lord] had to work [in my life this way]."

She describes her own physical abilities and limitations. She takes one or two steps and then sometimes she can't move. She attributes this to God. "I walked around the building once but then [God] won't let me go again." And later, "My psychologist calls it stress. He sees it all over me."

"What does he tell you to do?"

"He wants me to walk, to exercise."

A week later, we return to this topic of living between life and death. This time Miriam emphasizes life rather than death. "You have to be grateful for life because life is given to you, given to all of us."

"No matter how hard it is?"

"No matter how hard it is. We should appreciate it, and somehow put our arms around it, or put your arms around yourself and just be thankful."

"How do you embrace life?"

Miriam wraps her arms around her body, reaching as far as she can in a partial embrace. "You can't get it all the way around there; you wish you could, but you can't. Hug life, and love life."

When Miriam describes her condition as "between life and death," she describes an embodied experience rather than a single word for her condition. She stresses the importance of those who address her and recognize her life rather than "throwing her away." She refers to multiple powers involved in naming her experiences of her life: the Lord, a psychologist, a priest, and staff members. In other conversations, she refers to housemates, fellow congregants, and family members. Each one plays a part in determining the experiences that congregants like Miriam offer to or withhold from one another. Each offers a different set of names to help Miriam interpret her sorrow and her desire.

Multiple Frameworks for Naming Mental Illness at Sacred Family

Like Miriam, Sacred Family as a community is an interstitial space that holds multiple frameworks for interpreting the losses and desires of congregants. Sacred Family congregants often describe their community through the general category of mental illness or mental health challenge or mental health disorder. At the same time, specific diagnoses are rarely given or known in regards to each individual congregant. Within a medical framework, staff and congregants often interpret themselves and one another through the lens of medications. Certain behaviors may be attributed to a change in medications; if someone is acting in a way that is unusual for them, others might wonder if they quit or changed medications. Frequently in and out of hospitals, some congregants compare hospitals and medical care as others compare restaurants or grocery stores, evaluating the treatment they receive and the quality of food they get at each place. In addition to mental illness, many parishioners suffer from other serious health conditions. Most congregants assume the importance of regular medical assistance and treatment in navigating day-to-day lives even as they often fail to receive the medical attention and recognition they require.

Sacred Family also names needs and desires through a recovery framework, even when that term is understood in different ways. If Aisha refers to recovery from mental illness as doing things that people without mental illness don't think you can do, another congregant talks about his recovery as learning not to do things that are harmful to himself. When congregants offer a recovery story, they often narrate a transformation in lives and relationships as they learn to name and live with a mental health diagnosis. Naming and understanding one's mental illness is pivotal to such a narrative of transformation. Recovery language connects Sacred Family to other day programs that many Circle participants attend on days when they are not at Sacred Family. Although other programs are often referred to as school whereas Sacred Family is the church, implying the different roles these institutions play in congregants' lives, the church, like other kinds of mental health programs, is understood to offer a kind of therapy through its programs.

Mason describes Sacred Family as therapeutic when he tells me his story. He began coming to the church after he experienced some "issues with [his] mental health" and lost an apartment that he had lived in for more than ten years. He moved in with his family, and they recommended that he come to the church because they knew it had mental health programs. Now he participates in all that the church has to offer: arts, bingo, yoga, support groups for individuals with diagnoses of mental illness and addiction issues, Wednesday evening church services, social time with interns on Wednesdays, meals, morning prayer, and a NAMI Connections group. He explains:

> [T]he whole program is beneficial to me, because being bipolar you have a manic episode, and then you have a depression episode. And coming here after a manic episode, it somewhat prevented me from going into a depression by interacting with the people that [have] mental health issues. Even some of the staff deal with issues, and so that was good. And being involved in art programs, it's somewhat like a group therapy. To a certain extent, it keeps your mind occupied, rather than just sitting and dwelling on your problems and your issues. Last year I had a lot of trauma, you know. I had some events that took place that led up to me coming completely off my medication. And being bipolar, when you come off your medication, you really go into a manic state or high, that brings about euphoria and then it leads to confusions and that leads to hospitalization or institutionalization or incarceration, which this time, I went through the incarceration problem. Before that it had been a long time, since the '8os, that I'd been hospitalized.[13]

He goes on, "Over the years, I've been participating in mental health programs, group therapy, stress management, anger management, substance abuse programs and things like that, and dealing with the thought process, and being bipolar." As a person with bipolar disorder, he finds that "coming to Sacred Family . . . it just gave me something to look forward to the days that I came here, to be active and be around people that can remind me that I could be worse or I could be better, but I'm just grateful that I'm alive. Some of the staff who have [mental health] issues are actively working to provide services to people who do need help."

While mental illness and communal participation are often interpreted though language that is not explicitly religious or Christian, these frameworks are also used alongside ecclesial claims that emphasize the inherent equality in those who gather. Sacred Family and its members refer to the transformation of loss through liturgical rhetoric: restoration of dignity, conferred through baptism and through the love of God; the relational obligations of children of God and the unity of a community of people who share love and friendship with one another and with God. Likewise, congregants may refer to their losses as caused by mental illness, but they also attribute suffering in their lives to the will of God. As Miriam remarks, God saw fit to work her life this way even if she doesn't understand why. Circle participants are often willing to attribute their hardship and hopes to divine agency. At the same time, therapists, doctors, caseworkers, and caregivers are frequently cited as important agents in the navigation and interpretation of everyday obstacles and choices.

Such varied frames for naming human experience provide different tools and lenses for those who use them. While they are often used in complementary ways, competing references also create uneasy coalitions, particularly as one congregant names another's experience in relation to their own. Is this person I am speaking about my brother, a patient, a client, the poor, or crazy? Is she part of them or one of us? Is she low-functioning, or is she a gifted child of God? Am I a friend in mutuality or a staff person who enforces community rules? Is she a priest who buries one of her beloved congregants, or a fundraiser who supports recovery of people marginalized by mental illness and poverty? Are Circle participants teachers who help to shape and guide the interns who learn from them, or are they a demanding crowd from whom church workers, as disciples of Christ, need to seek rest from time to time? This plurality of references provides a window into the multiplicity of roles assumed by those who come to the church, different frames for naming and knowing another's life. They mark the ongoing struggle of a community that resists practices of segregationist charity but is also embedded in systems that interpret poverty, blackness, and mental illness primarily in terms of lack or deficit, and poor people with mental illness as unfortunate, needy recipients of charitable services.

Implied in a variety of overlapping discourses are also visions of what kinds of transformation a congregation desires for itself and for those who gather. Restoration of community, recovery from a mental illness, cure of a disease, and healing in response to suffering offer different paradigms for tracing the trajectory of a human life. Sacred Family is a coalition where the struggle for names adequate to each person is essential to its aesthetics of suffering, healing, and claiming one another.

Christian liturgies both invite and anticipate names for those who suffer. Liturgical impulses that reach back deeply into the traditions and texts of the church encourage prayers to God for the transformation and alleviation of suffering. They offer patterns, gestures, and language for the naming and anointing of those who are sick. Thus, in his meditation on the liturgical imperative to bring human pathos to the divine ethos, Don Saliers recalls a fifth-century petition from St. James's liturgy: "Remember, Lord, those in old age and infirmity, those who are sick, ill, or troubled by unclean spirits, for their speedy healing and salvation by you, their God . . ." The prayer goes on to ask that God "disperse the scandals, abolish wars, end the divisions of the churches." Commenting on this prayer within the scope of the church's liturgical work, Saliers argues that "to pray with the people of God is to remember the world, to be in dialogue with God about the sufferings and yearnings of the whole inhabited world."[14] Such dialogue requires the church to name these sufferings and yearnings. The conundrum of a community, where loss and pain are disproportionately experienced by some through experiences of mental illness, ableism, poverty, and racism, is that the naming of suffering and yearning can evoke pity, condescension, and stigma. Petitions by and for some kinds of people both mark divisions and erase differences among a congregation.

At the heart of Miriam's reflections on her own struggles is the thought that she might be thrown away by those who regard her suffering but disregard her struggle to embrace her own life. Like Miriam, theologian Simone Weil reminds us of the difficult and powerful asymmetries inherent in situations of affliction. In Weil's view, "the strong" are likely to perceive "the weak" as "things." Those who suffer often lose their relational identities as subjects or persons when beheld by those who fear or pity them. Claiming relationships of solidarity across vast differences of experience and asymmetries of power is practically impossible. Weil frames this impossibility as spiritual opportunity when she describes both "the preservation of true self-respect in affliction" as something "supernatural," and "love for our neighbor, being made of creative attention" as something "analogous to genius."[15]

Absent the genius of creative attention that is true love of neighbor and the supernatural self-respect that is true love of oneself, to misname a human life is commonplace. Indeed, the typical turn to pity or charity as response to disability has often resulted in the misnaming of disabled lives as either tragic or inspirational rather than ordinary.[16] In light of such misnaming, Eiesland argues that we need to pay attention to the creative means through which ordinary people "incorporate contingency and difficulty" into their lives and hold themselves together through relationships, technologies, and forms of expressions.[17] Such creative attention requires naming the human body as both "habitable and inhospitable—a body of plenty and privation."[18] It also supposes communal practices by which ordinary people are enabled, through the support of others, to hold themselves together and to act out against discrimination. Creative attention names not only individuals but also coalitions that are both erotic and political, whose struggles involve desire for one another rather than pity or condescension.[19]

With such modes of condescension and creative attention in mind, in what follows I investigate three rituals of Sacred Family's typical weekly liturgy that explicitly invite the community into the arts of naming: rituals of healing, health care, and friendship. By rituals, I mean patterns of repeated activities that require communal participation and involve constellations of words, gestures, and responses that shape the community of Sacred Family over time. Such rituals illustrate the struggle for adequate names for one another and for God, names that are essential to the work of those who worship God together. A consideration of the repertoire of names used in these rituals reveals the tensions between multiple frameworks and discourses for naming persons and relationships at Sacred Family. Each set of rituals anticipates particular kinds of needs and desires that another might have and uses a set of names to respond to it. But each also reveals limits in the language it employs, and thus echoes the struggle for adequate names for oneself and another that such rituals perform.

RITUALS OF HEALING AND THE DESIRE TO BE KNOWN

At a Thursday morning staff meeting, Father Brian begins with a prayer for the healing of the world. After the prayer, Eve asks, incredulously, "Healing of the world?" as if she's overwhelmed with the thought of such an impossible task at the beginning of a staff meeting. "One germ at a time," Father Brian jokes. After an update on the status of picnic tables and path maintenance, the staff name particular Circle participants about whom they are concerned. One by one, they offer names to the Circle staff for additional wisdom or more information: Edgar is in the hospital, Nicholas has a brain tumor, Tanya is looking fragile, Denny has been losing weight, Raymond has been acting inappropriately with the nursing students and has been asked to stay away until he expresses desire to change this behavior. In many of the situations named, the one doing the naming neither suggests nor intends intervention, but rather attention and regard for each person.

Such naming of community members and their needs is not only the work of the staff but also the regular work of the community. Sacred Family's weekly liturgy differs from many other churches in its regular emphasis on healing services and prayers as practices in which congregants can name their lives before God. Every other Wednesday, a liturgy of healing and anointing takes place. After scriptures are read and prayers for healing are spoken, two long lines form in front of the priest or a deacon or pastoral intern. Many congregants wait their turn to offer their concerns and to allow another to pray for and anoint them. Additionally, most Sundays, optional prayers for healing are offered in the back of the church after communion: a few congregants kneel at a wooden bench near the door during the service while another congregant faces them, naming them, hands resting on their shoulders, to pray for them.

As a researcher, I come to these healing rituals aware of the criticism and suspicion that many disability scholars, activists, and theologians bring to the Christian church's rhetoric of healing and the misnaming of disability as tragic through such practices. Many disabled persons remind us of their experiences of the violence of healing rituals: experiences of being publicaly prayed for again and again in the desire for eradication of disability; moments of being approached by strangers in public spaces, who desire to lay hands on a disabled body and pray for their bodily transformation; and language that imagines the healing of the whole world through metaphors of blindness, deafness, and brokenness transformed.

Disability studies scholars Snyder and Mitchell, reflecting on biblical motifs of healing, argue that Christian desires to imagine a body-mind healed and restored diverts attention from the more difficult work of imagining a world with adequate social supports for persons' well-being:

> the restoration of bodies to normative health through acts of faith
> healing ultimately devalues our commitments to the demands of
> embodiment overall. Miracles of the body (that is disability cures, the
> alleviation of chronic illness, resuscitation of the organism from non-
> being etc.) function as a form of *deus ex machina* in stories hard-pressed
> to resolve corporeal crisis in any other way.[20]

Theologian Sharon Betcher punctuates the bitter effects on those often targeted for such attention and healings: "The Spirit and its healing efficacy? Believe me, most disabled persons have been exposed to the fervor of its promise and the bite of its rejection when our bodies proved heretically resistant to cure."[21] Betcher also criticizes the trend in modern, liberal, Christian theologies to turn away from ideals of supernatural power to heal and toward the wonders of modern medicine: "While liberal theologies set aside supernaturalism, our close alliance with the miracle of modern medicine leaves us with a comparable anticipation of health as normalcy. But to wish me normal is no kindness, no generosity of spirit."[22]

Eiesland describes her own experiences with faith healing as more ambiguous. While she acknowledges the negative effects of many healing rituals, she also claims the power of laying on of hands "as restorative and redemptive. These physical mediations of God's grace have often kept me related to my body at times when all of my impulses pushed me toward dissociating from the pain-wracked, uncomfortable beast." She points to a charismatic meeting when a group of nuns responded to her pain, alleviated her isolation, and revealed her "spiritual body" through the laying on of hands.[23] Thus, while Eiesland invites a critical stance toward the desires instantiated and expressed through healing liturgies, she also recognizes their potential in claiming persons as desirable within Christian communities. Healing rituals might likewise name belonging and intimacy within community and provide some relief from pain.

At Sacred Family, congregants heartily embrace the optional Wednesday healing ritual. In a liturgical community where congregants are often selective about the elements of a liturgy in which they participate, such ready responses signal a compelling resonance between the formal gestures of the liturgy and the desires of congregants. I entertain multiple interpretations for such eager participation: the depth of concern that congregants experience for their own well-being or the well-being of those they love, their desire and faith in God as an agent of change in their lives, a moment when the official liturgy acknowledges the sacredness of touch and gesture that unofficially play out within this community at other times, and a unique Sacred Family ritual that encourages one-on-one interactions and that invites each voice to name something about themselves in the formal liturgical space. Because this ritual of healing is simultaneously public and also private, within the eyesight but out of the earshot of other congregants and researchers, I have limited access to the healing configurations that take place.

Then one Wednesday evening Wallace suggests that I go forward to participate in the healing and anointing ritual myself. While I intended to participate at some future time, I am caught off guard. What should I bring to the front? When I equivocate, Wallace urges me on. I'll go if you go, he suggests. I ask if we can pray for other people, and he assures me that we can. He tells me he is going to pray for his family. We stand one behind the other in a long line of congregants. While we wait, we greet the people beside us in line who are waiting for Father Brian. A few of those who wait for prayer embrace one another.

As I get closer to the front, I can see Deacon Elizabeth place her hands directly on each person's head. In contrast, those who face Father Brian put their hands out, he touches his hands to their hands or shoulders and asks: "Anything special?" but their responses are inaudible. When I reach Deacon Elizabeth, I name a friend, Sophia, who has cancer. I haven't seen or talked to Sophia in years; I have heard about her health struggles through a mutual friend. Yet in this moment I name and claim her as a friend. The deacon's prayer for me emphasizes healing in body, mind, and spirit both for me and Sophia and ends with a prayer for our joy.

Standing in front of Deacon Elizabeth, I recognize the intensity of this work of praying for each person one by one as we bring a motley diversity of concerns and petitions to the front. On another day, when I ask the deacon about her participation, she emphasizes the non-verbal communication rather than the spoken request: "Sometimes they don't even need to tell, it's just, when I make eye contact with someone in that setting, they are coming to me because they feel they need something, and they think I can help them access that. It seems like an enormous privilege to me."

Ginny, another congregant who works for a disability advocacy organization, offers prayers for healing on Sundays after communion. In her description, healing prayer forms an intercessory triangle that is mysterious and intimate to both persons involved in the effort.

> It is a very private, a very confidential moment, but it's where I get to know people and where people get to know me, and where . . . I don't say, 'oh my goodness. what am I going to pray?' It's like we're in communication with God, and I can pray for things, and people say 'oh, thank you!' so it's a very three-way thing. I'm there to pray because I believe prayer changes things. The person is there to pray because they believe prayer changes things. But half the time we neither one know what we want, or I don't know what they want.

"So there's a mysteriousness to it?"

"Yes, there's a mystery."

"This is something I can do. I think this is something a lot of people feel uncomfortable doing." She goes on to describe the language she uses to name those for whom she is praying: "Often when I'm praying for someone, I'm praying for my friend, my sister, or my brother, but it's very meaningful, and I have seen the depth of love for each other, love and trust in God that I don't see any place but that kneeling bench." She clarifies that she is not the healer. "People ask, 'Are you going to do healing this morning?' and I say, 'I am going to pray, and God is going to do the healing.'"

Knowing that Ginny advocates for people with disabilities, I bring up the ways that the disability community challenges religious and Christian discourses of healing. Ginny responds:

> Well, let me make this personal. People will say to me of Belinda (the young woman of whom she is a friend and guardian), 'What's wrong with her?' And my answer is: there is not a thing wrong with her. Not a single thing! Do I pray for healing for Belinda? No. I pray for blessing. I pray for continued health. And I have that struggle, my mom had cancer. Did I pray for healing? I, I remember saying to God, 'I don't know, you know. You're in charge. I love her. I don't want her to hurt.' You know. So all I can do is bring this concern. You know, I heard a sermon . . . that the Scripture doesn't say, 'Now organize your prayer concerns. Get them organized. Make *sure* they're organized. Make *sure* they're legitimate. Then prayerfully on your knees, in quiet, take them to God.' It says, 'Cast your cares upon him!' which kind of means as you're running, you're throwing 'em in God's direction. (We both laugh.) And so I do pray for healing if people ask for healing, you know, but often times I find that in the prayer I'm saying, 'Lord we don't know what healing means, but *you* do. So *whatever* that means, please grant it!' You know, who are we to say that having schizophrenia is a problem? Society has made it a problem. For my beautiful [relative], it's not schizophrenia. But we don't see that he has a problem; we wouldn't want him *any other way*, you know. I'm just so glad when he reached the point of his life of saying, 'God made me this way, and God doesn't make mistakes. I don't understand, but isn't that good enough?' So do I want Omar [a congregant] not to hear voices? It's fine with me if he does, but I can ask God to keep him safe and to help him know when he's being tempted to do things that aren't safe.

In Ginny's analysis, rituals of healing name human fears and desires before God for God to sort out and to work with as God sees fit. Healing prayer does not seek to remove disability but plays a role in the radical acceptance that congregants claim for themselves and for others. In a highly organized formal liturgy, Ginny imagines healing prayers creating a safe space for potentially disorganized desires, desires that neither the petitioner nor the one who speaks a prayer fully understands. Such forms of healing suggest that to offer one's anxieties and desires to God is more easily done with the accompaniment of another's voice, touch, breath, hope, trust, and imagination.

Having taken up this discussion with those whose acts of naming guide the healing prayers of this community, I also explore its perceived meanings with those who come forward to name their needs and desires before God and the intercessor. One morning at the art program I bring up Sacred Family's healing liturgy with two of the artists. Kayla tells me that when she goes forward to ask for prayers for healing, she prays for marriage for herself and for the whole world. She goes on to explain the role that marriage plays in healing: "You can be healing anything that needs healing. I chose to pray for not only myself but [for] everybody [who] needs it, like the world . . . everything would be better. I don't know how they feel about this, but this is my opinion: if everybody would get married and let marriage grow."

"Hmm," I make a surprised sound, pondering what it means to let marriage grow.

In response, she continues: "They don't know how to do it? I could tell them."

"So why would marriage make the world better?" I'm trying to understand.

"Because two care more."

"Care more?"

"Yes, care more. There's two in the house. One gets sick, the other one can pour the bread, pour the food. And it's a lot that each, that both of them could do together. They could clean up the house together and never get tired. They could go to the movies; that way one person ain't got no business sitting up in a movie by hisself. And if you get a partner to go with you, it's okay, but you never know what's going through their mind just as well as you know what's going through your mate's mind. But your mate is always a gender to you. Nobody knows like a mate know another mate."

"So it's about being known?"

"Yes, and loved," she concludes.

Rose, sitting next to Kayla, insists that marriage is more complicated than this: "You can't just count on the marriage because lots of times, things change with the marriage."

"I pray for that too," Kayla interrupts.

Rose talks about the possibility for betrayal that exists in marriage, but Kayla sticks to her position: "I need to have marriage because I need somebody that is strong there with me. I need some love from that person and give that person back love. I understand I can find another friend to do it, but another friend isn't going to get to the nitty-gritty with you. (We both laugh.) You know what I'm talking about." Kayla goes on to explain, "They (friends) have their own life to live, and when you're married, the life is combined."

From a disability perspective, we might conclude that Kayla's dream of healing, while not a dream about her individual body-mind, nevertheless assumes the power of normalcy. She imagines the best form of community, love, and social support through the institution of marriage and through the name of wife or mate. Kayla dreams of marriage, when marriage is a form of community in which many at Sacred Family do not currently participate even as they desire romantic partnerships. At the same time, Kayla's description of marriage resonates with an ideal of companionship that the church names as one of its most important responses to the needs of those who come: supporting friendships and loving relationships that are life-giving to those who enter.

As I listen to Kayla and Rose debate and disagree about the healing efficacy of marriage, I find it appropriate that the healing prayer invites us to bring these disparate, even discordant, desires and to name them to God with the help of another. I compare Kayla's desire for marriage to the way Rose describes healing at Sacred Family during a different conversation: "If we get sick, we can be healed. Yes, we see lots of healing. When someone needs help by getting somewhere to stay, that's healing." She goes on to enumerate other examples of healing, such as when Beatrice brought a blind man, whose name she has forgotten, chocolate milk. "That's healing, that's helping that person out, that's giving a helping hand." Later in this conversation, she comes back to this topic of healing: "People come there with no clothes, no shoes, and they will go and get shoes and clothes from the clothes closet, to go on people's feet, coats to go on their back, clothes to put on their body."

"And that's healing?"

"And that's healing . . . that will keep them from getting sick."

Kayla and Rose map the church's work of healing through different kinds of knowledge, ways other than diagnosis of illness or the identification of a cure from disease: healing comes from good caretaking and companionship. Kayla imagines the healing of the world as one in which each person shares a name and is therefore deeply known by the one with whom life, work, and play are equally shared. Rose, too, imagines the church's participation in healing as its ability to know and name what each one needs: clothes, food, chocolate milk, preventing sickness. To be able to participate in the work of healing, one must not only call on the name of God but know the needs of those in whose healing one participates.

Rituals of Health Care and the Desire for Dignity

Weekly rhythms at Sacred Family are defined not only by rituals of common prayer but also by health care practices: checkups, health screenings, consultations, and educational workshops provide a different set of practices and words with which to identify one's needs and desires. Many congregants value the fact that health care professionals attend to them during their time at Sacred Family. Many eagerly dialogue with nursing students about their own health issues, whether or not they follow the advice set forth. While not overtly liturgical, these rituals nevertheless shape an ecclesial space in which people are known as more than patients or consumers. Such relationships between Circle participants and those who offer medical advice take on a tone that is shaped by the possibilities of ecclesial rather than medical space. A nurse, for example, describes the church as a place where she can only make recommendations; she cannot prescribe medications. She is limited in what she can do for congregants, but she also embraces a space where she can foster relationships of trust and respect based on a community of joy rather than self-improvement. Thus, she urges a congregant to see a medical doctor at a hospital for high blood pressure and also to write poetry again. Naming him as poet rather than patient fosters a different set of relationships (mentor and artist rather than nurse and patient) that helps them both pay attention to his overall stress and well-being. Likewise, she expresses pleasure in being known at the church not only as a healthcare worker but also as "the nail lady"—the one who selects an assortment of nail polish for foot clinics and pedicures.

Such multiple frameworks for relationships can also cause tension. One afternoon, Lamar, another health care worker who also experiences mental illness, stops me in the hallway to tell me about saving a church member from choking during lunch the previous day. After saving the congregant, he later went to document this event, describing what had just happened to "Patient 57." In the process of writing, he suddenly stopped himself and wondered how he could write about a human being, whose life he had just saved, in such a cold and detached way. Later he would explain that the church gives him a way of engaging people "human to human"—a kind of interaction he distinguishes from his former work in the hospital. In such human-to-human relationships, he plays the serious role of helping to save lives at the church and is also an entertainer and a clown. He wants to become a better advocate for congregants and to fight against the neglect he worries that some of his patients/fellow congregants experience in their personal care homes. As he searches for other ways to name the people for whom he provides medical care, he also takes on other names and roles, keeping fluid the relationships that might ossify between medical expert and mentally ill patient. At the same time, he also names some of the people he sees as "doomed," as those for whom there is no hope because of their mental capacities and poor health.

While Lamar describes his relationship with congregants through multiple roles and names, those who come to the church, particularly those who spend short amounts of time within the community, struggle to establish relationships beyond a medical model and to respond to the health concerns that clients face. For example, one group of nursing students lectures the community on topics related to health: good exercise, nutrition, and bedtime routines. Their advice for self-improvement assumes a level of autonomy that appears dissonant with the everyday worlds that many congregants negotiate. Many live in group homes with limited control over the food they consume, the shoes they wear, and the bedtime routines they choose within regulated communal spaces. Some of the pleasures that may be essential to the passing of time each day—a walk to McDonald's or a walk to the corner store for chips and a soda—conflict with the ideals for healthy living proposed by the medical students. One group implicitly names another as free agents of their own health and wellness without acknowledging the financial resources and the institutional structures and strictures within which patterns of eating, drinking, bathing, dressing, and exercising are constrained.

While many Sacred Family congregants struggle to retain the tips for healthy living nursing students offer them, for their part students also struggle to acquire the relational knowledge necessary for interaction with congregants. For example, one morning I notice a group of the nursing students standing together talking; only one of them sits down near Circle members. She clearly desires to interact with Circle participants but does not seem to know how to initiate such interaction. Engaging her in conversation, I discover this is the second part of her group's clinical rotation in mental health; their first took place at a psychiatric hospital. She comments on the differences between the two settings. In the psychiatric hospital, people are in crisis and on more medication. At Sacred Family she witnesses more compassion for people. But here she finds it more difficult to get to know people. It was easier at the psychiatric institution where they had charts, and she could read people's diagnoses and ask them about details on these charts. However, she thinks that if her group came more often, participants might recognize them, and it would be easier to interact. She imagines the medical tools of chart and diagnosis as social tools to facilitate interactions, but she also acknowledges that more time might produce different social tools, such as more adequate names to foster dialogue.

I recall her comments some months later when another volunteer and longtime Sacred Family church member also articulates a desire for knowledge of congregants' diagnoses. Unlike the students, Melanie has considerable experience with mental illness, both as a parent and as a health care professional who enjoyed spending time with her schizophrenic patients. During home health visits, she was troubled by the very brief amounts of time other nurses spent with their mentally ill patients: just enough to take blood pressure, pulse, and give medication, but not enough to interact with them, or to ask about their housing situation, or to attend to other health concerns. In contrast, she enjoyed spending time with her patients, with whom she got along well: "Maybe it was that they sensed that I didn't fear them. A lot of people do fear people with mental illness."

She is also now a parent with a child who has mental illness and has struggled with the stigma they experience, for a time keeping her child's mental illness a secret from the neighbors for fear of their reactions. Nevertheless, even with her own intimate knowledge of and experience with psychiatric disability, she recalls a time when she was shocked when a Circle regular turned around and hit her after she touched him on the back. She has since come to understand that he does not like to be touched except from the front; she attributes his response to a diagnosis she did not know about at the time. She imagines that if she had known his diagnosis or knew the diagnoses of others, it might enhance communication across difference. As it happened, this congregant was suspended for a time for hitting her. He never apologized when he returned, but now they shake hands during the passing of the peace, which seems significant to her. Thus, Melanie refers to both the medical (diagnoses) and the liturgical (sharing peace with one another) as frameworks for maintaining healthy relationships between members at Sacred Family.

But Melanie also describes for me other ways that Sacred Family encourages its congregants to know one another and to support one another's well-being through frames that do not rely on medical diagnoses as mediation. She describes her relationship with Henry, a congregant who often experiences intense anger. "I'm really having a hard time," he might say when he comes to help her with daily tasks at Sacred Family. When she asks him about his bad day, he describes the voices that talk to him. Henry gets tired of trying to argue with these voices because they want him to do bad things; he doesn't want to do bad things, so it gets him down. He also tells her how voices "got to him" a couple of times, and he had almost committed suicide. When he is upset, she and another longtime volunteer and congregant reassure him and make him a hot beverage. He then sits by himself in a corner of the parish hall for a time. According to Melanie, by the end of the day, he often says, "I'm feeling really great." She concludes this story by expressing a desire for more opportunities to exchange stories with congregants who come. Sometimes she feels that completing her volunteer work at the church limits the amount of time she listens to stories of struggle that congregants might otherwise share with her.

Melanie imagines that the challenge of relating well to one another at Sacred Family church is affected by North American society. "We tend to look at people, and think 'are you better than they are' or 'are you less than they are,' and you have to fight that all the time." She recalls the gradual communal acceptance of a trans woman who comes to the church, as well as more and more openness around members who not only have mental illness but are also gay. Sacred Family, like other communities, is a place where those who attend continually compare themselves to one another through a variety of different statuses both within and outside of mental illness. And yet, she claims, the church is a place where congregants are named and known in ways she has never experienced in other contexts. She describes it as "learning to love the smallest thing in people, you know, it may be that the constituent has a particularly nice dimple or . . . a good smile, or the way that they come up, and say, 'Hi Melanie.' It's little things like that. It's the only world where, where, little things like that mean a lot, at least to me. It's very important."

Melanie's description resonates with other descriptions I have received of Sacred Family—ones that name another congregant's face or laugh or smile or tone of address or walk or irritating habit as essential to an image of what Sacred Family is. A bodily mark or gesture or the face of one is named as an image for the church as a whole. The power of such naming on a communal level resonates with the similar work of identifying that goes on in the easy yoga circle as we seek healthy bodies and relationships through stretching and breathing together. As yoga practitioners, we name together the different parts of our anatomy in order to become familiar with our body-minds. Invariably, anatomical names give way to other more playful names, such as naming the spine as a slinky toy. Each name focuses our attention on both the wonder and the pain of our bodies as we move and breathe. Just as attention to the small, repetitive movements of yoga helps practitioners move more easily through their own bodies, so attention to the small repetitive sounds and sights of community invites more fluid interaction than those prescribed through other kinds of roles and designations. Such names that require creative attention to our own bodies and to the bodies and gestures of others anticipate a greater degree of intimacy and belonging than the sole knowledge of a proper name, given upon introduction. At the same time, such attributions (such as associating Wallace and Joshua with their remarkable, jubilant, raucous laughter among other descriptors of them) also evade the hierarchies and statuses of other designations such as titles like volunteer or categorizations such as "people with mental illness" through which relationships can be circumscribed and negotiated.

RITUALS OF FRIENDSHIP AND THE DESIRE FOR EQUALITY AND MUTUALITY

During one Advent, I sit beside Daniella on the bus ride back from an outing to see the Christmas lights. We discuss the pleasures of the outing and of the Christmas season. Eventually, she talks about the house she lost, a three bedroom near downtown, with a backyard where she liked to sit outside and watch the squirrels and the birds. I imagine aloud that it might be hard to go from having your own house to living with a lot of other people. She says it was hard at first, and she used to stay upstairs most of the time, but now she comes downstairs more. "I have learned that to have friends you got to be a friend," she concludes. She says that it has helped coming to Sacred Family and to another program on Mondays and Wednesdays. She likes coming to Sacred Family better than the other program because of the art and because "more people here know my name, and maybe I don't know their names, but I recognize their faces."

Of all the rituals that Sacred Family emphasizes as central to its response to the marginalizing effects of poverty and mental illness, informal liturgies of play, work, and friendship are central to its vision of healing. Such healing through friendship is intended both for the scars of stigma and for the prejudice of those who fear psychiatric disability, for naming loss or desire implies and requires a relationship, a condition for entrustment through which one can expect help or recognition from another. Not everyone is baptized or even a member of the church, yet those who come seek a relation to one another mediated through the church, a relationship that is not familial in a conventional sense but that nurtures a sense of interconnectedness and belonging. When congregants come from worlds where they are not claimed or cannot claim a relationship with others in conventional forms of family and friendship, Sacred Family offers a common name. At times this common name feels sufficient to those who claim it; at times it feels inadequate.

Lillian, for example, describes the struggle of identifying with a church community as she once did with her own family. She tells me that my name is the name of her sister. "I don't see my people," she remarks. Her people are scattered. She lived in the same house for thirty-two years until the house went into foreclosure. It was a house she shared with her mother and son. Her son was shot when he was twenty-two. Five years ago, her mother died. When she lost the house, she lost pictures of her grandmother and her great-grandmother and her great-great-grandmother. It was hard, but "God saw fit this way," she concludes. "I try not to live in the past." She begins to sing, "One day at time." And then concludes, "It's hard to live without family and get used to being alone. It's hard to know other people the way you know your family."

Rituals of friendship at Sacred Family involve the struggle to learn and remember another's name. Rev. Jess begins and ends each Sunday school class by asking us to say our names aloud to remind us that we are known and loved by God. Likewise Laura, the yoga teacher, begins each class by asking that we go around and say our names; she tests our memories, explaining that it is important that we remember each other's names. But many in this community know each other's faces but struggle with first names. It is easier to remember the closing phrase of each yoga gathering, "*Namaste*, the light in me sees the light in you," than to keep track of the names of all the people who come and go from the circle. Yet even when community members forget each other's proper names, even when congregants are irritated with or belittle one another, they also know those who claim Sacred Family as their community. Congregants name when a van mate is missing or when someone has a doctor's appointment and is absent from the circle at yoga. They claim their relationships with and through the church as an important condition for being able to ask for help from another person. Sacred Family offers relationships, through which congregants identify their responsibilities to one another.

Some congregants regard Sacred Family as a form of kinship in light of absent or faraway blood families. Tanya, for example, describes Sacred Family as those who visit her when she's sick in the hospital, as the people you can call when you have a problem. She also wishes that it were possible to sleep at the church sometimes when you need a break from your home life. Aisha wishes the church gave driving lessons. Sacred Family is also a place where many celebrate the holidays or mark a birthday or a graduation. In celebratory moments, conventionally familial moments, there is often a hope and expectation of recognition from and by others at the church. In some cases, to be church family is to provide a relational space that is not so complicated by past relationships.

This is true not only for Circle participants but also for some interns and nondisabled church members who have had difficult relationships with mental illness within their own families. Sacred Family responds to their losses by offering a different set of close relationships within which to claim those who have psychiatric disabilities and to reimagine psychiatric disability itself. Aaron, for example, describes his strong reluctance to intern at Sacred Family because of a challenging situation with his own parent who has mental illness. He did not want to engage mental illness because he was tired of dealing with his parent's condition. But through the Wednesday evening rituals of hanging out with congregants, chatting and playing games, he discovered that his familial experiences aided him in developing life-giving friendships with Sacred Family parishioners.

Aaron describes a friendship with a woman at the church. He found her to be quiet, almost unapproachable until one day she was listening to the radio and they discovered their common love of music. Now every Wednesday, when he comes, he seeks her out. "There's some days she wants to talk, and some days she don't, but I believe what started off this genuine friendship is that although we are different, we have a lot in common, so we based our friendship off the commonalities, and the commonalties were magnified. So whether or not she understands me when I talk, or I understand her when she talks, we have music in common, we laugh together, and we play UNO." The relationship has challenged him to extend himself to look for commonalities in those he sees through difference. Such relationships have also given him more confidence to talk to people he meets on the street.

These friendships have, in turn, informed his relationship with his parent. He has started to listen to and understand her better. He had been raised in a church tradition that viewed his parent's illness as a spiritual illness, a tradition that prayed out of her the demons and "all this craziness." He now claims healing through a church that names mental illness as "a serious condition that needs to be evaluated by a licensed professional not by a reverend." Because of his experience at Sacred Family, he feels she shouldn't be "ostracized and crucified again. She's been crucified enough. This is a medical condition! So I've been offering: 'Do you want to go to therapy? Do you want to go to counseling? Do you want to talk to someone? Maybe I'm not the person to talk to, but you need to talk to someone.'"[24] He has encouraged her to leave her own church and to go to a place that is more welcoming and has more of the support she needs.

Sacred Family has also been important to him because it is a place where he spends time with other black men. At the university where he is a student, he is often made to feel like an outsider, that he is not as desirable or adequate as his white counterparts. At Sacred Family he encounters a sense of home and peace through a solidarity and camaraderie with other black men who attend. He names his relationship with others at Sacred Family as a "brotherly or sisterly experience not as a[n] 'oh, this is them and this is us' but as a unified sector." It has also been an eye-opener for him to see so many black men dealing with a mental illness. He feels grateful for a place that is welcoming and open to them in a way they would not be welcomed in other church spaces. At the same time, Sacred Family is also a place where racism results in forms of address that condescend or belittle black congregants in actions that have been upsetting to him. He recalls guest churches that come to serve meals "where you have a white superior who may be trying to give instructions or giving out food or whatever, talk down [to] or talk at a parishioner at Sacred Family." He questions the origins of this condescension but also identifies its emergence at the intersections of race and mental illness.

Sacred Family provides a place to name and claim mental illness outside the intense context of immediate family. It creates coalition through common identification with those in very different circumstances. At the same time, intersections of black and disability identities result in misnaming; forms of address belittle or condescend to those who struggle for respect. Unlike Aaron, many Sacred Family congregants are more willing to talk about the challenges and power asymmetries of ableism than to talk about the racism embedded in the poverty through which many congregants experience mental illness. Sacred Family is thus both a site for black solidarity and a location for wealthy white condescension and for obliviousness in regards to the effects of racism in situating manifestations and experiences of psychiatric disability. Across these divides, rituals of friendship heal some inadequate names but do not eradicate others.

Another intern named Simone recalls her own struggle to regard the dignity of persons with mental illness, especially in light of her past. Even though she is someone who has experienced the effects of poverty and abuse, she describes the initial prejudice she felt for the kinds of people who gather at Sacred Family. When she first came to Sacred Family,

> [T]here was just something here that uncovered something within myself. I was crying the entire time . . . it really took me back to what I was experiencing in my youth and some of the things I haven't dealt with. I think that's what made Sacred Family one of my first options. I have two family members; we have a history of schizophrenia in our family. . . . But I know that upon finding out about that, I was kind of distant, and I did develop or already had a prejudice that I never really recognized.

"A prejudice?"

Toward the mentally and physically disabled. And which I didn't, it left me feeling really inhospitable and unopen, and it's been interesting how since I've been here, my level of engagement with people in general has changed, not just with marginalized communities but just like with people, I'm able to see past who are you to see who you actually are . . . I've stopped putting my own standard [on] people and [telling them] this is how you should live. It was done to me, and this is where I am.

In contrast to putting up a standard for people that they cannot meet, Simone names the goal of Sacred Family as she comprehends it: "Here they're not made to live the life that we feel that they should live. We're just trying to help them live a more full and dignified life." She sees this dignity in the hope that parishioners have for their own lives and the ways "they love on each other." As part of the church leadership, she describes the relationship of staff and interns to the congregants who come to the church:

We're not here to fix people, but we're just here to listen to their stories and to affirm that they are beloved members of God's community and to lay power at their feet. We're not the ones in power, [but are here to remind them] that they hold power; it's not often that they're reminded of that. I like that here there's no contrast between those that are consumers of the services and those that are providing it, that we're all, we're all equally growing, no one's better than another, no one's able to give more than another, cause I don't think I've given as much as I've been gifted—really encouraging words and wisdom and it's just nice to be somewhere where you're not put in such a place where you constantly have to be a provider, like that you're not held to such a high standard that you can't meet it, that you're welcomed as you are, and I wasn't used to that.

Simone's description of Sacred Family reveals both the ideals of Sacred Family as well as the struggle for language that is part of everyday interactions. The church offers a set of relationships within which to overcome past prejudices but also offers competing frameworks for understanding relationships of mutuality and hierarchy—us and them, consumers and providers, beloved of God, those who are recognized as powerful and those who need to be reminded that they hold power.

While it is common for Sacred Family congregants to celebrate the bonds that emerge as they share space and time together, there is also a limit to what this community can do and be for each other. Sacred Family cannot play the roles that family members often play for one another. When congregants leave the boundaries of the church for a long period of time, they often lose track of one another. A parishioner moves or is moved by a family member to a new home or setting, and Sacred Family no longer knows where they are. While a constant stream of newcomers brings fresh energy, insight, and friendship into community life, these ever-shifting relationships also create waves of loss.

Aisha engages this loss when she describes both her enjoyment of and her frustration with the interns who come and go. Such newcomers are vital to the energy of the community as their intense interest and enthusiasm are important catalysts for fresh ideas, activities, and conversations. On the one hand, Aisha confirms Sacred Family as important to her well-being because of its friendly, familial relationships, and yet she mourns the different statuses that people within the community occupy. "On the one hand, there are no doctors or therapists here. They actually educate you about your illness, which other places, they educate you but they don't educate you enough. They treat you like children. But [at] Sacred Family they treat you as if you're family or a good friend. They'd do anything to help you."

When I ask her what makes it hard to be a community here, she also talks about relationships: "I like that people are coming here to intern, but then it hurts when they leave. Because, you know, you kind of build, maybe not always a friendship, but you grow kind of fond of the person, so it kind of hurts when they leave. I don't like when they do that!"

She laughs, and explains further:

> I'm the type of person who kind of, I have a wall because I don't want to get close to someone, and then they leave, and I never get to see them again. That's one of my issues that I need to work with, and I don't think the Sacred Family is helping that much with that because they come and go, and they never come back. I don't like how you may build a real friendship, but there are statuses, and when the person has a certain status, you can probably keep up with them, but it's not the same as a true friendship where you could go and have dinner or lunch or hang out. It's not that type of friendship. It's more like I care about you, but we're a different status, so that hurts.

She goes on to imagine occupying a position where she could maintain ongoing friendships with interns outside the boundaries of the church: "I feel like I could be in that place one day but it takes time."

I ask her to talk about her conception of status and what values are behind it. She responds:

> For instance, it's kind of like when a person is just there for interning, or something like that, and they can't really have a real friendship with you or anything else like that. They can't really hang out. It kind of hurts. I kind of look for people who are my age or maybe fun or something so I kind of want to keep in contact with them, but you can't really if they're . . . Facebook them or anything like that, but I guess it's like a rule here, or everywhere, that you can't be a real friend to the person who is a client here. And that goes everywhere.

I tease this out: "It's interesting because it's both a church and a community but you also feel you have this client status where you can't have that kind of relationship."

She acknowledges the boundaries of church space as the boundaries of some friendships: "I feel like the people I come to see, as long as I come here I get to see them, but if I don't come here, I don't get to see them." She wants to name them as true friends but is frustrated by the implicit rules that govern rituals of friendship here.

"So it's a friendship that is very contingent on this place? Do you feel like other friendships you have are not as contingent on a particular place?"

"Probably . . . I have plenty of friends who are not connected to this place." She points out that she might have a relationship outside the space with someone who has a mental illness (someone whom she understands to have the same status as she does) but not with someone who does not. Still, even with this experience of different statuses, she wants to make sure I capture that

> [T]his church is a real blessing to many people here. They get a different experience. People who don't have a mental illness get a perspective of what we're really like as people: that we have feelings and that we can love and that we're human beings. And people with the mental illness here, we grow here together, even if we don't really talk much, we still have an understanding that there's love here and understanding . . . [this place] helps you more to cope with problems. I think I've changed over time because I've become more responsible.

"How does it help you to cope with your problems?"

"We go to community meetings on Thursdays, and you talk about your problems, and you can talk about anything that is of the here and now, how you're feeling, and they'll give you advice or make you feel like you're not alone. I went from not being able to take care of myself to being able to take care of myself 100 percent on my own."

"You live on your own, right? And that was just being able to talk with people about what you were going through?"

"I think I just grew up on my own, but the coping skills help me manage staying on my own."

"What is growing up? Is growing being responsible?"

"Yeah."

"'Cause you said that in another program they treat you like children, and I wonder what the differences are between being treated like children or being treated like an adult."

> Like, for example, the other place they would . . . they basically gave out a paper and asked you what type of tropical fruits have you tried, and that was like for maybe third graders or something. I'm pretty sure, well, I guess not all of us, I guess I should be more considerate of the people here who may not know a lot, but I feel like that was an insult to my intelligence . . . Or coloring and stuff, which—I guess coloring is fine, but I don't want to do it 'cause I've done that.

"Being an adult is having options?"

"Yeah," she laughs.

"About what you do and don't want to do."

"Yeah."

Aisha cherishes Sacred Family as a place where she is named as an adult and as a person worthy of true friendship; but she also continues to struggle with the statuses assigned to her through her mental illness and the ways these statuses are performed within Sacred Family's weeklong liturgy. To be named and regarded as a person rather than a client or an adult rather than a child is not something she takes for granted, and that affects her perceptions of herself. To be named by another as a friend she often experiences as genuine for a time and as deception when other paradigms come into focus.

The Struggle for Names and the Christian Church

Inserted into the Christian church, the struggle for good names is both personal and ecclesial. In evoking the rituals and rhetoric through which Sacred Family responds to congregants' desires and losses, I have attempted to show both the desires and the struggles for adequate names and lenses through which to view one's own experience, as well as another's. As

congregants employ different frameworks for their relationships with others, they often hesitate or pause, searching for words that convey truths
about themselves or about the people with whom they pray.

It is possible to interpret this struggle as a failure of the community to
claim the fullness of theological or liturgical language: a failure to manifest
true spiritual friendship, or sibling love in Christ, or to demonstrate the
bonds between children of God who are one body in Christ. Rather than
interpreting such dissonance as a failure, I find it productive whenever this
gap allows those who hesitate to pay creative attention to the powers and
assumptions at play in any one frame. As Aisha notes, one cannot free oneself of condescension by employing the word friend, or rid oneself of status
by claiming the ideal of unity. Rather, congregants must continue to name
the hierarchies that separate them from one another and to imagine the
conditions for entrustment that would allow them to claim a life together.
On the other hand, as Aaron and Simone testify, the desire to call another
person friend might also facilitate a renaming of relationships outside the
community, ways of regarding familial relationships or encounters with
strangers, certain irritations or prejudices associated with disability, illness,
and poverty. In the failure of adequate names and in the simultaneous
desire for better conditions through which to ask for help and to respond
to another's concern, suffering, loss, or oppression, some relation that cannot yet be named or fully imagined is held in the contradictions. In the
hesitations and in the silences a name is given and then retracted or replaced
by another.

How, then, might the struggle to name human lives relate to the church's
work of naming God as part of its Christian worship and to the knowledge
and love of God that is required? Following a divine name into a world in
order to explore that world is a theological task, according to Eiesland.
"The challenge for the Christian is to engage one or more 'names' of God
and to follow these images into the worlds they open," she argues.[25] It
requires those whose experiences and frustrations illumine the terrain of
inhospitable or habitable spaces for lament, petition, and praise. Certain
names for God might open into violent landscapes for human life. For
example, Eiesland argues that living with Jesus as the suffering servant or
conquering lord has often created a difficult space for disabled to emerge
as an adequate name for one who would follow that Christ. On the other
hand, naming the disabled God as the one who returns to the disciples
after his crucifixion with scars on his body opens a more habitable world
for people with disabilities. The disabled God incarnates hope as one who
returns without pity or condescension to engage the losses experienced by
friends in the aftermath of his crucifixion and resurrection.[26]

One morning, I chat with Aisha and Andie as they weed a flowerbed at Sacred Family. They ask about my teaching, and I describe to them my struggles to teach Eiesland's *The Disabled God* to a small group of students at a nearby university. They resonate with the image and do not find it hard to follow.

"It's like the song, 'What If God Was One of Us,'" Andie suggests.

I agree with her, repeating the lyrics of the 1995 hit by pop artist Joan Osborne: "What if God was one of us/just a slob like one of us/just a stranger on the bus/trying to make his way home?"[27]

"I love that song!" Aisha chimes in. "Many people get mad all the time [about the song], but I like it. If Jesus walked the earth once, why he can't do it again?" Andie murmurs her agreement. Aisha goes on, "That song makes me cry every time. It makes me be kind to all the people on the bus," she adds and then repeats, "It makes me cry every time."

In this very short conversation, Andie and Aisha have managed to illustrate Eiesland's argument with which my students struggled. The disabled God matters because a name for God, a symbol for the divine life, deeply affects our everyday religious practices and the ways we perceive ourselves and one another. Aisha's desire to be kind to people on the bus is summoned through a name for God.

Andie, Aisha, and I enjoy our common love of this song as we contemplate the disabled God. Then Kayla comes over. Hearing the last part of our conversation, she joins in. "I know where Jesus is," she tells us. "Have you heard of Japan?" We look at her in surprise. She tells us that if she had plane tickets, she would take us there.

We are at a loss for words. Then Aisha says, "Cool!" as if she is perfectly fine with the idea that Jesus is in Japan. Kayla continues our conversation by adding another song to our theological reflection: "Do you know the song 'Jesus is on that mainline/Tell Him what you want'?" Later I ask Kayla why she thinks Jesus is in Japan. She has a persistent interest in Japan, sometimes evoking it in her paintings. She says because they have a lot of problems in Japan. She heard they eat dirt there.

What if God were one of us? Aisha imagines a scenario in which we can see all the strangers on the bus as deserving of kindness and in which we are moved to tears by a God who chooses public transportation as her way of travel. I imagine a context in which Kayla follows the disabled Jesus to Japan and finds the Japanese to be other than the people with the problems she has imagined. Sacred Family reveals that even in the space and time of a liturgy that claims God's infinite love for each one, the church struggles to manifest and articulate this reality. It is difficult to name a world where God is with everyone we meet. It is hard to imagine because we are often strange to one another and to ourselves. It is much easier to pray for the poor and the disabled and the Japanese than to invoke the vivid and manifold array of individuals and relationships summoned through such phrases. Yet to claim God's name as intimately connected with people we name as other demands creative attention to both God and others. Where God is named as present, those who worship this God must pay attention and homage. When God is named in association with unlikely people and places, this name arouses curiosity. Who is the God who rides the bus? Who is this Jesus in Japan? Who is this One whose holy name evokes curiosity and compassion but resists pity and condescension?

At Sacred Family, multiple interpretive frameworks laid on top of one another blur an image of mental illness, of poverty, of church membership. The blurred image, the dissonant sounds that accompany them, hover beneath the dis-ease of some congregants in describing their relationships with others. Language betrays the inherent difficulties in imagining and cultivating relationships amidst the dynamics of power and privilege that constitute Sacred Family. While at times its members ignore such dissonance, there are moments in conversations and interactions when the inadequacy of terminology reminds those who attempt to speak through them that they require better words than those most immediately available. Such dissonance reminds us that the disabled God, or the mad God, who might also be the poor, black, queer, Asian God, is not often named as such within the walls of Christian churches. If Christ is the one in solidarity with those who have mental illness, then this God is not often in the pews, but is on the bus, on the street, in the psychiatric ward, at McDonald's, in the corner store, and outside the group home. Christ rises elsewhere. Into the struggle to name God's location, imaging and relating to Christ though the peace of the Spirit marks a recognizable path of love to what is not yet known.

Meditating on the same New Testament Easter texts in which Eiesland discovers and names the disabled God, theologian Rowan Williams names this Christ a "familiar stranger." Christ as "alien friend," whose life opens a new world for the Christian church, is never the possession of the disciples or of the church. The church is continually reminded of the strangeness of the Christ who comes again to speak the name of those who thought they already knew him but realize they do not. Jesus returns to the disciples after his resurrection as one who recedes from the grasp of any who would claim him:

> The risen Jesus is strange and yet deeply familiar, a question to what
> we have known, loved and desired, and yet continuous with the friend

we have known and loved. His strangeness and his recognizability are both shocking, standing as they do in such inseparable connection. . . . The risen Jesus returns as a loved friend and brother, and at the same time holds us off: he shows the marks of familiar human pain, yet refuses to be only a consoling mirror-image of our suffering.[28]

The Christ who appears in the gospel texts is a surprise to the disciples who believe they possess the requisite knowledge of him. Coming to and receding from the church's grasp, the risen Jesus, the disabled God, calls for the church to journey. In following the stranger, those who seek Christ cannot escape the "consistent echo of disorientation and surprise" that hovers around these stories of Jesus's return to those who are his followers.[29] Or, as Wallace, joking, once put it to me during a church service, in his playful reformulation of a eucharistic response: "Christ has died, Christ has risen, Christ is gonna get you!"

Reading Sacred Family through the Easter texts, in the company of Eiesland and Williams, we might say that human lives are often got or caught or found in the gaps and beats between the names, the terms, the tensions in what is articulated (a place of unity and belonging premised on the dignity of each one) and what is manifest among those who gather (a place where true friendship feels impossible). Here there is a family that is not and cannot be family. Here friendships nourish some, and many fall short of lasting relationships that work with the nitty-gritty of love over time. Here adults claim one another as children of God and address one another, condescendingly, like small children. There is a patient who is also a poet and gardener. There is a medical expert who has mental illness and is a comedian. There is a nurse who is a nail lady. There is a woman who lives constantly in the struggle between death and life and still embraces her life. In the building and witness of this community, even imperfect names hold the hope for more and better words with which to name another. The dissonance between one name and another sounds and arouses the desires of congregants for a different understanding of themselves in relationship with themselves and others. There are questions to be asked: Which names are harmful? Which names give life? Which words are adequate to the task at hand?

BETWEEN DEATH AND LIFE: THE EMBRACE OF MANY NAMES

To discern the right names for relationships in our liturgies is never easy, for our language for human life is halting and impoverished. Some names we must throw away in order to regard the person whom we address with the honor they deserve. Some names, however, can lead us into life together, and we must pursue, try on, and find these names. If God calls Sacred Family as the church, as a beloved community, as a circle of friends, this God must name and nurture desire not only through tension but also affirmation, claiming those who gather as those who belong to one another and who respond to one another's needs in recognition of this belonging. If dissonant names signal confusion and desire, what then is the sign that any name resonates with the relationships that arise among a group of people that gather in Jesus's name in the invocation of the Spirit?

Occasionally, at Sacred Family, the liturgy invites such moments of illumination, not as single names, but as a crescendo of names performed by the whole community. One Wednesday evening, for example, on the celebration of the Eve of the Ascension, the church gathers to remember the life of Albert, a community member who recently died. Before the sermon, as is the Sacred Family tradition, the priest gives an opportunity for congregants to share memories and stories about Albert. One young man begins by saying what a nice guy he was. Kayla remembers how he used to stroke her chin and teased her about having a beard. She says she is really going to miss him. Another man remembers that he was a great artist. Shonda recalls his classy dress and his classy smile. Deacon Mac appreciates that Albert could trash talk with him. Father Brian reflects on the kinds of suffering Albert had experienced and the ways he treated others with respect even when he was suffering. Hannah stands up and holds a colorful painting that Albert made of a small bird sitting on a barbed wire fence. The community breaks into a spontaneous round of applause for this work of art, a physical reminder of Albert's life and work. In the course of this service, Albert's life, his struggle and his hope, is named in many different ways, refusing one-dimensional portraits that might be summoned through names like mental illness or program participant, or even child of God.

If there are moments of dissonance that are part of Sacred Family's frames for acknowledging relationships, then there are also resonant refrains when an accumulation of names responds to the question of how one will know when a name is adequate to the person who is loved. Such moments more fully name the life of the person they symbolize and thus generate an experience of beauty within Sacred Family as community. The performance of such names reflects the artistries of social interaction that give rise to them. They amplify the desire of a community and of God for a person who might otherwise be thrown away.

Adequate names matter. They matter to the embrace of the beauty of human connection and well-being, even when those connections involve a struggle between life and death. They require many different relationships over time. They matter not only to the ones whose lives deserve many more words than poor or destitute or bipolar or client or constituent or staff or vicar or us or them; they also matter to the naming of God, who is addressed through language that connects God to and through God's relatedness to the creation. Christians often name God—know God—as one who heals disability or illness, or as the one who loves the poor and destitute, or the one who reconciles black and white people, or as Salvation or Love. But the arts and struggle of naming at Sacred Family reveal that God is only known and loved when those words themselves become flesh, again, so that the complex lives they symbolize become shape and sound and relation rather than stereotype or caricature. For, if God is the One who loves the poor and destitute and heals the sick, then this God is known only when the lives of "the poor" and "the destitute" and "the sick" are not reduced to one-dimensional symbols of complex human experiences and Christians begin to know the multifaceted people who elicit such depths of divine love and the coalitions that help God's people in the struggle for life. Words become flesh when there is sufficient time and ample space to know and love another human life in multiple forms. Thus, the work of the people in a liturgy is not only to name God but to name well those with whom and about whom Christians pray.

Taking on the particularities of human flesh, such names both touch this God we name and reveal their own limits, especially when Christians pray for healing and transformation of the world. God's name is not known or loved apart from the creative struggle for adequate human names. This struggle to find good names and pay creative attention to relationships of difference is the journey of those called to discern and name Christ's presence among us. Such naming occurs through desire, rather than an illusion of control: a desire to know where God is, with whom God sits, how God heals, and through whom God befriends those who hope and struggle to embrace their own lives.

Row of chairs in the sanctuary sit empty between services. A painting of red tulips hangs on the wall. (Photo credit: Cindy M. Brown)

CHAPTER 5

Sending: Aesthetics of Belonging

This little light of mine, I'm gonna let it shine . . .
Everywhere I go, I'm gonna let it shine . . .
Jesus gave it to me, I'm gonna let it shine . . .
—A favorite spiritual of Sacred Family congregants

Sending the Church, Empowering the People

One Sunday in early February, a bishop comes to visit Sacred Family. It is a morning of celebration: Andie's baptism, Jack's confirmation, and Belinda's reception into the church. The community first gathers for a festive breakfast and conversation with the bishop and then reassembles in the sanctuary for the formal service.

Before the rituals of baptism and confirmation, there is a homily. The bishop begins this sermon with a question: "So why are you here this morning? Why did you come to church?"

"Praise the Lord. Praise Jesus!" a chorus of voices responds.

The bishop offers another possible answer: "To be together. To not be alone, right? To be in a place where you have value and worth, where you are important to someone, where somebody loves you. Jesus loves you."

"Jesus loves you," Forest affirms.

Jesus loves you, but isn't it important that others love you? That's what it means to be a family. So today, we celebrate the sacrament of baptism. We're going to publicly say that this person is now a member of

our family. We will love them, give them value and worth, and think
that they're important. And we'll miss them when they are not here
for whatever reason. We will help them when they need help. We will
gather together and give strength to one another.

The bishop goes on to describe the church as a place where people
gather not only to be loved and to belong but also to be sent, to be light and
salt for the world. He connects this to the ritual actions of the community
that morning.

> We're going to confirm somebody and that reminds us of our job as
> followers of Jesus. Confirmation is not about being together; it's about
> being sent. It's entering into apostolic ministry. The word apostle
> from the Greek has a very simple meaning. It means one who is sent.
> To be a Christian isn't just to come together to get good things for us.
> Coming to church isn't just about what you get. Coming to church is
> about what you get so you can give it away. And so if you listen to the
> words, our deacon will send us into the world. We come together to
> gather the light that is in this building, but our job is to take that light
> out into the world of darkness. And to be light to other people. Our
> job is take the light into the world where the darkness lives, so that
> some others can see that light. . . . If you find something that is good
> for you in coming to this church, ask yourself who you are going to
> give it to. Because what happens if you hold on to the light? And you
> hold it so tight you don't want to let it get away?

"You extinguish it," Jack, the one to be confirmed, responds.

> You extinguish it. Exactly! It's like putting a bushel over it so that no
> one can see the light, but if we do that, the light in us goes out. So that
> when we're trying our best to hold on to something, we're losing it.
> The truth of the gospel is that the light only grows if you are willing
> to take the risk to give it away. And it is a risk isn't it? It's scary. . . .
> You put out your hands again, empty, and Jesus fills them with the
> light of his presence. You get the light again and again and again. This
> is why we come back every week. To get more light so that we can give
> it away. You, you, you, and I are the light of the world. If the world is
> dark, it's not because there is not enough light; it's because we're hid-
> ing it in places like this and not sending the light into the places where
> it is needed. You and I, you and I, normal, ordinary people, or maybe
> we're not so normal, none of us is, but God has chosen us to be a light
> to the world.

Yes! There is a chorus of affirmation to this word. At the end of the sermon, the bishop encourages us to look to the Spirit's work among us:

Look at the rays of light. The Spirit is among you today. You are living light. That's you. Those rays of light. Take them out of this place. Make a difference. Change the world. Jesus did that with twelve disciples. Think what we could do if we all did that together.

This bishop's sermon has a rousing effect on the congregation. Although this occasion affords him a unique opportunity to speak about the power of liturgical sending, his invocation also echoes an already familiar pattern repeated within the weekly prayers and gestures of the sending of the congregation after communion. Embedded in these words and gestures is an assumption: To know and love God, a Christian community not only gathers together in a physical location but is also sent out to take whatever is found, revealed, and shared there out beyond the boundaries of a building and space to those who are not present.

The sermon on this celebratory Sunday punctuates the weekly petitions of the post-communion prayers that congregants say together at the end of every service before the dismissal. The prayers imagine a similar trajectory to the one offered in the bishop's sermon: the community gathers to be nourished and claimed by God and other Christians before being sent to love and to serve others as "faithful witnesses" and as those capable of "gladness and singleness of heart." Such prayers echo a favorite song of Sacred Family congregants: "This little light of mine I'm gonna let it shine, everywhere I go, I'm gonna let it shine."

At Sacred Family the sending involves the ritual action of turning away from the focal point of the altar and toward the back doors of the sanctuary. The priest, the acolytes, and the deacon process to those doors and stand in front of them during the final hymn. As the community turns, following the procession, the doors are opened wide to reveal the world beyond. When the final hymn has ended, the deacon commands the community: "Go in peace to love and serve the Lord!" The congregation responds, "Thanks be to God!" The doors open onto the Sacred Family gardens and the walkway that leads to communal meals. Just out of sight, beyond the beautiful flowers and trees, are the vans that will soon take some congregants out of this neighborhood to other parts of the city.

If gathering requires a faith that a community of difference can come together without violence or coercion, then sending involves a faith that a love and protection of these differences can be carried back out into a segregated city. As the bishop imagines it, there is a world in need of this church as it is sent in the lives of those who gather. Mapping the sending of Sacred Family congregants, we might ask: what is this world into which the love and service of the faithful witnesses brings light?

Sending a Church That Is for, within, and of the World

Liturgical theologians often posit necessary relationships between the church and the world. Alexander Schmemann, for example, argues that the church is given "for the life of the world." The sacraments reveal the meaning of the world as gift through adoration and joy: "the Eucharist is the entrance of the Church into the joy of its Lord. And to enter into that joy, so as to be a witness to it in the world, is indeed the very calling of the Church, its essential *leitourgia*, the sacrament by which it 'becomes what it is.'"[1] The church is a sacrament given for the life of the world to reveal the sacramental nature of all creation through the church's praise and adoration: the world is not an object to be used but a gift through which human life is given ultimate meaning. Thus to worship God as the church is the most profound public, political, or social action that one could take. The Eucharist—as joy and remembrance of the reality of the world—transforms human relationships. While Schmemann resists dualities of sacred and profane in terms of elevating the church over the world, he nonetheless believes a clear distinction is possible: "The liturgy begins then as a real separation from the world."[2] Such separation is important so that the church may be sent back into the world "as witnesses of this Light, as witnesses of this Spirit," testifying to the possibilities of salvation and redemption which previously seemed impossible.[3]

Theologians like Andrea Bieler, Luise Schottroff, and Mary McClintock Fulkerson trouble such clear distinctions or relations between church and world by speaking of what Fulkerson calls a "worldly church," one whose sacramental nature is embedded and shaped within the often invisible and complicated histories of place.[4] In their meditation on the sacredness of holy and ordinary meals, Bieler and Schottroff emphasize both the reality and imperative of "sacramental permeability." The task of liturgical imagination is to see one thing as another or in relationship to another: "Sacramental worship embraces a permeability in which the bread we consume at our kitchen tables, the bread we steal from the poor, and the bread that is consecrated and consumed during Holy Communion are related." Thus, the "celebration of the sacraments is a place full of conflict; [the Eucharistic life] creates presence and absence, love and alienation, hunger and abundant life."[5]

Fulkerson also warns about too broadly sketched maps that fail to account for the complicated relationships between congregations and the places that shape them over time: "The very conviction of God's redemptive presence tempts the theologian to map sense and order onto the worldly. The zeal to find good news can slip easily into the desire to smooth out the tangle called 'community,' rendering it amenable to the correct theological categories."[6] In her mind a "theology for a worldly church" attends carefully to ambiguity, banality, and opacity in light of ordinary existence.[7]

The Church Is Sent to a Gentrified Neighborhood

Part of the tangledness of Sacred Family as a community and congregation is its permeable relationship to an ever-changing neighborhood. At one time, congregants from personal care homes came to the church because they lived in the same neighborhood and were welcomed into its worship. But now, these same congregants with psychiatric disabilities are often strangers, persons out of place in a gentrified neighborhood. They are no longer part of the neighborhood except for their participation at Sacred Family. The current neighbors, who walk by the church with their dogs or as part of daily exercise routines, often appear friendly and only occasionally display anxiety in the presence of those whose dress and behavior mark them as other. Some come to plant sales or other Sacred Family community events. A few go so far as to associate Sacred Family congregants with crimes or identify them as a threat to the very neighborhood where some members once lived.

In the midst of this complicated relationship with those who live closest to the church, clergy often encourage Sacred Family members to consider the ways they might love and serve their neighbors—with particular emphasis on those who live closest to the church, the neighborhood. The thrust of sermons like the bishop's is to empower each one who gathers; for each one holds the light and has something we must give. Each person can minister to another, no matter their income or social status. As one priest put it, "There are people who do not know that they are called to love their neighbor as themselves. People who need to be saved from their lack of compassion. We need to invite them to Sacred Family where they can experience a laboratory for the development of compassion and empathy." Many of these invocations implicitly or explicitly assume the God-given ability of each individual to transform their neighbors and neighborhood. They allude to a pattern in which God—through the church—infuses neighborhoods with love. In this particular neighborhood, people from

Sacred Family, as light and salt for the world, have something to teach their wealthier, abled neighbors.

Alongside the goals of theological transformation, the parish desires that neighbors with incomes might come and share the financial responsibilities of sustaining this community in ways that unemployed congregants cannot. Such desires are not stated explicitly in church services but often surface in meetings. Sacred Family staff members desire the support of the neighborhood—or those with incomes like those in the neighborhood— in order to have the resources it needs for Circle programs. A relationship of potential mutuality exists with people whose homes surround the church: the parish's neighbors need the good news of Sacred Family's vision of community, and Sacred Family desires more financial resources and support to enable this vision to flourish.

One afternoon, I discuss these complicated relationships between parish, neighbors, and neighborhood with a retired priest, who frequently attends Sacred Family. Abe and his spouse, Esther, choose Sacred Family for its liveliness. Finding themselves bored or restless in other parishes, there is life within Sacred Family's gathering that draws them in and keeps them coming back. Over lunch one Sunday afternoon, we talk about the history of the parish. Abe describes how it was a failing church until group home congregants living nearby came to fill the pews at Sacred Family and helped to keep its doors open. Poor, disabled congregants in the neighborhood came to share meals with members of the church. Gradually these congregants transformed the community into a parish that welcomes people with mental disabilities.

Abe points to a pattern of similar developments in other congregations that are compelled to change in response to demographic shifts in neighborhoods. It is not that a congregation desires to change, but when the demographics of a neighborhood change, the congregation is forced to change as well or close its doors. Esther wonders out loud what will happen to Sacred Family as the neighborhood around the church transitions again, this time to a wealthier neighborhood. Will Sacred Family change again?

Her comment reflects current demographic shifts spurred by the desire of middle- and upper-income people to live in denser, urban neighborhoods, as well as municipal efforts to encourage this kind of development. One result of these shifts is that those marginalized by poverty are further displaced from their homes and neighborhoods and, increasingly, pushed further and further from the center of the city. In the past ten years, group homes have moved further away from the parish's immediate neighborhood due to rising property values. During my time at Sacred Family, the costs of housing in the surrounding neighborhoods—both rental rates and purchase prices—steadily rise. Echoing Esther's fears, I can imagine a time when Sacred Family as a church with and for poor people with mental illness ceases to exist.

The parish might then transition again to reflect the wealthier neighborhood or close its doors for good, as it almost did before group home residents helped bring it back to life. According to one Sacred Family vicar, many of the neighbors are friendly but not interested in attending church on a regular basis. When those who love and need this community live too far from it to be gathered to it, will there still be Sacred Family congregants for this parish to send? Such trends suggest complex dynamics between parish and neighborhood. Those who live nearby might reconfigure the neighborhood so as to deprive the parish of those who are currently at the heart of its congregational identity.

Rituals of sending such as those named in the bishop's sermon thus require sustained reflection on the particular persons sent and the kinds of relationships into which they are sent. Rather than assuming that the church is able to transform the neighborhood, one must ask what kinds of communal and economic arrangements might allow the church to sustain and foster its particular theological understanding: the significance of persons with mental illness to its mission and its vision of community. Asking these kinds of questions reveals the violence of the city within which faithful witnesses carry the good news they find within the parish.

The Church Is Sent to a Segregated City

While configurations of sending emerge from shifting patterns between Sacred Family and its immediate neighborhood, congregants are most literally sent to many different neighborhoods across the city of Atlanta. While they do not live near one another, many face similar conditions in the homes to which they return. During the initial months of my research, one of the Sacred Family interns collects stories about personal care homes from Circle regulars. He then assembles a list of common characteristics to help educate church leadership and others who come to the church without an understanding of the places from which people come and to which they return. While congregants rarely complain to me about the places where they live, the list helps to illustrate the challenging circumstances in which many of them abide.

Life in a Personal Care Home

BASED ON THE TESTIMONIALS OF CIRCLE PARTICIPANTS

The quality and structure of life vary a great deal between personal care homes. That being said, the following is true of all personal care homes in which our participants live:

Living in a PC costs $625 a month . . . at the most inexpensive. Generally, but not always, this is paid for with Social Security Disability.

Everyone has a roommate. Some share a small single bedroom. And some folks have two or more roommates. But no one has his or her own room.

Three meals a day are provided. They are never highly nutritious. In some cases the meals are decently nutritious, but in many cases white bread, bologna, and potato chips are staple foods.

Almost always, residents rise early and go to bed early. I think it is mandatory to get up by 7 am or so, and often residents go to bed at 8 or 9 pm. In at least one instance, a man had extreme difficulty sleeping because his roommate slept with the lights on and the TV on at full volume, but this situation seems rare.

Residents rarely come and go as they please. In many cases, the residents are forbidden to leave without permission, which is rarely given. In other cases, inability to pay for MARTA [the public transportation operator for metropolitan Atlanta], lack of anything within walking distance and lack of anywhere to go, keep residents in the house or yard all the time.

Fighting, bickering, and interpersonal drama arise frequently at most homes.

Some homes limit the number of showers residents can take.

Some homes will punish residents by not allowing them to leave, if a resident mentions looking for an alternative housing situation.

Most personal care homes (that we deal with) do not provide regular rides to the doctor, dentist, or psychiatrist. Some PC homes charge $15–$25 for rides to a medical facility. Some other homes do provide rides free of charge.

Some residents become great friends with their housemates, and most develop at least some positive sense of community.

The most difficult questions and anguished conversations I witness and participate in at Sacred Family are about the parish's relationship with group homes. This complex relationship often entails the kinds of power that group home owners and managers wield over the people who live there. While a few of the homes are known to be supportive places to live, the majority are tolerable at best. Parish members often express the urgent need to advocate for better conditions for congregants. Yet they also fear that their advocacy only further isolates members from spaces where they might find help or have access to basic resources. If the church raises questions about conditions in group homes, the owners or managers of these homes may ask Sacred Family no longer to gather congregants from their homes.

In one of the most tragic events during my time at Sacred Family, a group of congregants is sent home from the church because the individuals are covered with bedbugs. For months the management at their group home attempts to rid the home of the bedbug infestation, but to no avail. Eventually, the home is sold, and the congregants are sent to new homes. Neil, a staff person at the Circle, works to find places in new homes where living conditions will be better for congregants and where congregants will still be able to come to the church. In this process of attempting to locate good new homes for congregants, he is incensed when he realizes that these parishioners have already been sold, as he describes it, to other homes for a small referral fee. A staff member at the closed home reports that the owner accepted around $100 for each client to be referred or sent to another home. It is difficult to know what role (if any) the residents themselves played in these decisions about where they would move and with whom they would live; however, typical patterns of decision-making within group homes would suggest that residents were not given options. While most of these congregants eventually return to the church and express relative contentment with their new living situations, such practices reveal the frameworks through which poor people with mental illness can become commodities.

In an even more tragic occurrence, the Sacred Family van arrives at a personal care home one day to pick up a group of long-term congregants, including Wallace, Joshua, and Victoria, only to find that they no longer live there. The story, as various congregants and staff recount it to me, begins with an act of hope. Two women from this home have found a better living situation. When they leave their personal care home, they are accused of stealing items from the home; the two women subsequently contact Adult Protective Services to report neglect at their previous home. Fearing closure by state authorities, management evacuates the premises and moves all remaining residents to a different city outside of metro

Atlanta. The priest and other staff attempt to find the congregants. They talk to the manager who gives a general location. However, the manager refuses to provide a specific address and instead promises that the congregants will return at some point. Eventually, the owner of the home is tracked down and arrested on twelve counts of abuse and neglect. She is accused of moving the residents from place to place and of leaving residents outside for a time without food or medication.

Weeks after the arrest, the staff and others at the church have no way to contact congregants who have been moved to new homes but do not have cell phones or other means of communication. They receive news that a number of congregants were malnourished, dehydrated, unable to speak coherently, and hospitalized before they were moved to other licensed homes. The priest contacts over fifteen different authorities involved in the case to try to find the congregants and visit them, but she is told that their location cannot be revealed to her unless congregants themselves contact the church. They can be given her information, but she cannot be given theirs. Over the months and years that follow, the priest along with other church members try again and again to locate the church members. Last time I spoke with the priest, she told me she had spoken with dozens of people in an attempt to locate the members and had even hired a private detective to search for them, all to no avail.

In each of these situations, it is possible to locate the evil of such forms of abuse and coercions with those who run these homes, referring to the managers and owners as malevolent human beings who take advantage of vulnerable congregants. Sacred Family staff frequently speak with anger about individuals who wield power in the group homes; they are justifiably outraged at the ways congregants are abused and mistreated. Yet, to locate evil on the level of personal care home owners and managers is to make invisible the larger structures and patterns through which people with psychiatric disabilities, many of whom are also poor and black, are deprived of basic rights of protection, treated like property, and segregated from social networks that might offer recourse for abuse of rights.

Harming Those Who Are Sent: The Violence of Institutionalization

In May of 2012, over a year before my research at Sacred Family begins, journalists Craig Schneider and Andria Simmons of *The Atlanta Journal-Constitution* (*AJC*) publish a series of articles outlining the scope of the abuse and injustice affecting people with disabilities in the metro Atlanta area (both physically and mentally disabled people in both licensed and unlicensed personal care homes). They report that in the five years prior to the publication of these articles, the state of Georgia had found 35,000 violations in personal care homes yet had only leveled 544 fines; the average fine was $600. Of the eighteen homes that had more than one hundred violations each, fourteen remained in operation.[8] Within licensed homes, violations included insufficient training and background checks on employees, as well as inadequate living conditions such as dirty floors, bathtubs and walls, soiled toilets, and live cockroaches in the kitchen. Violations also entailed more serious neglect and abuse, including the failure to give necessary medicines for diabetes and heart disease—resulting in the death of a resident—and patterns of physical abuse.[9] In unlicensed homes, the violations included such offenses as residents beaten with belts and burnt with curling irons, confined to a basement with a bucket for a toilet, robbed of their money, and moved from home to home as owners and managers sought to evade the law.[10]

One of the articles suggests reasons for such rampant abuse and neglect. First, state resources required to oversee and implement regulation—or to track and close down unlicensed homes—are lacking. The authors relate this lack of resources to a significant increase in the number of homes in metro Atlanta, which grew from less than fifty in the mid-1990s to more than 900 homes in 2012. Such growth is attributed not only to an increase in the aging population (the number of people 65 and older increased more than 44 percent in the same timeframe) but also to the federal government's push to move mentally ill and developmentally disabled persons out of mental hospitals and into community settings. The authors suggest three factors contributing to the rampant problems they uncovered: the increase in people looking for homes, insufficient government resources to provide oversight, and the impact of the 2007/2008 recession on household income. There are not enough good homes for everyone who needs them. Furthermore, some who provide the housing are ostensibly looking for ways to make a living, but they do so without the commitments or institutional capacities to provide adequate care. The result is that many elderly and disabled people are valued as commodities to be exploited for their Social Security and other entitlement checks.[11]

Sacred Family congregants who participate in Circle programs are not powerless in these situations; many of them tell stories of how they deliberately moved from one group home to the next in search of a better life. I am amazed at the complex maps that many of them narrate for me as they trace their movements around the city both as their group homes move and as they seek other arrangements. The challenge then is not that congregants do not desire or actively pursue something better for themselves,

but that when they seek a better life, there are few, if any, good and affordable choices, and there are no choices that provide the kinds of support
that congregants desire without impinging on their rights to make basic
decisions about their lives. Even in the best situations, poor congregants
with mental illness often live with numerous other housemates with psychiatric disabilities, people whom they did not choose and with whom they
may find it difficult to live. As I visit congregants in their homes, it is difficult
for me to imagine surviving in the circumstances that these congregants
are asked to tolerate. One local disability advocate summarizes: "They [the
homes] are crazy making!"

The *AJC* articles about personal care homes reveal the horror of living
in poverty with mental illness in a particular place and time. But disability scholars argue that such forms of incarceration follow an all too common and pervasive logic by which many people with disabilities are
deprived of basic rights: "Disability, situated alongside other key lines of
stratification such as race, class, nationality, and gender, is central to
understanding the complex, varied, and interlocking ways in which incarceration occurs and is made out to be normal, natural, politically necessary, and beneficial."[12] They question the "neoliberal policies that [have]
led simultaneously to growth of the prison system, the reduction in
affordable housing, and the lack of financial support for disabled people
to live viably in the community."[13]

Of the many complex and varied factors that result in such devaluing of
disabled lives, four are particularly salient to the home lives of Sacred Family congregants: institutional logics of control that continue to prevail in
the wake of "deinstitutionalization"; perceptions of disability as an individual and medical problem rather than a social and political issue; the
commodification of disabled lives within for-profit models of "care" and
"custodialism" in a capitalist economy; and the continued segregation of
persons with disabilities from social networks in many "community-based"
institutions.

Disability scholars question a common narrative about the "failure of
deinstitutionalization" that might emerge from stories such as the one told
by the *AJC*. This narrative suggests that the problem lies with inadequate
resources to provide sufficient oversight for group homes or independent
living. Such understandings fail to recognize the patterns through which
institutions like the personal care homes perpetuate rather than challenge
the logics of institutional care and, thereby, people with disabilities. Steven
J. Taylor analyzes deinstitutionalization in his work on the continuum of
care for people with developmental disabilities. The continuum of care
framework advocates for progressively less restrictive communities, with

public institutions at one end of the continuum, groups homes somewhere in the middle, and independent living on the other end. Taylor argues that the continuum of care framework's emphasis on finding the "least restrictive environment" perpetuates an assumption that restriction is necessary. The continuum conflates higher levels of care and services with the necessity of segregated living and in so doing sanctions the violation of basic human rights, such as the rights to movement, privacy, and choice.[14]

Considering the re-institutionalizing logic of deinstitutionalization, advocacy for more resources to enhance government regulation of group homes is an inadequate response to the problem. Certainly, better regulation and more resources for such forms of protection are important, but equally if not more important are resources required for transforming logics of institutional care that pervade many group homes, fostering power asymmetries between owners, managers, staff, and those who live there. Thus, Taylor and others advocate for innovative community-based models of integration that do not assume an exchange of rights for the relationships and supports needed to navigate daily life.

The continuation of an institutional logic for persons with disabilities is perpetuated by the second factor, a persistent pattern of interpreting disability as an individual or medical problem that is solved by "correcting, normalizing or eliminating the pathological individual."[15] Rather than transforming the social imaginations that pathologize disability, this emphasis on the individual's responsibility for the pathology means that the individual is in some way responsible for the needs they have and their own inabilities to meet those needs. Thus, those who reside in care homes can be expected to give up basic rights in order to receive care to ameliorate or correct their pathology. As Carey, Ben-Moshe, and Chapman point out, this desire "to individualize and psychiatrize what is properly a political, ethical, and socioeconomic issue," also directs attention away from the state and its policies for provision of care to a "human service sector who are charged with ameliorating the problem with individualistic mental health interventions and haphazardly available free meals or sleeping bags."[16] In this regard, persons with disabilities are denied the right to stable availability of basic services and, in order to secure basic services, can be expected to forfeit basic rights.

Third, in the context of personal care homes, disabled people are not only problems to be solved but sources of income to be exploited. Sacred Family congregants have enough money to make them valuable commodities as they are pursued by various group homes in need of constituents, but not enough money to give them other viable options about where they live and with whom. Many are regarded as a source of revenue within a capitalist and human service economy in which practices of care are profit driven, so that the meals and other services provided are minimal or insufficient in order that caregivers can maximize their profits. Furthermore, such caregivers may advise group home members to make choices that are economically advantageous for the caregivers or the group home rather than for the individual.

Fourth, while the personal care home might be understood as a community-based model of care, it is clear from the experiences of Sacred Family that the group homes remain highly segregated from the communities and people who surround them and thus deprive group home members of broader social networks of people that might advocate for them and bear witness when violations to rights do occur. While Sacred Family provides a social network and place of belonging for those who come to the church, the relationships are often limited to a particular "social geography"—the space and time of church gatherings.[17] Thus, when an entire group of people disappears from a neighborhood and community, it takes some time before the church, family members, or anyone else knows about it. Without reliable access to phones, credit cards, online accounts, or even online networks that might provide clues to their locations, it proves impossible to find those who have moved or been moved against their will even when church leaders put significant time and resources into locating them.

In light of such persistent devaluing of congregants' lives, how then does the church claim a truth about communal belonging through baptism and confirmation such as the bishop did in our opening story: that the lives of those marked through its rituals and sacraments are inestimably valuable both to God and to God's people? How can anyone declare that through the power of the Spirit at work within the church congregants are prepared to be sent back out into the difficult, even dangerous conditions they regularly face? The situations into which congregants are sent often contest the gestures and words that Sacred Family places upon them through sacramental blessing. In view of the desecration of life that many persons face outside the church, the flexibility and freedom of the space at Sacred Family also becomes a limitation, a source of lament and despair over the community's inability to protect clients from the degradation they encounter.

Losing Those Who Are Sent: The Fragility of the Worldly Church

One morning Neil and I discuss the perils of the loose weave of community that is Sacred Family: where people come and go as they are able, engaging as full participants for a time and then disappearing for a time to return later. While such flexibility facilitates forms of belonging that invite non-coercive participation, it also characterizes a community where many who gather are lost to others over time.

Neil reflects on the challenge of maintaining close relationships for those who come to the Circle. He describes two close friends who attended Circle programs for a time and then disappeared.

> They were gone for a few months and she came back. And they were like best buds, both homeless but in a very supporting relationship to one another. And I said, "Where is your friend?" . . . And she said, "Well, I heard he drank himself to death." And that was—I got the impression that that was his closest relationship in the world was his relationship with this woman, and his death was just through the grapevine to her.

Neil goes on to describe how such loss affects funeral and burial practices, the sacredness of human bodies after death, particularly as it affected a longtime Sacred Family congregant:

> When Marlys died, and the state, to do their due diligence, before they will do a pauper's burial, does a search for next of kin. And they hunt down basically anybody who they hope will claim the body and claim financial responsibility. I just feel a kind of spiritual unrest with the body of my friend being in a cooler in the city morgue for a month. I mean there is just something about that that just really bothers me. . . . And people here have fluid loss in their lives, where they just lose so much of family and supporting relationships that they die, and because there is nobody who can claim financial responsibility, their body just stays frozen for a month until they get a pauper's burial in an unmarked grave. I mean the pauper's field is a beautiful field, but I don't know, it's just something about it (his voice trails off).

I respond, reflecting on Sacred Family as a place that works to cultivate a community without the coercive rules and regulations that mark group homes: "It strikes me: one of the things I think is beautiful about Sacred Family is the flow, the fluidity, people can come and go, and they don't have to show up and sign something, or do whatever, but I do think it makes, I can see that it would be hard because then . . ."

"People get lost!" Neil interjects with vehemence.

Neil offers another example of a year in which there were not enough church staff, in the form of interns, to do home visits. The following year, he sent interns to follow up at nursing homes with a number of people who could no longer make the journey to Sacred Family. He discovered that Sacred Family no longer had correct addresses for four people who had once been regulars in the community. He was particularly concerned about a former congregant who had Alzheimer's and couldn't engage in conventional conversation; in her situation, it would be difficult, if not impossible, for her to contact the church. He concludes this story with how terrible it can feel to know that people who were claimed by the church community might be lost and unable to be found by the congregation: "I have lost so many members of our community to the wind. I don't know if they are alive or dead, and that's the painful side of having such fluidity in this community, and that's also the fluidity of poverty."

In this community, congregants are often displaced when a neighborhood becomes too expensive for a group home to exist there, or because home managers are attempting to evade closure, or because congregants move from home to home in a search of better conditions. Any one of these congregants might be sent from the parish on any given day without assurance of their safe return. Thus, congregants' abilities to be light for their neighbors and advocates for themselves are limited by the violence of social spaces within which they might love and serve the world around them. It is not that congregants are unable to let the light of their lives shine in the world and to build community among those with whom they share home. In fact, such forms of support (or lack of support) are palpable at Sacred Family when group home mates seek out and advocate for one another, or have disagreements and become frustrated with one another. Nor is it that they are unaccompanied by divine love; the church claims that they are marked as beloved in life and death, whether or not the church knows where they are. Yet relationships outside the bounds of the church often appear threatened by coercive living spaces in which only fragile forms of community can be sustained. These relationships are affected by spaces that anthropologist João Biehl identifies as "zones of social abandonment,"[18] where what it means to be human is contested. In these zones, societies come to relegate certain persons as "ex-human" through repetitive practices of neglect, abuse, or indifference.[19] Those whose lives do not make "common sense" to others are excluded from what counts as reality.[20] Those considered "good for nothing" are sent to spaces where their deaths become inevitable yet appear "self-generated."[21]

When I map the sending of Sacred Family, it seems to me that relationships formed within the congregation do little to disturb forms of segregation or zones of abandonment in the broader city or to create new patterns of living together outside the space of the church. If ostensibly distinct spaces are always overlapping and intersecting through the memories, histories, and bodies of those who gather and create a place together,[22] then the place of Sacred Family is continually informed by the ways in which those who are sent, myself included, do not share space and time outside the church gathering. A liturgy decentered and inspirited out to the boundaries of the congregation is often circumscribed by the physical boundaries of the church property, outside of which forms of belonging to one another are more difficult to imagine.

One of the priests often emphasizes the mission of the church made explicit in the church's prayer book as being "to restore all people to unity with God and each other in Christ." Such images of unity resonate with refrains in the eucharistic prayers that talk about gathering those who are scattered from the nations as one people. Yet when I imagine the promises of sending each one, the hope is that those who are gathered might then be scattered not alone but *together* across the dividing lines of wealth and mental ability. The hope is that the differences gathered might also be mirrored in new patterns of intimacy, solidarity, and creativity in the particular places in which people live around the city. Such scattering might perform the theological work that theologian M. Shawn Copeland describes as "eucharistic solidarity" where the "dynamics of domination" are countered by the "dynamics of love"[23] and through which those who are sent by the church recognize the truth of the fact that they are created for communion with one another and belong to one another.

Sending as Solidarity and the Aesthetics of Interdependence

The sending prayers at Sacred Family claim that all who are sent are "faithful witnesses to Christ our Lord" through the love and service rendered. As I ride the vans and occasionally visit personal care homes, I come to understand the struggle to witness to the difficult realties of group homes, both for those who live there and for those who might visit from the church. Here, the possibilities for human flourishing and the material conditions under which poor persons might live well with mental illness are not yet imagined or felt. One volunteer describes the group homes as "too depressing," especially in light of difficult circumstances she has in her own family. Yet she also dreams of a day when every person in the congregation has an advocate in the form of another person who would actively and intentionally intercede on their behalf for the resources they require.

Even in cases where Sacred Family congregants attempt advocacy on behalf of one another outside the boundaries of the church, relationships are troubled by histories of racism and ableism that inhibit acts of solidarity. When Sacred Family is sent out to other churches for outings, where they are now in another congregation or community's space, many Sacred Family members celebrate the rare opportunity to be treated as invited and honored guests. But here, too, it is clear that they are recipients of gifts not their own, in places in which they do not make decisions about the structures and patterns of giving and receiving that take place. Invitations and relationships with other congregations often appear fragile and conditional. Sacred Family depends on gifts from people who may or may not be invested in the kinds of community that Sacred Family envisions and struggles to maintain.

Even when church members share a common vision, histories of oppression mean that well-intentioned support fails. For example, a young, white, abled woman tells me the story of how she struggled to advocate for needed medical resources for an older, disabled, black man. He came to resent the assistance she was trying to give him, and he thus resisted depending on her to fill out the necessary medical paperwork. He felt belittled rather than empowered by her desire to remain by his side in the hospital, even though he required help to navigate a system that would not recognize his needs and that he could not navigate on his own. To remain together and to advocate from within such spaces reflects the deep challenges of solidarity across histories of oppression and condescension and the well-founded suspicions that some have of others' motives and commitments.

As Neil and I reflect on patterns of dwelling and belonging together across the spaces of the city, we imagine the practices and conditions that disability scholar and community organizer Mia Mingus describes as moving from "forced intimacy" to "access intimacy." Forced intimacy operates on a transactional model of access: people with disabilities must accept terms of intimacy and forms of vulnerability they may not choose in order to gain access to the spaces and relationships they need or desire. Forced intimacy assumes that because some are dependent on others, they must consent to a proximity with others they would not otherwise choose.[24] In contrast, Mingus describes access intimacy as consensual practices of interdependence among those who create access together, forms of access that may be imperfect but that are also not conditional: "when access intimacy is present, the most powerful part is having someone to navigate access and ableism with. It is knowing that someone else is with me in this mess." Such interdependence involves a transformation in social imagination and power dynamics: "The power of access intimacy is that it reorients our approach from one where disabled people are expected to squeeze into able bodied people's world, and instead *calls upon able bodied people to inhabit our world.*" Disabled people aren't expected to "shrink" themselves into able-bodied and able-minded worlds but non-disabled people are invited to transform their own habits and practices to cultivate interdependence. Such intimacy is sometimes intuitive and often hard to build and sustain, particularly as those who are abled have less to lose when access to intimacy is not sustained or cultivated and as white supremacy and ableism function so as to isolate disabled people of color.[25]

Sending then might be the promise to cultivate access intimacy among those who are sent together so that all those who sent are accompanied in these liturgical acts of sending. Those who are subject to the marks of social death cannot be held solely responsible to shine a light on the injustice of their own home situations and of the body practices of incarceration they experience. In this case, rituals of sending might proclaim a form of ecclesial solidarity and name a practice of attention to the conditions and relationships necessary for art forms of interpersonal relationships to continue outside the church grounds. As a practice of interdependence, sending has both ecclesial and political dimensions and calls attention to the interrelationship between the two.

Such a connection is evident in Lloyd's reflection on life at this parish, a place where he is certain that God has called him to be. He wonders whether the church could play another role outside the boundaries of the church. Perhaps, he suggests, "we could do more . . . like when they do things at the Capitol, try to sign people up, there's one in January . . . a mental health day, not raise hell, but silently raise hell. I read a lot about these silent protests, they don't cause trouble, they're there." He reflects on how his anxiety around crowds prevents him from taking part in such protests. Like Sacred Family, Lloyd struggles to imagine a way to transform public regard of himself, and other congregants, whose beauty might remain hidden within the parish grounds. Both he and I have to try to imagine what public and communal forms this act of sending might take in light of the already fragile community struggling to sustain the space and time of its own identity.

Political action—and its relationship to ecclesial belonging as Eiesland defines it—begins with the fragile yet ordinary interdependence of human bodies. To be embodied is to be held together and to act out in love of one's own life and the lives of others. "Acting out" is the refusal to accept the roles and places assigned people with disabilities. "Holding our bodies together" evokes those practices that enable solidarity with one's own body and with others who are marginalized.[26] For many people at Sacred Family, the struggle for life in group homes and in the broader space of the city shapes how they hold together body-minds or how they act out against injustice.

On the one hand, disabled congregants are remarkably resourceful in claiming their own beloved lives and in manifesting a strong resistance to whatever would mark them as "ex-human." On the other hand, those who live in group homes often cannot afford to act or speak out against those on whom they depend for survival. Yet without social protest of such zones of abandonment, or without moral imagination to envision an alternative, congregants' lives and relationships remain at risk of real abuse and literal death. Some congregants are sent out again and again without the hope of conditions in which the light of their lives is not under threat of being extinguished by forces beyond their control.

The liturgical act of sending at Sacred Family requires forms of sending that resonate with both the beauty and the fragility of a disabled church. Sending as belonging to one another must, then, take clues from patterns familiar in the gathering of the congregation: from the practices of consent that help to hold its communal life together. How, for example, might the pleasures of eating together shape the protest of the community against the degradation of some congregants? Such a question emerges from another sermon, which links the acts of sending with the work of theological imagination.

Perils and Promises of Sending: Imagining a Future for All

On the twenty-fifth anniversary of the Americans with Disabilities Act, a visiting preacher reads this landmark piece of legislation through the lens of a gospel text. The disabled preacher invokes the feeding of the five thousand as a parable about eschatological imagination. Describing the ADA as a work in progress, he notes the disciples' inability to grasp the provision for the crowd that Jesus intended. "It's really important to begin to believe in a world that God dreams, and that world is a world where everyone has access to the means to live," he urges the small group gathered in the sanctuary. As I listen to him, I have difficulty imagining the real possibility of a world in which these congregants are regarded with both dignity and desire and, therefore, have access to the resources they need. I find it almost impossible to believe in a soon-to-be world where they would have adequate protection.

Claiming the good news of the text, the preacher reminds us not to give up hope:

> Our role as a people of faith is to claim God's vision and to claim that the history of God is to claim a history of bread. It's a history of feeding people *and* taking seriously that people have what it takes to make it through the night, *and* using that vision of the world to ask good questions of lawmakers, *and* to push forward when we don't quite have what we need, *and* to be persistent about this idea that people should not have to live on less than is livable. People should not have to make it on just a portion of what they need! And so it becomes important to ask ourselves and to ask the church: what is it we're going to do to continue to push for a future where everyone has what it takes to make it through the night?

After the sermon, the community celebrates a sacred history of bread, of feeding, as we do every Sunday: an enthusiastic passing of the peace, prayers of the people, a gathering of offerings both monetary and vegetable, and a eucharistic prayer that recalls salvation history. As we eat together, I am left with the preacher's questions. How do we come to believe in a world that God dreams? What kinds of belonging to and intimacy with other people both within and outside the physical boundaries of the parish does this require? What do I need to know of another to dream a city and world where she has what she needs or where they can claim from me what they need?

Liturgical theologians often emphasize the communion table as a site of such theological imagination. Bieler and Schottroff, for example, trace eschatological motifs woven through the history of eucharistic prayers and texts: a gathering of those who have been scattered, a feast for the nations who have gathered, an end to violence in the remembrance of the death and resurrection of Christ, and a reminder of the covenant God has made with God's people.[27]

With similar hope, theologian M. Shawn Copeland argues for the possibility of eucharistic witness to transform community. Identifying her theological task as one of "re-membering and remembrance,"[28] she remembers the body of Jesus—"marked by race, gender, culture and religion," "by refugee status, occupation and colonization"[29]—as one who regularly ate with other people, in intimate practices that were interpreted by some, according to the gospel accounts, as strange and scandalous. Copeland interprets the sharing of an open, common table as an imitation of Jesus and a faithful witness to the community of desire and resistance of

which he was a part.[30] In Copeland's argument, we must mark the flesh of
Christ through a communion table where all are welcome. Gathering
human differences, marked, despised bodies, around a communion table,
Christians resist the devaluation of human flesh.[31] Interpreting Eucharist
as a resistance to the "anti-Logos" and "antiliturgies" of globalization and
racism that debase human life, she envisions a "welcome table" as an
embodiment of new loyalties and resistance to empire.[32]

At Sacred Family the congregation eats together at an open table in the
ecclesial spaces of the church, a place where all are explicitly welcome to
partake of the holy meal and of any church meal that precedes and follows
Holy Communion. Yet such intimacies emerge in sharp contrast to the
many tables that are not shared at other times in home spaces, where the
closest friendships and familial bonds are manifest. The holy table stands
apart from the ordinary tables of home and group home, not only because
congregants that do not live together spend little time in one another's
home, but also because a mutual sharing of home spaces is difficult for
many to imagine.

Even within a congregation like Sacred Family, which expressly desires
mental difference to be at the heart of its eucharistic celebrations, there is a
danger of segregationist charity. What might it mean for congregants, volunteers, and visitors to share not only the common tables of altar and church
dining room and picnic table but also the personal spaces of homes scattered across the city? What might it mean to share Thanksgiving Dinner
and Easter Feast and wedding showers and birthday parties, not only within
the moderated space and time of a church gathering but in the intimate
spaces of home and group home, with family and friends across a table?

Such questions are occasioned by an invitation to a home. I am welcomed to a private celebration in the church to which both church and
non-church guests are invited. It is a festive sharing of food and friendship
that takes place in a member's house. The gathering is characterized by
different kinds of eating (no lines, no long tables) and socializing (min-
gling, moving in and out of small groups in the kitchen and living room,
touring the home) than is possible with such a large group in a parish hall.
While I am grateful to be present and enjoy the festivities, I find it significant that although not everyone in the church could be invited, no Circle
participants are present. While this absence might well result from the
difficulties of transportation from a different part of the city, it appears as a
clear divide within an ecclesial community, a divide made palpable in social
interaction that would likely differ in its form if group home congregants
were present.

Such an event compels me to ask questions about the people I invite into my home and whose homes I visit. Many of these people share something in common in terms of wealth, ability, education, and race. I consider inviting even just two or three Circle congregants to parties and dinners with my own friends, particularly those Sacred Family members with whom I most enjoy sharing pleasures within the space and time of the church, as well as those who express desire for more opportunities for social interaction during the week. Such an invitation would necessarily entail arranging transportation. Such an invitation would also result in different kinds of social interaction than might otherwise occur at the gatherings my spouse and I host.

I also imagine accepting invitations to celebrate holidays and important occasions in personal care homes. How might people who live in different parts of the city, with different aesthetics of interaction over food and conversation, commit to share and consent to space and time together? What arts of social interaction might be summoned forth by such occasions? While many Sacred Family congregants are supportive of my research and writing, some are far less concerned with written representation than with sustained social interaction. Will I continue to spend time with them, even when my project is over? Will I return to the church? Entertaining this question, I envision new relationships this continued commitment might entail, post-research and writing.[33]

If I imagine a time when everyone at Sacred Family has access to the means to live, it begins with a scattering of those who gather, a scattering out into one another's lives across the lines of ability, wealth, race, and security, to share the desires, aesthetics, pleasures, and discomforts of many common tables. Such a sharing of pleasure and deprivation would occur outside the safe spaces and the moderated liturgical time of the church through invitation by small groups or individuals. Such a liturgy of sending would begin with relationships made possible through the gathering of Sacred Family but also extend the physical boundaries of the community. It would entail smaller configurations of relationships that might be sustained over time. It would not consist of one group (volunteers) helping another (participants), but a few people together at a time helping to rearrange the spaces of the city with and through others.

The Arts of Sending a Disabled Church

I began this chapter with a sermon about a theology of sending; yet in the bishop's own homily, the sending presumes another act: the gathering and blessing of those who belong to one another. When Jack, Andie, and Belinda go forward to receive the marks of baptism, reception, and confirmation, they are claimed as "God's own forever" with and through those who gather. They do not stand or sit alone near the baptismal font. There is an immediate circle of some family members and friends and those from the congregation who "sponsor" them. And there is the congregation, who strain from the pews to catch a glimpse of each one and who speak on behalf of the church to promise to love and support them. As the bishop claims, "We're going to publicly say that this person is now a member of our family. We will love them, give them value and worth, and think that they're important. And we'll miss them when they are not here for whatever reason. We will help them when they need help. We will gather together and give strength to one another."

In light of the suffering that sending might entail, these claims and these concentric rings of people around the baptismal font—touching, blessing, promising, claiming these lives—appear fragile. Yet Bieler and Schottroff remind us that sacraments have the potential to make visible to us the love that often remains hidden, as well as to reveal the experiences of God's absence in the world and the church.

What I have hoped to show in the prior chapters are the artistries of shared space and time that are sometimes hidden when congregants are sent outside the bounds of the church. Belonging to one another, the aesthetics of consent is made visible through art forms and through the slow time and decentered space of Sacred Family, for the truth of these sacraments remains: none of the people who gather are worthy of social death, nor are they worthy of wealth or inheritance or privilege or ability that divides them from others. Rather, all who gather deserve the means to live together, to belong to one another, and to have power to renounce the forces that proclaim otherwise. In the language used for baptisms, which rings oddly in a congregation that does not often talk about evil powers or the devil: those who are baptized "renounce the evil powers of this world which corrupt and destroy the creatures of God." Those who gather vow to "do all in [their] power to support these persons in their life in Christ." The divided spaces into which people are sent often belie this truth. And yet it is manifest in the space and time of Sacred Family, albeit in fragile ways that are difficult to sustain.

Sending cannot be an ableist imperative for each one to overcome the circumstances of their life by God's grace. Rather, sending entails the promise that the palpable belonging experienced within the time and space of the assembly at Sacred Family is the more profound truth of these relationships than what often appears when the congregation is sent. Other patterns and practices of witnessing, belonging, and dwelling together can exist. And that possibility is experienced again and again not only in the communal acts of baptism, confirmation, and Eucharist, but also in the jokes, conversations and silences, touch and gesture, in the struggle for adequate names, and in the pleasures of eating together. When the congregation consents to such ways of being together, it mirrors the possibility for a broader consent to a life together outside of the time and space of the parish gathering.

As researcher, I return again and again to Sacred Family. It is here that my desire and ability to imagine a good future for all, especially for the most minoritized in the city, is stoked and refined. Such desires are aroused by the unconventional beauty and the persistent hope of the people who summon and demand it. When I want to imagine a more just city than the one I now live in, I spend time at Sacred Family with the people whose liveliness and lament evoke this urgency for me. Even the fragility of the relationships at Sacred Family calls forth and makes manifest hope for a different social geography. Those who are marked for social death refuse those marks in the fragile beauty and consent to life that persist. Through art forms, congregants insist that even in the liminal, provisional space and time of a congregation, something new can be created and held out as a witness to other social arrangements. Such hope insists that something impossible be understood as possible; a different way of dwelling together as both church and neighborhood can be imagined.

In Sacred Family's case, such hope makes visible a connection between a set of tables: the communion table, the many tables in the parish hall, and all of the tables around the city where people sit down to eat together in places where others could not comfortably dwell. The arts of Sacred Family draw communal attention to the permeable nature of liturgy: "Does this life-meal proclaim the death of Christ? Does this death-meal give life to the community? Does this community meal open toward needs beyond this circle? Is this table set next to other tables in the world?"[34]

Sending, then, is the hope that the community might hold together and perceive together that which is often divided. When Sacred Family is sent into the world, the good thing that is sent is the *we* that emerges through artistries of connection. This *we* might be sent because it is the we that has eaten side-by-side, has shared and multiplied laughter, and has sat together in silence. Thus, the art forms of sending must contribute to other kinds of arrangements of social flesh. Different social arrangements might also call forth different political arrangements, different dreams of the common good, different felt senses about what material conditions for life are required beyond the bounds of the congregation. Such arrangements are not only desirable but also necessary for the artistries of belonging to take place within the church.

The call then is not to send each enabled individual to be a bright light in a troubled world. Rather, the goodness of these eating and belonging practices might extend the liturgy, stretching it out into the places outside of the parish walls, so that new aesthetics of belonging can be learned. The lines that divide some people from one another in the city can be troubled, revealing a failure to manifest both Christian and human belonging. Such practices of intimacy cannot cure the structures of ableism, racism, and income inequality that prevail. But such patterns of dwelling and remaining together bear witness to the forces of social death, so that desires for other kinds of political, economic, and ecclesial arrangements might be deemed necessary. They might foster a dream of a common good—one that would make possible an alternative mutuality of relationships between those who call themselves the church.

Such a common good must include Rose, a congregant with mental illness who lives on her own, in spite of the fact that some friends and family think she should not. When Rose asks me to come to her home to conduct a formal interview, I gain a new understanding of her life in that space. When I get lost finding her apartment in the affordable housing complex, I learn that hers is the balcony filled with plants. I know Rose as an artist but not as a gardener. As she shows me around her house, she talks about how much she loves to cook but also about the dangers of cooking given certain health conditions. Her frequent complaints and concerns about her caregivers become more palpable when I can visualize her reliance upon them to occupy this place on her own. She tells me stories of people in her neighborhood who watch out for her, and people who take advantage of her. There are pictures everywhere of her family, and she tells some of their stories, both happy stories and ones that trouble her. There is a large photo album filled with pictures that document her many years both at Sacred Family and at another church she attends, a history of relationships. At the end of our conversation, she walks me to my car and points to a gazebo in her housing complex. She describes a time when two women at Sacred Family, Shonda and Beatrice, came on their own time to share a celebration with her in that gazebo. It is a memory that she cherishes. Thinking about Rose's relationship with Beatrice, I recall a time during the art program when Beatrice helped Rose navigate a problem she had encountered in maintaining her food stamps. As I perceive it, Beatrice's ability to advocate and watch out for Rose comes from interactions that Beatrice and Rose have both within and outside of Sacred Family. Spending time with Rose in her home, I glimpse the possibility of ecclesial relationships that might respond to Rose's needs and dreams outside the time and space of the church. Likewise, Rose's love of planting, cooking, and singing might enliven the spaces of some with whom she might consent to share her time, transforming certain stereotypes of mental illness and poverty as constituting an uninhabitable life.

With words like *beloved, friendship,* and *advocate,* Sacred Family sends people outside the bounds of the parish. It imagines the conditions in which these names, these words, these symbols, might find an adequate form in the neighborhoods, the city, and in other parishes. When Sacred Family welcomes, in the name of God, it names those who gather as those who belong to one another. Sending then is an invitation to reveal those marks of belonging through recognizing one another in spaces where some congregants are most likely to be feared or disregarded. Such an invitation is manifest not only in the ritual words of the priest but also in the invitations and dreams of congregants whenever the we of desire for companionship and adventure appears as an invitation to one another. We should go for a hike in the woods. We should go to the movies. We should do yoga together. Can I have your number? Such proposals echo the desires for different configurations of relationships to extend beyond the physical boundaries of the parish, marking and revealing other patterns of belonging.

Such desired intimacies challenge in profound ways the dividing lines that remain in fragile communion at Sacred Family and between many congregations. They also make apparent the different material conditions of congregants' lives and the struggle to inhabit shared spaces across experiences of wealth, poverty, mental illness, and racism. To be sent is not only a mandate to proclaim good news; it is also an invitation to seek out new patterns and more truthful arrangements for dwelling together and belonging to one another. New ecclesial choreographies are called forth by the Spirit whose fire and light frame the sanctuary doors at Sacred Family, by these symbols of unquenchable vitality and luminosity. Sending requires trust that the Spirit who amplifies sacred space within the grounds of Sacred Family also gathers God's people in the places from and to which the church is sent, restlessly rearranging zones of security and abandonment, creating the conditions for beauty where social death might otherwise prevail.

A Circle artist's self-portrait in progress sits among piles of painted canvases lining the studio walls. (Photo credit: Cindy M. Brown)

The Disabled Church: Beauty and the Creation of a Community of Difference

Together, with little or nothing in common, we pray and sing
and walk and talk and believe and lose our beliefs, we understand
and have no idea, and practice with one another what we have
received from the traditions and that which we invent
and add to the traditions.

—Cláudio Carvalhaes, *Eucharist and Globalization*[1]

One morning in Sacred Family's art studios, I wander into Kirby's room, piled high on all sides with his remarkable art. There are paint bottles strewn over the rug and floor, which themselves have become canvases mottled with blotches and swirls of paint. As I stand beside Kirby, he touches a blank canvas, putting four or five globs of each color in a circle moving inward toward the center of the painting—white, blue, green, yellow, and red. He then swirls the paint to create a movement of gentle wavy color; the edges of the canvas are earth tones with brighter colors at the center. He looks down over his painting for a time. Then, surprising me, he dramatically alters it; he dabs black paint around the outside and then swirls dark swaths of liquid around the edges. The mood of the painting has changed. It looks like a storm. Standing up and looking at it from a distance, he discerns what else is needed, then gets down on his knees, close again to the painting, to add an intense and highly textured patch of red here, some green over here, swirling down through the center, some more intense yellows at the center. Occasionally he murmurs, apparently dissatisfied with a turn in his work, but more often he appears satisfied, yet unsure if there is more to add. At one point, he asks if I think the work is done. I find it beautiful, but I cannot say whether or not it is finished. He stares again for a time, and when I ask him if he is done, he tells me that he is still thinking. He props it up so that he can get a different perspective on it. He seems reluctant to judge his creation. Then, abruptly, he is finished.

My experience of the painting changes over the course of the hour I watch Kirby; each dab of color changes the way I interpret the artwork. Yet I am aware of the lack of specific criteria available to me to decide whether the painting is finished or whether a certain color enhances or diminishes the painting. There is a sense that Kirby has developed as an artist, something that makes a change in the painting agreeable or disturbing to him. At the same time, the colors he uses also surprise him. Kirby and I discuss how the changes in the painting affect us, but we have limited language with which to describe or evaluate it.

As I watch Kirby paint, I think of Sacred Family as something like this canvas, a community created continuously as different people and personalities are added to the art of the liturgy and participate in the color, mood, variation, and texture of community. Unlike Kirby's other paintings—scenes, where lifelike figures sit, read, and converse—in his abstract paintings, forms of life are focused into colors that function by virtue of their necessary relationship to one another. Kirby attends to different corners of the painting, thinking about how a patch of red changes the line of blue beside it. The colors themselves are not able or unable, virtuous or deviant, good or evil, but necessarily constitute the painting. A pattern on the edges shifts the mood of the artwork, what it is able to name or evoke as a whole, and how each part of it fits together.

As I consider the portrait of Sacred Family that I have drawn in these pages, I consider criteria for evaluating any liturgy. Who is to say that any particular rendering of Christian worship is beautiful or inadequate or that its relationships of difference are hopeful or harmful? Who is to say that the liturgy of any congregation is pleasing or troubling to God?

In her analysis of the tensions between art and theology/philosophy, philosopher and novelist Iris Murdoch articulates the potentially competing commitments of these disciplines. According to Murdoch, whereas artists are invested in rendering an interpretation of the particular and in conveying the ambiguities of "the whole [person]," theology tends to elevate that which it understands to be good and to be fearful that art might distract from the mind's pursuit of divine truth or reality. In pointing to truth or wisdom, theology and philosophy render judgment about what is good, beautiful, and real in ways that artists often consider unnecessary. Comparing the "purist" tendencies of theology and philosophy with art as a "shameless collaborator,"[2] Murdoch reminds her readers that "the artist is a great informant, at least a gossip, at best a sage, and much loved in both roles. He lends to the elusive particular a local habitation and a name."[3]

In focusing on the artistries of Sacred Family, I have rendered one of many possible portraits of the church called Sacred Family. In doing so, I have sought both to capture the ambiguities of the whole congregation and to encourage an appraisal of its beauty and fragility. In describing Sacred Family, I have drawn attention to the subjective nature of my interpretation, of its location at a particular point in time, of its view from a very particular perspective. Yet I also maintain its relevance for other religious communities who seek to inhabit a good life together that names God as the one who makes common prayer and communal love necessary, possible, and hopeful.

I have attempted to show how the particular artistries of connection at Sacred Family give an encounter with God "a local habitation and a name." Yet that particular habitation and name make Sacred Family no less relevant for those who occupy other particular theological locations. The God who unfolds, weaves, disrupts, and names Sacred Family offers something to other congregations and communities through the gathering and sending of this parish. The questions that emerge from Sacred Family's life together have vital significance beyond the place and time of Sacred Family, for other religious communities invariably require space and time for the differences and disabilities of those who constitute them. Prayer that assumes the power of a unified choreography of human bodies always emerges from a range of human embodiment and the limitations of uniform participation. The question is not whether such differences exist in other communities but whether these differences can be desired and acknowledged rather than tolerated or ignored there.

I have proposed that an aesthetic frame might help theologians pay attention to a liturgy that does not assume a normative set of abilities or body-minds. This frame might also encourage us to appraise or understand a liturgical choreography on its own terms and in terms of the particular people who gather. It might be used to discuss the adequacy or inadequacy of liturgical forms inhabited by a congregation as it lives out a relationship with the divine in patterns that do not presuppose uniformity or conformity. Furthermore, a theological aesthetic might illumine if and why a particular liturgy is beautiful. And beauty matters because of the faith that difference can be gathered without coercion, for from a theological perspective beauty both accompanies and testifies to the importance of consent.

*Consenting to Be with Another
through the Beauty of Difference*

What does it mean to consent to another? As a researcher, I engage a careful process by which I collect informed consent from those who contribute to the knowledge I gather and create. I must be mindful about consent both as a carefully delineated process that is part of my research protocols, and consent as a fluid, interactive process by which I discern a person's discomfort or dis-ease in the presence of certain topics or questions or in certain spaces or in the presence of certain other people.

Such a process of research discernment has parallels with the discernment involved in consenting to participation in forms of congregational belonging. There are clearly delineated protocols for joining and belonging as a church member, but there are also subtle practices through which recognition and belonging are performed and negotiated by those who gather. When I discuss my research with people unfamiliar with Sacred Family, I sometimes encounter a stereotype that people with psychiatric disabilities must be joining a church out of either coercion or delusion. Such suspicions raise broader questions about what it means for any human person to inhabit a religious community consensually and truthfully. What does it mean to join a Christian church willingly? How does one consent to time and space and prayer together in light of the challenges of access and desire? How would one track that consent and understand the freedom it entails without losing sight of the constricted choices that any congregation and any congregant encounters every time human differences are gathered into a common time and space?

By choosing theological aesthetics and ethnographic methods as tools for analyzing Sacred Family, I have departed from a frame for consent to community that would mark belonging to a Christian church solely in terms of explicit theological discourse about the identity of Sacred Family, or in common beliefs about God that must be claimed by those who come to church. Rather, I have argued that a weeklong liturgy anticipates God as the one who requires and creates the possibility for relationships and connections between those who gather. The conditions for consensual belonging to Christian community are performed through the amplification of spaces for differences and the disruption of linear notions of time, through artistries that weave congregants together, and through a struggle for language and recognition with which to claim oneself and others. When and where consent rearranges the possibility for relationships at Sacred Family, those who gather find beauty.

For in a strain of theological thinking, the categories of beauty and consent are interrelated in a mutually dependent way. Beauty accompanies transformation as a way to map a person's consent to their transformation through immediate pleasure or delight that works non-coercively with human embodiment in all its variations and social constructions. For example, in a community like Sacred Family, as one transforms one's ableist assumptions about the way that productivity and efficiency determine the possibilities for a worthy human life, one is also drawn by divine love through desire and pleasure into the life of the community; such a transformed relationship to oneself and others may entail sacrifice or resistance, but it is not inherently destructive or harmful to the one who engages in it. Beauty marks the possibility that transformation does not entail the destruction or harm of the person one once was; a person might change and still be truthful to who they are in the divine light.

So beauty functions as a witness to the non-coercive nature of God; the divine does not force human transformation or destroy something of the human person in order to make them good. Rather, the beautiful accompanies a consent to an alignment of the desires of the human person with the desire of God for that person. Various theological accounts of beauty name it as an intimate relationship between the accessibility of the immediate pleasures of human life and the horizon of what a person might become.

In order to trace some possibilities of this relationship between beauty and consent, I turn now to three theologians who analyze beauty differently and yet help me to articulate the importance of its presence and absence at Sacred Family. I briefly explore these articulations of beauty first in order to investigate its role in the creation of Sacred Family. Because Sacred Family also manifests aspects of beauty that are not emphasized in these accounts of the beautiful, nor in many theological accounts of a desire for God, I then examine how beauty extends liturgical surfaces and confuses accustomed liturgical borders or boundaries of ecclesial belonging and identity.

My first theological conversation partner, twentieth-century French philosopher and political activist Simone Weil, describes the love of the order and beauty of the world as that which prepares a human person for direct contact with the divine. This is what Weil terms one of four "form[s] of the implicit love of God" along with love of neighbor, love of religious ceremonies, and friendship.[4] As Weil puts it, "At the moment when it touches the soul, each of the forms that such love may take has the virtue of a sacrament."[5] Weil associates beauty not primarily with human others in neighbor love or friendship (although justice is beautiful, she claims) or with religious ceremonies, but with the created world. Like the other forms, the beauty and order of the world is a form of love for God because it elicits the creative attention that expands the abilities of a human mind toward God.[6]

Weil describes beauty as both a surface and as "the mouth of a labyrinth" by which God lures human beings to God's self. Because there is something infinite and impenetrable to the beautiful order of the world that humans cannot control, manipulate, or use as a means to an end, even if they so desire,[7] beauty prepares humans for the love of God by teaching a divine form of renunciation. Such renunciation is the love by which God consents not to manipulate or coerce God's own creation.[8] Thus, we might say that beauty is the quality through which God regards humankind as theological subjects beautiful in their own right rather than as objects to be used as a mere means for divine purposes.

Beauty for Weil is not only readily accessible to all who encounter it but also transformative. It might release a human person from the illusion that they are the center of the universe and so create an opening for divine love to enter the depths of the soul of that person and to admire the beauty of creation through that person's soul. Beauty is not inherent within matter but is possible through a certain kind of perception. Thus, beauty involves attention to that which is not the self in a way that is also truthful and thus makes the soul more virtuous.[9] Beauty prepares the soul for God by helping to increase human virtue.

Another theologian, the eighteenth-century preacher and philosopher, Jonathan Edwards, also associates the theological category of beauty with "the nature of true virtue" by which humans consent to the being of any and all others, not only those they know personally or to whom they are related through kinship bonds. Like Weil, Edwards emphasizes a depth that beauty invites because of its impersonal dimension; it is that which cultivates human desire for that which is not us or ours, or immediately related to us, because through it we come to understand our unity with all that exists. As Edwards explains, "Beauty does not consist in discord and dissent, but in consent and agreement. And if every intelligent being is in some way related to being in general, and is a part of the universal system of existence; and so stands in connection with the whole; what can its general and true beauty be, but its union and consent with the great whole?"[10] For Edwards this consent is only possible through an intelligence and a love that is like God's, an indiscriminate love for everything that exists and a benevolence toward it. Edwards contemplates how this kind of love might go against human nature, as he considers human proclivities to protect and love that which is dearest, most proximate, and most familiar at the expense of a more general consent to any and all beings. It is only by loving God, who loves and consents to all that exists, that such far-reaching and public love grows within life.[11] Yet God has made the world and humankind in such a way that what is good for us (love for all that exists) is also beautiful to us, bringing some immediate sweetness and gratitude, even if such consent and beauty is also difficult and impossible without divine redemption.[12]

While Edwards identifies beauty as consent to the lives of all others, Edwards himself participated in the violence of slavery: both enslaving black people and defending slavery. Edwards's apparent Universalist ethic is called into question by his practice and defense of slaveholding, revealing the logics of white supremacy that mask oppression through the legitimatization of inequality. How can one consent to the beauty of another and still view them as not equal to one's self? Historian Kenneth P. Minkema identifies:

> [a] paternalistic outlook that saw black and Indian adults, before conversion, as little more than children in the extent of their innate capacities. To be sure, both blacks and whites were equally in need of the means of grace and of salvation, but that was as far as equality went. Edwards and his fellow colonists lived in a hierarchical world, including racially, and that hierarchy was to be strictly observed; even in heaven, as Edwards conceived it, there would be "degrees of glory."[13]

Edwards's theology of beauty can support an ideal of unity with all others without interrogating the racist, ableist hierarchies that brutalize or colonize people without their consent. Edwards both baptized black people and welcomed them as full members of his church and enslaved black people throughout his life, including the sale of a Titus, an enslaved person listed under "Quick Stock" in Edwards's will.[14]

More than two centuries later, in his meditation on the cross and the lynching tree, black liberation theologian James Cone's theological aesthetics confronts the sins of white theologians and theologies in perpetuating white supremacy and in supporting either explicitly or implicitly "white America's crucifixion of black people."[15] If Weil and Edwards trace the pleasures of the beautiful as necessary accompaniments to the challenges of truth, virtue, and justice presented by divine love, then Cone writes of the discomfort and anguish of beauty as an accompaniment to the unimaginable suffering in black existence.[16]

Describing black artists as "society's ritual priests and prophets, seeking out the meaning of black experience in a world defined by white supremacy," Cone writes about the moral imagination to make explicit connections between the cross of Christ and the lynching tree in American history.[17] He argues that by conveying the beauty in black bodies lynched and beaten, these artists refused the supremacy of white brutality: "The beauty in black existence is as real as the brutality, and the beauty prevents the brutality from having the final word."[18] Such beauty is made evident through attention to black subjectivity, dignity, communal suffering, and spiritual agency rather than interpreting suffering as the helplessness of black victims.[19] Cone rejects atonement theologies that would make sense of white violence or black suffering through virtuous or necessary sacrifice; consent to black suffering is antithetical to the liberation God desires. Yet recognition of the beauty of black people who suffer is imperative. While Cone does not use the language of consent, focusing instead on the deep disruption and outrage that such beauty in brutality brings, he describes beauty as that which must be acknowledged in order to bear witness to the truth of black suffering. The moral imagination required to see the lynching tree as the cross, and vice versa, emerges from the black artist's ability to expose the hideousness of white brutality through the beauty of black solidarity. Cone links the beautiful in black life with a transformation of perception and imagination that enables black artists to see the world as subversively as God does, whether or not they profess explicit Christian practices or commitments.[20]

Thus in different and dissenting ways Weil, Edwards, and Cone evoke the power of the beautiful as a relational quality that connects the one who perceives with the one perceived. Consent to the love of God through nature, consent to the love of God for all that exists, and consent to engage the divinity and humanity in black suffering and liberation all require the recognition of belonging to another whose right to existence is marked as beautiful by divine presence. All three theologians describe the work of beauty as a catalyst in the moral transformation of those who consent to their own lives and to the lives of others through the desire of God for what God has created. Beauty animates connection through desire and respect rather than pity or charity. Beauty is thus the principle by which God weaves human desire, wonder, or anguish into divine desire for God's creation to struggle and dwell together in light of a common life. Following Weil, Edwards, or Cone, we might ask whether the liturgy at Sacred Family affects greater human connection through obedience to and love for God, or compassion for others, or an altered moral imagination that rejects the powers of white supremacy and the ableist logics that it assumes.

Beauty and the Surfaces of Space, Time, and Form

The earlier chapters bear witness to Sacred Family as a place of hopeful transformation for some who are a part of it, yet it is difficult to offer a consistent narrative of transformation. As an ethnographic theologian who has spent three years with this community, I find it difficult to map the kinds of transformation over time that some theological or liturgical anthropologies imply, for those who gather were and are complex narrators of their own experiences, as are most human beings. The same person who tells me how much she loves Sacred Family suddenly stops coming or offers a contradictory narrative at another time. Another has little to say about what they find in the community but returns again and again to be part of it. Some who have been at Sacred Family the longest are also the ones most willing to treat others in ways that appear condescending rather than beautiful, even if they are also the most sacrificially committed to the well-being of those who come. Narratives and behaviors may be difficult to integrate into any kind of coherent witness or evidence to a depth of individual or communal moral formation over time. For I have limited access to the range of encounters across ability, race, and class that occur outside the space and time of Sacred Family.

While I do not doubt that the diverse beauty of Sacred Family affects the formation over time of some individuals, Sacred Family's life together has drawn my attention to a different work of beauty. Rather than contemplating human relationships through metaphors of depth, I have been compelled again and again by the surfaces of interaction that make Sacred Family possible. While these surfaces reveal beauty in ways that resonate with aspects of Weil's, Edwards's, and Cone's descriptions, they also help to capture a different theological aspect of beauty. Rather than focusing on the transformation of individuals or communities through a focus on the interiorities or growing capacities of persons, I have discovered theological significance in the relational surfaces between and among those who gather, as together they alter liturgical choreographies of space, time, and form. I have attempted to convey how social artistries extend the sensory surfaces of a liturgical gathering and stretch out the forms of encounter, making them more accessible.[21]

For Sacred Family members to create more accessible liturgies requires consent to the differences in the body-minds who gather. Such interactions may not have an ethical or moral intention, or demonstrate a studied self-awareness by those who pursue them, or require a focused attention often attributed to those who most manifest the goodness or virtues of one transformed by love of God. Yet, they are no less important for thinking about the relationship between beauty and consent to a divine love that binds together those who might otherwise not recognize or acknowledge their belonging to one another. In other words, eating hot dogs side by side or sharing a cigarette or talking about pop songs by the church entrance or weeding together in the church garden or drawing pictures together during a church service may or may not make the individuals who partake in these interactions wiser, freer, more generous, or more compassionate human beings than they were before these actions; nonetheless, those actions are significant in the relatedness they bring about and in their creation of access to relationships, which is fundamental to Sacred Family's life together. The artistries of interpersonal connection are beautiful because they consent to common space and time and persistently invite others into the creation of a life together that I have been calling liturgy.

I think, for example, of a conversation I had with Mother Daria about a sermon she gave on Easter Sunday. She began the sermon with an invitation to name one's favorite dessert, an activity that would seem to require little spiritual depth, attention, virtue, or moral imagination. She remembers her dessert illustration eliciting an intense and active response from the whole congregation. Through this illustration congregants with and without mental disabilities eagerly identified a point of access to her sermon and actively engaged one another through each one's sensory experiences. Might then her opening illustration have been as important as the body of the argument, a careful and creative interpretation of the Easter text for that day about the different ways we experience God through different senses and sensibilities? She voices this question to me when we talk about the sermon together. She reasons aloud: "at its core, worship is about common prayer so if the prayer cannot be commonly held, then it's missing the point. It's not meeting the needs of the community. I don't think that means that we do whatever and just anything. It has to be intentional, but I think there are ways it can meet the needs of the community and make sense, ultimately, and if it's not making sense, then there's a question." At Sacred Family, the artistries of interpersonal connection help to make sense of human difference. One consents to particular others within the community through amplifying embodied surfaces through which different congregants are invited, known, and held within the larger common prayer.

At the same time, any beauty at Sacred Family appears fragile in light of the structures outside the church that limit consent to a common political and social good. Thus, any false assumptions about autonomy are called into question by the sending that is assumed to be beautiful in its empowerment of each individual to change their world for the better. There is no beauty in sending if sending does not acknowledge the sometimes brutal or abusive circumstances into which congregants are sent. Beauty attends to such suffering and fosters a dream of rearranging the conditions, the commodification, and the devaluing of human life, under which such brutality and neglect persists. In this sense, beauty is what black humanist Anthony Pinn names a "creative disregard" for the hierarchies that elevate the worth of some lives over others.[22]

Borders of Belonging, Circles of Consent

How then to think about the beauty and fragility of Sacred Family? If the consent to extending the surfaces of common space, time, and form is limited by the violence of surrounding spaces, is it still possible to name Sacred Family as beautiful? To assume that beautiful consent is important and even essential to this church's life requires faith. It is not evident from the pleasures of manicures and pedicures that very different congregants actually consent to another's way of being in the world. To use theologian Mary McClintock Fulkerson's term, "obliviousness" to the hierarchies of wealth, whiteness, and ability persists.[23] Furthermore, such hierarchies, and the artistries that interrogate them, occur among people who have very few choices about where and how they can live and with whom; to describe beauty as consent to being together must take this systematic oppression into account. Disability scholar Sharon Betcher reminds us of the challenge to Christian practice if our work is not always pleasurable but also requires us "to live with pain in such a way that it does not sever or cut insurmountable chasms through the city but might support the emergence of social flesh."[24] Any account of beauty must acknowledge the need for dissent from the subtle logic of segregation and degradation that are also fostered through the assumed peace and safety of shared spaces, times, and forms.

As a participant-observer, I have faith in the beauty of Sacred Family. I have also nurtured doubts during the years of my research. I have asked: What makes significant these sensations, enjoyed in common, in light of a city where some are kept at a distance from others, and where cities are made beautiful by obscuring the perceived ugliness of those considered undesirable and unproductive? Is the church another place to hide the sensations of people that others would prefer not to encounter? How does the church reveal the beauty of its congregants? Many at Sacred Family desire to transform public perception, but beauty often remains hidden within the church grounds.

Yet, to use Lloyd's phrase, "silently raising hell"[25] at Sacred Family begins with small, elusive circles of consent to interdependence. These circles trouble the boundaries in cities and churches that mark which kinds of lives and minds are worth loving and protecting. By occupying a rare relation in this city, Sacred Family congregants not only help one another, but sit down and enjoy space and time together. They take uncommon pleasure in the everyday objects, encounters, and relationships they hold up to the light.

When I sit with Pete during a service of Holy Eucharist, he grabs my hand, rocks back and forth, crying and laughing over a familiar hymn. He stares straight at my lips as I sing, standing close to me so that he can feel my singing even though he does not sing. Most of our communication involves gesture because I struggle to make out the phrases he speaks to me. One evening, during the eucharistic prayer, I hear his words with remarkable clarity. "I can smell the beans cooking!" he announces with a mischievous smile. Pete smells the ingredients of a common meal wafting up from the basement through the sanctuary floor and shares his pleasure with me. In doing so, he broadens my own sense of what prayer to God should entail. The arts of becoming a disabled church at Sacred Family suggest that these expanding surfaces of shared relationship and communication are a pleasure and a struggle. The stretching of such beautiful social surfaces requires those with and without disabilities, a work of extending community that is unfinished but possible.[26]

Sacred Family sheds light on this struggle because of the way its fragile beauty draws attention to the importance of that which might be taken for granted or judged as superficial rather than essential to Christian liturgy: both what may be held in common and the unconventional differences that accentuate common forms. When I recall Sacred Family, the images that first come to mind are sharing a bench, eating across the table from another person, whispering with another during church, holding a hymnbook with another, waving across the sanctuary, or sitting with a vague awareness of another sleeping beside me. Like an attempt to grasp the beauty of the world and hold it, the search for accessible forms is both elusive and essential to community at Sacred Family.

The range of differences gathered at Sacred Family exhibit humanity "at full stretch" to borrow Saliers's description of Christian liturgy.[27] Actions and relations that can be held in common become beautiful even if they do not contain the same associations of depth often used to describe profound and meaningful human interaction or virtuous Christian identity or good liturgy. Thus, as I look forward to conversations or interactions that might have felt strange or superficial to me in another context, these encounters become easy and pleasurable because, through them, those who gather experience and manifest a connection to others. Might God be as present in such interactions as God is in a time of reverent, sustained prayer, or in a complex and attentive theological discussion with a wise friend, or in a contemplative reading of the Bible, or in the gathering of those mobilizing for justice work?

"What do you need in order to have church?" In *Holy Things*, liturgical theologian Lathrop reminds us that the central rituals of Christian worship—baptism, communion, the reading and proclamation of scripture—are intimately connected to the most ordinary actions and objects in human communities—water, a bath, a table, a meal, a loaf of bread, wine, storytelling, clothing, a candle.[28] The liturgical task of those who gather, he argues, is to unfold (or break open) the meaning of common things, common both in the sense that they are ordinary and that they are sacred because they are given by God as a center of human interaction to be animated by divine love through a worshipping body: "The gathering is to do something, to set these symbolic objects in motion, to weave them into a pattern of meaning. People do not gather at water only, but at a bath, and a bath interpreted by words and by other things set next to the bathing—anointing oil, a burning candle, welcoming hands, new clothing."[29] In Lathrop's understanding the objects gain new depth of meaning as they are juxtaposed and reanimated by other people and objects in a traditional yet creative liturgical pattern.

And so I return to the question with which I began: What do you need in order to have a church that assumes difference at its heart? At Sacred Family the water, the table, the bread, and the word are given life by artistries of connection that expand the surfaces of an extended liturgy. Jokes or commentary interpolate the sermon, which functions better as an interactive story than as a lecture because of these patterns. A service of Holy Eucharist is most often set alongside another meal happening outside of the sanctuary doors, which is as significant as the meal inside the sanctuary to those who gather. What animates these basic actions, these "holy things for holy people" are the differences, both the remarkable and ordinary stories of the lives of those who gather. By drawing attention to such basic objects and gestures, these patterns also suggest the intersections of pleasure and discipline that might help to decenter Sacred Family's liturgy yet further: the ongoing creation of public spaces for common acts of sharing food and storytelling and the sharing of private home spaces for these same pleasures. The beauty of shared surfaces at Sacred Family both blurs the borders of where liturgy begins and ends and, at the same time, invites the community who gathers to stretch out liturgical time and space in order to nourish and protect the lives of all who gather and are sent.

While Sacred Family is not ostensibly involved in the direct transformation of political and social structures that affect the daily lives of those it gathers, it bears witness in important ways to the value and devaluing of the lives of its congregants. In its life together, it traces the importance of both access and consent in the ongoing creation of space and time for those who gather and in the calling into question of liturgical aesthetics used to mark those not fit for any ecclesial choreography. In this way beauty helps to illumine what liturgical theologian Cláudio Carvalhaes names the "borderless border" of Christian liturgy: that place recognizable to those who worship God within it and to those who seek a place of welcome from outside it and yet a place flexible and creative enough to respond to the differences of those who enter.[30]

The borderless border of Christian worship is an elusive space because liturgy is always embodied and therefore inherently bordered. Carvalhaes names five different kinds of borders that mark any Christian liturgy, with a particular focus on the eucharistic table: ecclesiastical borders that articulate the norm and standards of who belongs to the church; theological borders which give content to any given definition of Christian church; liturgical borders which locate worship of God in particular time and space and dictate shared rituals; social/economic borders where social class often determines who is found within a given liturgical border; and political borders which reflect economic, social, and political commitments that affect liturgical identity.[31]

Given these multiple borders in any liturgy, a primary task of Christian liturgy is to work with and around the borders, to negotiate them and breach them continually in memory of God who becomes "our permanent home" and in whom those who might lose themselves in the negotiation of these borders will always be found and held.[32] A God who is not contained or limited by liturgical borders is nevertheless found within them and is known in exploration of the borderless border of that which is

God, for belonging to those who are God's is both impossible to define and always defined in some way by the words, gestures, silence, and practices of those who gather. Even if all are welcome, as so many Christian churches proclaim, the theological aesthetics of a community, or what Eiesland calls the "body practices" of a liturgy, create and maintain a "physical discourse of inclusion and exclusion."[33] These borders also provide connection to God and to other Christians across time and space and make possible a prayer to God with other bodies in meaningful, intimate, and familiar ways.

Yet liturgical borders are and always have been contested by the differences of those who gather. Carvalhaes reminds us, "It is within these blurred, complicated, and interconnected borders that liturgical practices and spaces must engage and be engaged. The messy, nervous, and uneasy interrelations of these borders are a challenge to every Christian believer and privileged place for the field of worship."[34] These uneasy liturgical boundaries are also an important place for tracing the work of beauty and disability. Where a liturgical border might result in coercion or refusal of difference, the artistries of relationships and improvised collaborations must emerge to acknowledge and incorporate human variation across these possible divides.

I am reminded of this blurred, messy, beautiful border one Sunday morning when, after almost a month of absence from the congregation, I walk to Sacred Family for the baptism of a young child. I walk past the smoking benches and greet an unfamiliar man standing there alone outside the church. He turns his back to me, refusing my greeting, preserving his right to the silence of that space. Once inside the sanctuary, by contrast Forest rushes back to greet me with a bump of his fist, refusing any distance I might preserve around myself, announcing my return to the church.

I notice that the church is filled with strangers; the family and friends of the one to be baptized fill the front section in places of honor. These honored guests struggle to keep up with the songs, hymns, and prayers in the same way that many of the regular disabled congregants do. I witness a common struggle between guests and Circle congregants to participate fully in the standard forms of the service. At the same time, the dress and comportment of these guests also mark them as distinct from Sacred Family folk; a socioeconomic border appears in the differing aesthetics of those who gather. Sacred Family congregants must share a liturgy with no assurance that those who gather do not regard them with pity or condescension.

As I listen to the sermon and witness to the baptism of a child of God, on one side of me sits Mr. Davis. He tells me he is sick and proceeds to fall asleep. On the other side, Debbie shares a book with me and follows with me as best she can. But when the sermon feels long, she seems to register the restlessness in the congregation, stands up, and begins to sing a solo during the sermon as she might during noonday prayer. Someone from the back rushes up to quiet her. I pat her back.

Debbie is not the only restless one; in front of us four small children, guests of the church, crowd into three seats. One of them covers all the words in the bulletin with a purple crayon, making it impossible to read the order of service. Two others begin to measure each other's faces with their hands. They whisper to one another; they arrange their toys over the seats and on the floor. Eventually, because they cannot see the front of the sanctuary, they spill out into the aisle to get a better look at the baby; they are then invited to the front so that they can witness the baptism up close. I look at those who surround me, Mr. Davis, Debbie, and the children, and acknowledge that we have no direct access to the sermon, the baptism, and the Holy Eucharist except with and through the border of those who help to constitute the liturgy with us. Such interrelations can be difficult, distracting, or distancing, but they can also become beautiful in a consent to each other's right to occupy a shared space and time and to do so in a manner befitting each.

Whom do we need in order to have a church that assumes difference at its heart? I have proposed an answer to this question: at the heart of any Christian liturgy are people whom we would not otherwise choose to surround us and a fragile system of human communication by which we consent to or dissent from the relationships that are a given of any religious ritual. At Sacred Family, mental disability makes clear both the fragility of human connection that is a requisite for any love of God and the persistent beauty of this connection as the gathered ones find, create, and manifest forms for communal love and knowledge of God. Thus, access is sacred and essential, not just something it would be good to have if possible and feasible: the access of one to and through another reveals the sacred arts of being human in relationship with the divine. In the creative disregard for certain borders (silence during the sermon, wakefulness as essential to presence in worship), the community consents to the possibility of different kinds of human beings creating and sharing a common space and time. Thus, mental differences reveal the elusive spaces of the borderless border and its ongoing creation and animation through artistries of connection that are essential to any worship of God.

The God for whom human difference is ordinary rather than aberrational makes possible the elusiveness of an accessible life together, one that we share not in spite of but thanks to human differences. The animate border of the liturgy, possible in and through creative, consensual relationships, is beautiful as a community consents to an understanding of divine love manifest not only through what is held in common but through what diverges, distracts, and extends the surfaces of hospitality and community. That the access of one might not limit the worship of another is a testament to the nonviolence of the beauty of God. Borderless borders become beautiful, rather than frightening or irritating, when those who gather consent to one another through their creative disregard of the segregationist charity that would separate them not only from other humans or from the rest of creation but also from access to the beauty of God.

Thus, for example, Kayla's and Rose's solo performances at noonday prayer bring the most delight to the congregation when they appear at ease within a form of love for God that fills them with pleasure. Even when this singing appears disruptive to some people in some contexts, it still carries a beauty for many in the congregation because of the way it both creates access for Kayla and Rose to the community's common prayer and gives access to Kayla's and Rose's worship for those who witness their singing. Performances like theirs help to rearrange the meanings not only of noonday prayer but of any space where they assume the roles of those who can offer something pleasing to God.

To meditate theologically on the permeable or borderless border of the disabled God in Christian thought is to follow a Trinitarian aesthetic. Incarnate God takes a particular human shape and time, assuming and requiring an imperfect body. The memory of Jesus led by the Spirit lends a particular shape to worship and informs the prayers and embodiment of a church as the flesh of Christ. At the same time there is no life without the Spirit of Christ, the breath, the flame, the ghost, the advocate, who animates the body of Jesus and the flesh of the church, creating new possibilities for human life and for access to God and human community. The Spirit moves freely and with ease across the permeable border of Christian communal gathering, animates its beauty in the bodies of those who gather, and informs the consent to one another and disregard for the ostensibly impermeable liturgical borders of those who gather. To acknowledge such inspirited, interanimate borders is necessary because Christian liturgy requires an "endless preparation with those who are there and those who are yet to come" as one "made of connections with what we know, what we have and what we find around us. In this sense, to create a borderless border hospitable liturgy is a theological Sisyphean task of creating, relocating, connecting and dismantling borders."[35]

Creating Space and Time for the Beauty of Belonging

What does it mean to consent to participate in a community, parish, or church—to belong to what is both bordered and in flux and in which access is both continually created by those who gather and also frequently denied? Such questions often characterize the Circle community meetings that take place two to three times a year. In addition to welcoming new participants, making general announcements, fielding complaints, and resolving conflicts that arise, at such meetings church staff often facilitate time for a discussion about what it means to be the Circle of Friends of Sacred Family. Such guided discussions are intended to improve weekly programs and to help those who try to raise funds for those programs; the dialogue that emerges is energetic and participatory if also meandering and circuitous. The results, some of which are captured on a whiteboard by a volunteer scribe, are more like Kirby's process of creating an abstract painting than like a focused mission statement or set of program goals that clearly define the church and its objectives.

Where would you be if you were not here? Neil asks one Thursday morning of the group gathered in the sanctuary. The answers are multiple: in bed, at work, sweeping at Goodwill, watching Western movies, at home calling friends, trying to get out of the house, thinking about coming here to do something, at school learning life skills, at home, reading the Bible and praying, at the library trying to get a job, at an amusement park, visiting friends, going to another church, at a peer center, or bored and helping other people. Such answers do not provide clear evidence that coming to Sacred Family is better than doing something else, although one woman insists that this is the place she wants to be. Will the Circle ever be five days a week? she wants to know, wishing to be here every day.

Neil then asks the community to compare Sacred Family's programs to other programs they have attended. At first the responses are more focused, moving toward a definition of Sacred Family. Wallace suggests that there are new experiences in life here; you get out what you put in it. Marji talks about nutritious meals rather than the bologna sandwiches. Lucille names church and prayer as unique aspects of Sacred Family. Aisha talks about the fact that although there are no doctors here, she is treated better here than in other places and has more chances for success. Norah suggests that this community is about finding joy rather than meeting goals.

But quickly the discussion turns to the topic of whether or not Sacred Family is a cult, as some outside the church have described it, according to one of the participants. There is then a vigorous refutation of Sacred Family as a cult based on the diversity of those who gather, which leads to a process of self-identifying among those present. Most identify as Christians, but Marji describes herself as an atheist turned deist who really loves Rev. Jess's sermons. Lucille admits that you could call her a Baptist, but she identifies as a follower of Christ. Chad suggests that God, not people, makes Sacred Family what it is. As participants negotiate their relationships to Sacred Family and to the Christian church in multiple ways, there is no clear definition of who is inside and outside of what makes Sacred Family its own unique place, both a church and not a church.

As we begin to discuss the third question about how Sacred Family has impacted your life, Annie leans over to me and expresses her delight: "I like this!"

"What do you like?" I inquire.

"Everything that they're talking about. I thought I would be bored but I'm not. Friendship. Love. The clothes closet." I suddenly notice that she has put her drawings and writings away, those tools that usually help her to access and navigate most church services and meetings. She responds to this community meeting with a direction and intensity that I find unusual. Later I surmise that somewhere in this circuitous conversation, concerning the myriad ways that those who gather consent to a shared community with one another, Annie discovers a space and time for her own mental patterns, for her frame for belonging at Sacred Family, and she is drawn into the energy of this discussion. Through Annie's delight and curiosity, I witness something beautiful about the controlled chaos of community meeting and the resonance it creates in her and others. Together we marvel at the beautiful opening of an accessible space for bearing witness to what kind of world one comes from and what kind of community one imagines creating alongside others.

In the fragile hope for a capacious and beautiful liturgy that assumes and desires mental differences like those of Annie's and my own, I offer this limited and imperfect depiction of Sacred Family. It is my hope that this one portrait of Sacred Family, among the many other portrayals that could be rendered, will inspire those who read it to consent to the beauty of shared ecclesial and social spaces with those whose differences stretch their love and knowledge of both human and divine. I hope it may also inspire those with and without mental disabilities to participate in extending the breadth of the beauty of what counts as sacred liturgy, as Kirby's ever-changing canvas in the opening pages of this Conclusion extended my imagination. My desire is to contribute to the extension, creation, and preservation of spaces, times, and relationships within which we hold one another before God, in our communities, and in our dreams for the future.

ACKNOWLEDGMENTS

Support for the research and writing of this book came from The Louisville Institute and the Initiative in Religious Practices and Practical Theology at Emory University. Portions of Chapters 3 and 5 appear in my article, "Disabling Eschatology: Time for the Table of Our Common Pleasure," *Liturgy* 31, no. 3 (2016).

I would also like to acknowledge those whose wisdom, creativity, and accompaniment have contributed to this book. First and foremost, the people of Sacred Family Church generously shared with me their space and time, their food, their stories, and their creativity; they wove me into community and made my research not only work but also pleasure. Their beauty gives me hope and animates my commitment to work for a different church and world than the one to which I belong. This book, including its title, bears the imprint of the work of the late Nancy Eiesland and honors her remarkable book, *The Disabled God*, which has shaped this project and my theological imagination in myriad ways. This book also bears witness to the wisdom and generosity of excellent mentors and friends: Wendy Farley, who accompanied me and who nourishes safe and creative spaces for many women's theological voices; Don Saliers, who shaped and inspired my great love for the art of liturgy; Joyce Flueckiger, who taught me what it means to be an ethnographer; Rosemarie Garland-Thomson, whose passion for disability studies has nurtured many interdisciplinary projects, including my own; and Andrea White, who encouraged my theological fascination with bodies and flesh. Colleagues in the Disability Studies Initiative at Emory provided me with a collaborative space to grow my ideas and analysis of Sacred Family as did colleagues in the Critical Theories and Liturgical Studies group of the North American Academy of Liturgy. Ashley Graham gave insightful feedback and helped to smooth and clarify my prose in the early stages of this work as did Ulrike Guthrie in the later stages. I am grateful for the enthusiasm and encouragement of Richard Morrison and others at Fordham University Press. Last but not least, my partner and friend Silas Allard read every single word of this manuscript multiple times and made me believe it was possible. Without his tireless encouragement and his hours of editing, this book would not be.

NOTES

PREFACE

1. João Biehl, "The Right to a Nonprojected Future," *Practical Matters*, no. 6 (2013), http://practicalmattersjournal.org/2013/03/01/nonprojected-future (accessed May/06/2019).

INTRODUCTION: DISABLING LITURGY, DESIRING HUMAN DIFFERENCE

1. The name of the church and all names of persons have been changed to protect confidentiality.

2. Gordon W. Lathrop, *Holy People: A Liturgical Ecclesiology* (Minneapolis: Fortress Press, 2006), 1.

3. Ibid., 8.

4. Ibid.,13.

5. Ibid., 93–94.

6. Nancy L. Eiesland, *The Disabled God: Toward a Liberatory Theology of Disability* (Nashville: Abingdon Press, 1994), 94–95.

7. Identifying Sacred Family as a disabled church, I extend Eiesland's argument about naming Jesus Christ as the disabled God. I call for the use of the disabled church as a term to identify and interpret the meanings and significance of disability in and for the broader Christian church. As Eiesland argues for a contextualized Christology, so I argue for a contextualized ecclesiology that responds to "the particular situation in which people with disabilities and others who care find themselves as they try to live out their faith and to fulfill their calling to live ordinary lives of worth and dignity." Eiesland, *The Disabled God*, 98–100.

8. João Biehl, "The Right to a Nonprojected Future," *Practical Matters*, no. 6 (2013), http://practicalmattersjournal.org/2013/03/01/nonprojected-future (accessed May/06/2019).

9. Edward Farley, *Faith and Beauty: A Theological Aesthetic* (Aldershot, UK: Ashgate, 2001), 117. Farley summarizes these three different approaches to theological aesthetic/s. He focuses on the third approach.

10. Throughout this book, I also engage theologians who wrestle with what Mary McClintock Fulkerson calls "a worldly church": a church that is

participant in forces of oppression and injustice, as well as a people that embody the love and justice of God. Mary McClintock Fulkerson, *Places of Redemption: Theology for a Worldly Church* (New York: Oxford University Press, 2010), 6.

11. The church first met in a saloon and then in private homes for some time when the saloon burned down. It moved into its first church building in 1899. Later it would be forced to move again, to its current location, due to the City of Atlanta's plans to build an expressway through the neighborhood where it was located. Sources are on file with the author but not cited in order to maintain confidentiality.

12. I encountered different narratives about how demographic changes in Atlanta affected this particular neighborhood, but it seems clear that practices of racial segregation and integration were important factors in the parish's current identity.

13. For an account of the debates surrounding the City of Atlanta's treatment of homeless people and people on the streets in preparation for the 1996 Olympics, see Ronald Smothers, "As Olympics Approach, Homeless Are Not Feeling at Home in Atlanta," *The New York Times*, July 1, 1996, sec. U.S., http://www.nytimes.com/1996/07/01/us/as-olympics-approach-homeless-are-not-feeling-at-home-in-atlanta.html (accessed by author May/06/2019).

14. Staff Writer, "Atlanta Preview '96: The Olympic Games Begin in 2 Weeks," *Fort Oglethorpe Press*, July 3, 1996.

15. For a discussion of patterns, practices, and policies of de/institutionalization in North America, see Chris Chapman, Allison C. Carey, and Liat Ben-Moshe, "Reconsidering Confinement: Interlocking Locations and Logics of Incarceration," in *Disability Incarcerated: Imprisonment and Disability in the United States and Canada*, ed. Liat Ben-Moshe, Chris Chapman, and Allison C. Carey (New York: Palgrave Macmillan, 2014), 10–15.

16. During the period of my research, the church worked to establish the Circle as its own 501(c)(3) organization in order to secure funding and support that is not available for churches.

17. While a significant number of group homes were located near the church when its ministry to persons with disabilities first began, gentrification has increased property values, and many of these homes are now located in other parts of the city. Many congregants now travel into the neighborhood rather than being a part of it. The number of group homes fluctuated during my time at Sacred Family.

18. My research was approved by Emory University's Institutional Review Board on October 16, 2013. The Institutional Review Board aided me in establishing research and informed consent protocols that accounted for the mental differences that are present at Sacred Family.

19. Taking into account the differences of people with mental illness meant that I was always careful to make such options clear and to take note of any signs of discomfort during my interactions at Sacred Family, so as to do no harm through my research.

20. Eiesland, *The Disabled God*, 22.

21. Ellipses in material from field notes and recordings indicate omission, as well as incomplete thoughts expressed by the speaker.

22. Karen McCarthy Brown, *Mama Lola: A Vodou Priestess in Brooklyn* (Berkeley: University of California Press, 2001), 12.

23. Jean Vanier, "The Wisdom of Tenderness," interview with Krista Tippett, *On Being*, podcast audio, December 20, 2007, https://onbeing.org/programs/jean-vanier-the-wisdom-of-tenderness/.

24. For a discussion of the individual/medical model of disability, see Alison Kafer, *Feminist, Queer, Crip* (Bloomington: Indiana University Press, 2013), 5–7.

25. Ibid., 4–10.

26. For a brief introduction to the term "disability" from a disability studies perspective, see Rachel Adams, Benjamin Reiss, and David Serlin, "Disability," in *Keywords for Disability Studies*, ed. Rachel Adams, Benjamin Reiss, and David Serlin (New York: New York University Press, 2015), 5–11.

27. National Alliance on Mental Illness, *Mental Health by the Numbers*, https://www.nami.org/Learn-More/Mental-Health-By-the-Numbers, accessed May 6, 2019. According to NAMI's figures, one in twenty-five adults will be diagnosed with a serious mental illness, such as schizophrenia, bipolar disorder, or major depression.

28. Recent North American discourses about gun violence and public shootings illustrate this desire to distance and distinguish between normal and abnormal persons. As discussions focus on how to keep guns away from the mentally ill, persons with mental illness quickly become associated with a potential violence from which those who do not live with mental illness are automatically exempt. When I ask my students what they think of when they hear the words "mental illness," they respond with notions of instability and violence.

29. For an insightful reflection on the liabilities and benefits of different kinds of language used for mental disability, see Margaret Price, "Defining Mental Disability," in *The Disability Studies Reader*, ed. Lennard J. Davis, 4th edition (New York: Routledge, 2013), 298–307.

30. Karen Nakamura, *A Disability of the Soul: An Ethnography of Schizophrenia and Mental Illness in Contemporary Japan* (Ithaca, NY: Cornell University Press, 2013), 25.

31. For helpful introductions to mental illness from a disability studies perspective, see Nakamura, *A Disability of the Soul*, 35–69; Margaret Price,

Mad at School: Rhetorics of Mental Disability and Academic Life (Ann Arbor: University of Michigan Press, 2011), 1–24; Margaret Price, "The Bodymind Problem and the Possibilities of Pain," *Hypatia* 30, no. 1 (2015): 268–284. For a theological perspective on mental illness, particularly schizophrenia, from a practical theologian and former mental health professional, see John Swinton, *Resurrecting the Person: Friendship and the Care of People with Mental Health Problems* (Nashville: Abingdon Press, 2000).

32. Eiesland, *The Disabled God*, 67–70.

33. Ibid., 73–74.

34. Ibid., 72.

35. Ibid., 71–72.

36. Ibid., 70.

37. Ibid., 70–71, 75.

38. The author and date of the pamphlet are unknown but it was written some years prior to my introduction to Sacred Family. The terminology of "lifestyle preferences" does not reflect the congregation's current language regarding gender identity and sexual orientation.

39. The newsletter, which provides regular updates on the Circle at Sacred Family Church, was written by a staff member and circulated by email to the parish listserv, April 2014.

40. Potential divisions in the church are not primarily identified as occurring between those with mental illness and those without mental illness, but rather between persons from group homes and those who are able to live in their own homes and maintain full-time work. Some of the staff and committee members identify themselves as persons with mental illness but also identify their choice to "pass" as normal or to "come out" as a person with mental illness. Persons from group homes, who embody the intersections of disability and poverty, are often immediately identifiable as those unable to perform the activities, work, or social interactions of an abled person.

41. Sacred Family receives significant support from the denomination, which pays the salary of its priest in addition to other forms of monetary and institutional support. At the same time, Sacred Family must raise additional funds to support its Circle staff and programs. During my time at Sacred Family, raising such funds was a significant source of concern and stress for leadership at Sacred Family, most of whom were not people from group homes.

42. Eiesland, *The Disabled God*, 20–21.

43. Ibid., 112.

44. Ibid., 98.

45. Ibid., 105.

46. Tobin Siebers, "Disability and the Theory of Complex Embodiment—For Identity Politics in a New Register," in *The Disability Studies Reader*, ed. Lennard J. Davis, 4th edition (New York: Routledge, 2013), 279.

Siebers writes, "The ideology of ability is at its simplest the preference for able-bodiedness. At its most radical, it defines the baseline by which human-ness is determined, setting the measure of body and mind that gives or denies human status to individual persons."

47. Thomas E. Reynolds, *Vulnerable Communion: A Theology of Disability and Hospitality* (Grand Rapids, MI: Brazos Press, 2008), 59–63.

48. Molly Haslam argues that theological anthropologies often describe what it means to be human in a way that occludes the intellectually disabled. I would argue that liturgical anthropologies also often assume capacities that do not attend to mental disabilities in their descriptions of and prescriptions for individual and communal responses to God and one another. Molly C. Haslam, *A Constructive Theology of Intellectual Disability: Human Being as Mutuality and Response* (New York: Fordham University Press, 2011), 1–18.

49. Min-Ah Cho, "The Body, To Be Eaten, To Be Written: A Theological Reflection on the Act of Writing in Theresa Hak Kyung Cha's *Dictee*," in *Women, Writing, Theology: Transforming a Tradition of Exclusion*, ed. Emily A. Holmes and Wendy Farley (Waco, TX: Baylor University Press, 2011), 205.

50. Ibid.

51. Farley, *Faith and Beauty*, 6–12.

52. Ibid., vii.

53. Ibid., 117.

54. Ibid., 83–99.

55. Ibid., 98.

56. Serene Jones, "Glorious Creation, Beautiful Law," in *Feminist and Womanist Essays in Reformed Dogmatics* (Louisville, KY: Westminster John Knox Press, 2006), 22–23.

57. Ibid., 23–24.

58. I borrow this phrase from Rosemarie Garland-Thomson's description of disability activists who use their bodies to help us understand beauty in a new way. See Rosemarie Garland-Thomson, *Staring: How We Look* (New York: Oxford University Press, 2009), 188–193.

59. Sharon V. Betcher, *Spirit and the Obligation of Social Flesh: A Secular Theology for the Global City* (New York: Fordham University Press, 2013), 16.

60. Ibid., 17.

61. Ibid., 22–23.

62. See, for example, a theological interpretation of the arts and of beauty in James H. Cone, *The Spirituals and the Blues: An Interpretation*, 2nd rev. ed. (Maryknoll, NY: Orbis Books, 1992); James H. Cone, *The Cross and the Lynching Tree*, reprint edition (Maryknoll, NY: Orbis Books, 2013), 93–119. See also M. Shawn Copeland's focus on human beauty in theological anthropology in M. Shawn Copeland, *Enfleshing Freedom: Body, Race, and Being* (Minneapolis, MN: Fortress Press, 2009), 7–22.

63. Anthony B. Pinn, *Embodiment and the New Shape of Black Theological Thought* (New York: New York University Press, 2010), 38–52.

64. Ibid., 24–33, 123–41.

65. Sharon L. Snyder and David T. Mitchell, *Cultural Locations of Disability* (Chicago: University of Chicago Press, 2006), 8.

66. Siobhan Garrigan, "The Spirituality of Presiding," *Liturgy* 22, no. 2 (2007): 5.

67. Fulkerson, *Places of Redemption*, 19.

68. Ibid., 21.

69. Ibid., 17–21.

70. Eiesland, *The Disabled God*, 108.

71. Don E. Saliers, *Worship as Theology: Foretaste of Glory Divine* (Nashville: Abingdon Press, 1994), 22.

I. GATHERING: UNFOLDING A LITURGY OF DIFFERENCE

1. Teresa Berger, *Fragments of Real Presence: Liturgical Traditions in the Hands of Women* (New York: Crossroad, 2005), 6.

2. Gordon W. Lathrop, *Holy People: A Liturgical Ecclesiology* (Minneapolis: Fortress Press, 2006), 21.

3. Williamson notes the history and significance of the term: "The noun form of the word 'access'—meaning 'the power, opportunity, permission, or right to come near or into contact with someone or something'—first appears in published texts in English as early as the 1300s. It has been used to characterize the relationship between the disabled body and the physical environment since the middle to late twentieth century." She then describes the ways a broader set of meanings around inclusion and integration have become attached to this word in the history of disability rights. Bess Williamson, "Access," in *Keywords for Disability Studies*, ed. Rachel Adams, Benjamin Reiss, and David Serlin (New York: New York University Press, 2015), 14–16.

4. Nancy L. Eiesland, *The Disabled God: Toward a Liberatory Theology of Disability* (Nashville: Abingdon Press, 1994), 23.

5. Aisha was nervous about disclosing these beliefs, so I did not name them here.

6. While Fiona imagines that she could end up in a position like those Sacred Family congregants with mental illness who live in poverty, she does not speak about the intersections of whiteness and wealth that make it much less likely for her to experience the precarity that many people at Sacred Family experience.

7. Teresa Berger, *Gender Differences and the Making of Liturgical History: Lifting a Veil on Liturgy's Past* (Burlington, VT: Ashgate, 2011), 30.

8. Ibid., 40.

9. Ibid.

10. Ibid.

11. Khalia Jelks Williams, "Engaging Womanist Spirituality in African American Christian Worship," *Proceedings of the North American Academy of Liturgy*, 2013, 103.

12. Ibid., 99–100.

13. Berger describes "traditioning" as an "ongoing, situated, and interested mode of knowing that selects, orders, and interprets." Berger, *Gender Differences and the Making of Liturgical History*, 171–172.

14. Ibid., 166.

15. This Connections meeting is one of the few parts of Sacred Family's liturgy to which I do not have direct access: I do not have a diagnosis of mental illness, a strict requirement for participation.

16. I did attend one DTR meeting with special permission from the group.

17. During my research time, the landlord asked Sacred Family to move out of the space it rents for the art program, and so the art program was moved temporarily to the Circle hall, which limits the kinds and number of art activities that can be offered. Sacred Family considered buying a house next door, but it was too expensive. As I concluded this project, Sacred Family continued to dream of an adequate art space.

18. See, for example, Lennard J. Davis, *Enforcing Normalcy: Disability, Deafness, and the Body* (London: Verso, 1995).

19. See, for example, Rosemarie Garland-Thomson, *Staring: How We Look* (New York: Oxford University Press, 2009), 185–196. Garland-Thomson argues that starees, those regularly stared at, can, as visual activists, arouse our wonder and curiosity in order to engage us and move us to desire and political action.

20. Sharon V. Betcher, *Spirit and the Obligation of Social Flesh: A Secular Theology for the Global City* (New York: Fordham University Press, 2013), 14–25.

21. Alison Kafer, *Feminist, Queer, Crip* (Bloomington: Indiana University Press, 2013), 15.

22. Ibid., 14–17, citing Carrie Sandahl, "Queering the Crip or Cripping the Queer: Intersections of Queer and Crip Identities in Solo Autobiographical Performance," *GLQ* 9, nos. 1–2 (2003), and Robert McRuer, *Crip Theory: Cultural Signs of Queerness and Disability* (New York: New York University Press, 2006).

23. Sharon V. Betcher, *Spirit and the Obligation of Social Flesh: A Secular Theology for the Global City*, 22.

24. Ibid., 20–21.

25. Ibid., 23, 41.

26. Ibid., 165.

27. Ibid., 167–170.

28. Ibid., 167.

29. Ibid., 6. Imagining crip/tography as a religious vocation, Betcher recalls the work of medieval "seculars" who walked the city streets in order to occupy public spaces in a revelatory way: "uncloistered religious persons who carried their spiritual passion and sense of an obligated life into temporal concerns, specifically, their daily circumambulations of the city." Seculars were to walk and occupy the city on behalf of its inhabitants and to offer alternate visions of the materialism and the isolation that city relations often encourage and require.

30. Betcher, *Spirit and the Obligation of Social Flesh*, 7–8. Betcher builds on the work of Chris Beasley and Carol Bacchi who define social flesh as an "ethico-political ideal" with an emphasis on "*embodied* interdependence" and "the *mutual* reliance of people across the globe on social space, infrastructure, and resources." Chris Beasley and Carol Bacchi, "Envisaging a New Politics for an Ethical Future: Beyond Trust, Care, and Generosity Towards an Ethic of 'Social Flesh,'" *Feminist Theory* 8, no. 3 (2007): 280.

31. Betcher, *Spirit and the Obligation of Social Flesh*, 8. Betcher is drawing on Judith Butler, *Precarious Life: The Powers of Mourning and Violence*, reprint edition (London: Verso, 2006).

32. Betcher also writes of Spirit as "a necessary 'prosthesis,' an aid that might help us advance toward spacious and fearless empathy, toward forbearance amid messy entanglements." Betcher, *Spirit and the Obligation of Social Flesh*, 12.

33. Berger, *Gender Differences and the Making of Liturgical History: Lifting a Veil on Liturgy's Past*, 41.

2. WEAVING: AESTHETICS OF INTERDEPENDENCE

1. "Warp," *Merriam-Webster Online*, accessed February 7, 2016, http://www.merriam-webster.com/dictionary/warp.

2. Ali Smith, *Artful*, reprint edition (New York: Penguin Books, 2014), 65–66.

3. Ibid., 65–67.

4. Ibid., 67.

5. Ibid., 126–127.

6. Rosemary Crow, "Weave," in *Chalice Hymnal*, ed. Daniel B. Merrick (St. Louis, MO: Chalice Press, 1995), hymn number 495.

7. Jean Vanier, *Becoming Human*, 2nd ed. (Mahwah, NJ: Paulist Press, 2008), 128.

8. Ibid., 128–129.

9. A therapist once encouraged Annie to write, and there is now rarely a space or time, other than meals and bingo, when she is not engaging in one of these activities; worship services are no exception.

10. Andrea Bieler and Luise Schottroff, *The Eucharist: Bodies, Bread, & Resurrection* (Minneapolis, MN: Fortress Press, 2007), 4.

11. Nancy L. Eiesland, *The Disabled God: Toward a Liberatory Theology of Disability* (Nashville: Abingdon Press, 1994), 41–43.

12. Ibid., 47.

13. Eve Kosofsky Sedgwick, *Touching Feeling: Affect, Pedagogy, Performativity* (Durham, NC: Duke University Press, 2003), 8.

14. Anthony B. Pinn, *Embodiment and the New Shape of Black Theological Thought* (New York: New York University Press, 2010), 24.

15. Ibid., 26.

16. Ibid., 28.

17. Ibid.

18. Ibid., 24–25.

19. Ibid., 4–11. Drawing on the work of Foucault, Pinn dialogues with black and womanist theological discourse about black bodies. I extend his argument to consider disabled and abled bodies in dialogue with liturgical discourse and practice.

20. Ibid., 31.

21. Don E. Saliers, *Worship as Theology: Foretaste of Glory Divine* (Nashville: Abingdon Press, 1994), 27.

22. Ibid., 24.

23. Ibid., 24–25.

24. Ibid., 17.

25. Ibid., 27–28.

26. Ibid., 199.

27. Ibid., 211.

28. Ibid., 201.

29. Sedgwick, *Touching Feeling*, 8.

30. This observation is reconstructed from the author's notes on a lecture by the philosopher Lauren Berlant. Lauren Berlant, "Sex in the Event of Happiness" ("Strange Relations": Studies in Sexualities Graduate Student Conference, Emory University, January 24, 2013).

31. Alan Shain, "Comment from the Field: Perspectives on Comedy and Performance as Radical Disability Activism," *Journal of Literary and Cultural Disability Studies* 7, no. 2 (2013): 337.

32. Saliers, *Worship as Theology*, 27.

33. Aidan Kavanagh, *On Liturgical Theology: The Hale Memorial Lectures of Seabury-Western Theological Seminary, 1981* (Collegeville, MN: Liturgical Press, 1992), 42–49.

34. Ibid., 47.

35. Ibid., 62.

36. Ibid., 74–76.

37. Ibid., 91.

38. Ibid., 63.

39. Ibid., 74, 88.

40. Analyzing the work of a piece of photographic art by Lalla Essaydi, Pinn describes creative disregard as "those attitudes and sensibilities that run contrary to the normative workings of societal arrangements/regulations and are therefore considered problematic because they question what discourses of power and restrictions on life practices are meant to enforce." Pinn, *Embodiment and the New Shape of Black Theological Thought*, 21.

41. Romano Guardini, *The Spirit of the Liturgy* (New York: Crossroad, 1998), 7.

42. Ibid., 64–71.

43. Ibid., 69.

44. Ibid., 66.

45. Ibid., 77–79.

46. Ibid., 95.

3. DISRUPTING: AESTHETICS OF TIME AND WORK

1. Isaac Watts, "We're Marching to Zion," in *Lift Every Voice and Sing II: An African American Hymnal*, ed. Horace Clarence Boyer (New York: Church Publishing, 1993), hymn number 12.

2. During the years I spent at Sacred Family, each year there was a different full-time intern who participated in a year-long formation program. Unlike other interns, Marcus, and those like him, were at Sacred Family for almost every service, program, and event. While they worked at Sacred Family, they participated in an intentional community of other volunteers serving across metro Atlanta. Volunteers like Marcus attended staff meetings, drove vans, and became involved with almost every aspect of life at Sacred Family.

3. Eve Kosofsky Sedgwick, *Touching Feeling: Affect, Pedagogy, Performativity* (Durham, NC: Duke University Press, 2003), 16.

4. Ibid., 14.

5. Ibid., 15.

6. Ibid., 17.

7. I abridged this conversation from a longer time of reflection on the artwork to highlight different interpretations participants offered over the course of the class.

8. Mary Button, "Statement | Stations of the Cross: Mental Illness," MaryButton.com, accessed February 7, 2016, http://stations2015.com/statement/.

9. Siebers describes disabled bodies as essential to the work of modern art because of the sensations such bodies are able to evoke. Tobin Siebers, *Disability Aesthetics* (Ann Arbor: University of Michigan Press, 2010), 1.

Siebers is drawing on the work of Alexander Baumgarten. Alexander Baumgarten, *Reflections on Poetry*, trans. William Holther (Berkeley: University of California Press, 1954).

10. A Sacred Family staff member once said to me that it is the sign of a safe space when you feel comfortable enough to go to sleep, and sometimes it is enough for a church to be such a space.

11. For example, Thomas Reynolds's constructive theology on the vulnerability of God invites Christian churches to become more comfortable with their own vulnerabilities and, thus, be more hospitable places for people with and without disabilities. Thomas E. Reynolds, *Vulnerable Communion: A Theology of Disability and Hospitality* (Grand Rapids, MI: Brazos Press, 2008).

12. At the same time, Circle congregants are also likely to speak about hell, damnation, punishment, and graphic atonement theologies in ways that other congregants are not.

13. I introduce the concept of "loitering with intent" in Chapters 1 and 2.

14. Nancy L. Eiesland, *The Disabled God: Toward a Liberatory Theology of Disability* (Nashville: Abingdon Press, 1994), 89.

15. For a brief introduction to a Christian liturgical calendar, a calendar that is reflected in Sacred Family's patterns of worship, see James White's description of "the language of time." James F. White, *Introduction to Christian Worship*, third edition (Nashville: Abingdon Press, 2001), 47–80.

16. Ibid., 26. White construes this collective work to entail the vital participation of all worshippers: "To call a service 'liturgical' is to indicate that it was conceived so that all worshipers take an active part in offering their worship to God."

17. Ordinary Time designates liturgical time that is not set apart for other major liturgical seasons such as Advent, Christmas, Epiphany, Lent, Easter, and Pentecost.

18. Don E. Saliers, *Worship as Theology: Foretaste of Glory Divine* (Nashville: Abingdon Press, 1994), 217.

19. Button, "Statement | Stations of the Cross."

20. Saliers, *Worship as Theology*, 68.

21. Alison Kafer, *Feminist, Queer, Crip* (Bloomington: Indiana University Press, 2013), 27–28.

22. Eli Clare, *Brilliant Imperfection: Grappling with Cure* (Durham, NC: Duke University Press, 2017), 15.

23. Kafer, *Feminist, Queer, Crip*, 27–28.

24. Ibid., 27.

25. M. Shawn Copeland, drawing on a passage from Toni Morrison's novel *Beloved*, reminds us that for those who experience oppression "enfleshing freedom" often requires loving the parts of one's body that have been rejected or despised. She notes the significance of a ritual context for this form of black

"healing and re/sanctification" in community. M. Shawn Copeland, *Enfleshing Freedom: Body, Race, and Being* (Minneapolis, MN: Fortress Press, 2009), 51–53. In the context of Sacred Family, I think of this act of enfleshing freedom as claiming one's own life on the level of the body through pleasure.

26. Andrea Bieler and Luise Schottroff, *The Eucharist: Bodies, Bread, & Resurrection* (Minneapolis, MN: Fortress Press, 2007), 23.

27. Ibid., 167.

4. NAMING: AESTHETICS OF HEALING AND CLAIMING

1. Charles Wright, *Appalachia: Poems* (New York: Farrar, Straus and Giroux, 1999), 30.

2. Margaret Price, *Mad at School: Rhetorics of Mental Disability and Academic Life* (Ann Arbor: University of Michigan Press, 2011), 4.

3. Ibid., 9.

4. Ibid.

5. Ibid.

6. Ibid., 12.

7. Ibid.

8. T. M. Luhrmann, *Of Two Minds: An Anthropologist Looks at American Psychiatry* (New York: Vintage, 2001), 8.

9. Ibid., 23.

10. Ibid., 45.

11. Ibid., 10–12.

12. Ibid., 10, 34–35.

13. Some recent studies of mass incarceration emphasize that large numbers of people who are imprisoned have mental illness or mental disability. For further reflection on the troubled intersections of disability and incarceration, see Michael Rembis, "The New Asylums: Madness and Mass Incarceration in the Neoliberal Era," in *Disability Incarcerated: Imprisonment and Disability in the United States and Canada*, ed. Liat Ben-Moshe, Chris Chapman, and Allison C. Carey (New York: Palgrave Macmillan, 2014), 139–159. See also Nirmalla Erevelles, "Crippin' Jim Crow: Disability, Dis-Location, and the School-to-Prison Pipeline," in *Disability Incarcerated: Imprisonment and Disability in the United States and Canada*, ed. Liat Ben-Moshe, Chris Chapman, and Allison C. Carey (New York: Palgrave Macmillan, 2014), 81–99.

14. Don E. Saliers, *Worship as Theology: Foretaste of Glory Divine* (Nashville: Abingdon Press, 1994), 35. Saliers quotes "Liturgy of St. James," from *Prayers of the Eucharist: Early and Reformed*, ed. R. C. D. Jasper and G. J. Cumming, 2nd ed. (London: Collins, 1975), 60.

15. Simone Weil, *Waiting for God*, trans. Emma Craufurd (New York: Harper Perennial Modern Classics, 2009), 87, 91–92.

16. Bringing Eiesland and Weil into dialogue, we might say that to suffer is ordinary but to name and regard one who suffers rightly without pity or condescension requires extraordinary love and struggle. Love of neighbor requires both obedience to God and renunciation of self for Weil and, for Eiesland, an intentional transformation of theological symbols including names and images for God.

17. Nancy Eiesland, *The Disabled God: Toward a Liberatory Theology of Disability* (Nashville: Abingdon Press, 1994), 47.

18. Ibid., 42.

19. Ibid., 94–98.

20. David Mitchell and Sharon Snyder, "'Jesus Thrown Everything Off Balance': Disability and Redemption in Biblical Literature," in *This Abled Body: Rethinking Disabilities in Biblical Studies*, ed. Hector Avalos, Sarah J. Melcher, and Jeremy Schipper (Atlanta: Society of Biblical Literature, 2007), 178–179.

21. Sharon V. Betcher, *Spirit and the Politics of Disablement* (Minneapolis, MN: Fortress Press, 2007), 70.

22. Ibid., 71.

23. Eiesland, *The Disabled God*, 117.

24. Aaron suggests that a medical model is preferable to other kinds of religious names, such as "demonic," which might require a healing ritual (casting out demons). His story implies the destigmatizing power of naming something as "a serious medical condition," which doctors rather than pastors have the requisite knowledge and authority to treat. I do not spend time in this project exploring the religious name of "demonic possession" for mental illness in part because such a designation is not operative in Sacred Family's own way of naming mental illness or naming one another, although occasionally both demons and angels appear in a small number of narratives shared with me by congregants. In conversations at Sacred Family, I heard a clear preference for a medical name rather than any association of evil in relationship to mental illness. At the same time, in this chapter I want to raise the question of the limits of medical models for naming human lives and suggest other ecclesial and religious designations that are important to the healing and claiming of one another assumed in Sacred Family's liturgy. For an overview of different frameworks for describing mental illness within histories of Christian theology and practice, see Heather H. Vacek, *Madness: American Protestant Responses to Mental Illness* (Waco, TX: Baylor University Press, 2015), and Rosemary Radford Ruether, *Many Forms of Madness: A Family's Struggle with Mental Illness and the Mental Health System* (Minneapolis, MN: Fortress Press, 2010).

25. Eiesland, *The Disabled God*, 105.

26. Ibid., 98–105.

27. Joan Osborne, *Relish*, Audio CD (Mercury, 2015).

28. Rowan Williams, *Resurrection: Interpreting the Easter Gospel*, rev. ed. (Cleveland, OH: The Pilgrim Press, 2003), 67, 84.

29. Ibid., 88.

5. SENDING: AESTHETICS OF BELONGING

1. Alexander Schmemann, *For the Life of the World: Sacraments and Orthodoxy* (Crestwood, NY: St. Vladimir's Seminary Press, 1973), 26.

2. Ibid., 27.

3. Ibid., 45–46.

4. Mary McClintock Fulkerson, *Places of Redemption: Theology for a Worldly Church* (New York: Oxford University Press, 2010), 6, 30–31.

5. Andrea Bieler and Luise Schottroff, *The Eucharist: Bodies, Bread, & Resurrection* (Minneapolis, MN: Fortress Press, 2007), 5.

6. Fulkerson, *Places of Redemption*, 6.

7. Ibid., 7.

8. Andria Simmons and Craig Schneider, "Lax Enforcement in Personal Care Homes," *The Atlanta Journal-Constitution*, May 22, 2012, http://www.ajc.com/news/news/local/lax-enforcement-in-personal-care-homes/nQT2J/.

9. Ibid.

10. Andria Simmons and Craig Schneider, "Unlicensed Homes to Face More State Scrutiny," *The Atlanta Journal-Constitution*, May 31, 2012, http://www.ajc.com/news/news/state-regional-govt-politics/unlicensed-homes-to-face-more-state-scrutiny/nQWCr/.

11. Andria Simmons and Craig Schneider, "Perils in Personal Care Homes," *The Atlanta Journal-Constitution*, May 9, 2012, http://www.ajc.com/news/news/local/perils-in-personal-care-homes/nQTgL/.

12. Allison C. Carey, Liat Ben-Moshe, and Chris Chapman (eds.), *Disability Incarcerated: Imprisonment and Disability in the United States and Canada* (New York: Palgrave Macmillan, 2014), x.

13. Ibid., 16.

14. Steven J. Taylor, "The Continuum and Current Controversies in the USA," *Journal of Intellectual & Developmental Disability* 26, no. 1 (2001): 15–33.

15. Alison Kafer, *Feminist, Queer, Crip* (Bloomington: Indiana University Press, 2013), 5.

16. Carey, Ben-Moshe, and Chapman, *Disability Incarcerated*, 16.

17. For an exploration of the social geography of disability in relationship to social networks, see Pam Walker, "Community Based Is Not Community: The Social Geography of Disability," in *The Variety of Community*

Experience, ed. Steven Taylor, Robert Bogdan, and Zana Marie Lutfiyya (Baltimore: Paul H. Brookes, 1995), 175–191.

18. João Biehl, *Vita: Life in a Zone of Social Abandonment* (Berkeley: University of California Press, 2005), 2.

19. Ibid., 39–41, 52–53.

20. Ibid., 247.

21. Ibid., 52–53.

22. Fulkerson, *Places of Redemption*, 29–31.

23. M. Shawn Copeland, *Enfleshing Freedom: Body, Race, and Being* (Minneapolis, MN: Fortress Press, 2009), 124–128.

24. Mia Mingus, "Forced Intimacy: An Ableist Norm," *Leaving Evidence* (blog), August 6, 2017, https://leavingevidence.wordpress.com/2017/08/06/forced-intimacy-an-ableist-norm/.

25. Mia Mingus, "Access Intimacy, Interdependence and Disability Justice," *Leaving Evidence* (blog), April 12, 2017, https://leavingevidence.word press.com/2017/04/12/access-intimacy-interdependence-and-disability -justice/.

26. Nancy L. Eiesland, *The Disabled God: Toward a Liberatory Theology of Disability* (Nashville: Abingdon Press, 1994), 94–95.

27. Bieler and Schottroff, *The Eucharist*, 41–67.

28. Copeland, *Enfleshing Freedom*, 130.

29. Ibid., 58.

30. Ibid., 61–62.

31. Ibid., 82.

32. Ibid., 57, 127.

33. I look forward to learning more about the answer to this question after my formal research period under Institutional Review Board is over; it is my intention to pursue the formation of such relationships through the sharing of home spaces. During the research period, I felt it was important to be careful about maintaining my role as a researcher rather than a close friend, so that congregants did not share with me information that they would not have shared with a researcher otherwise.

34. Gordon W. Lathrop, *Holy Things: A Liturgical Theology* (Minneapolis, MN: Fortress Press, 1993), 171.

CONCLUSION. THE DISABLED CHURCH: BEAUTY AND THE CREATION
OF A COMMUNITY OF DIFFERENCE

1. Cláudio Carvalhaes, *Eucharist and Globalization: Redrawing the Borders of Eucharistic Hospitality* (Eugene, OR: Pickwick Publications, 2013), 31.

2. Iris Murdoch, *The Fire and the Sun* (Oxford: Clarendon Press, 1977), 72.

3. Ibid., 86.

4. Simone Weil, "Forms of the Implicit Love of God," in *Waiting for God*, trans. Emma Craufurd (New York: Harper Perennial Modern Classics, 2009), 83.

5. Ibid., 84.

6. Ibid., 102–103.

7. Ibid., 105–106.

8. Ibid., 99, 115–116.

9. Ibid., 99–100, 104–106.

10. Jonathan Edwards, *The Nature of True Virtue*, reprint edition (Eugene, OR: Wipf & Stock, 2003), 4.

11. Ibid., 14–18.

12. Ibid., 98–99.

13. Kenneth P. Minkema, "Jonathan Edwards's Defense of Slavery," *Massachusetts Historical Review*, no. 4 (2002): 35. I am grateful to Jeania Ree Moore for drawing my attention to Edwards's theology and practice of slaveholding.

14. Ibid., 34, 43–44.

15. James H. Cone, *The Cross and the Lynching Tree*, reprint edition (Maryknoll, NY: Orbis Books, 2013), 166.

16. Just as disability scholars and activists often warn against reducing disability experience to tragedy and/or inspiration, so there is also a danger in identifying black experience solely with suffering and resistance. See Victor Anderson, *Beyond Ontological Blackness: An Essay on African American Religious and Cultural Criticism* (New York: Continuum, 1995), 91.

17. Cone, *The Cross and the Lynching Tree*, 94.

18. Ibid., 95.

19. Ibid., 100.

20. Ibid., 94.

21. Betcher describes the importance of "a disability aesthetic that practices 'ethical width'" drawing on religious images of the width of divine mercy. Sharon V. Betcher, *Spirit and the Obligation of Social Flesh: A Secular Theology for the Global City* (New York: Fordham University Press, 2013), 67.

22. Anthony B. Pinn, *Embodiment and the New Shape of Black Theological Thought* (New York: New York University Press, 2010), 21.

23. Fulkerson calls obliviousness "a form of not-seeing that is not primarily intentional but reflexive. As such, it occurs on an experiential continuum ranging from benign to a subconscious or repressed protection of power." Mary McClintock Fulkerson, *Places of Redemption: Theology for a Worldly Church* (New York: Oxford University Press, 2010), 19.

24. Betcher, *Spirit and the Obligation of Social Flesh*, 77.

25. See the description of a conversation with Lloyd about participation in public protest in Chapter 5.

26. Ibid., 158. What I describe as extending and stretching the surfaces of a liturgy, Betcher might identify as social flesh. She identifies flesh as "a plane on which bodies encounter one another and become involved, entangled."

27. Don E. Saliers, *Worship as Theology: Foretaste of Glory Divine* (Nashville: Abingdon Press, 1994), 212.

28. Gordon W. Lathrop, *Holy Things: A Liturgical Theology* (Minneapolis, MN: Fortress Press, 1993), 88–97.

29. Ibid., 88–89.

30. Carvalhaes, *Eucharist and Globalization*, 13.

31. Ibid., 17.

32. Ibid., 33.

33. Nancy L. Eiesland, *The Disabled God: Toward a Liberatory Theology of Disability* (Nashville: Abingdon Press, 1994), 112.

34. Carvalhaes, *Eucharist and Globalization*, 17.

35. Ibid., 31.

Adams, Rachel, Benjamin Reiss, and David Serlin. "Disability." In *Keywords for Disability Studies*, edited by Rachel Adams, Benjamin Reiss, and David Serlin. New York: New York University Press, 2015.

Anderson, Victor. *Beyond Ontological Blackness: An Essay on African American Religious and Cultural Criticism*. New York: Continuum, 1995.

Beasley, Chris, and Carol Bacchi. "Envisaging a New Politics for an Ethical Future: Beyond Trust, Care, and Generosity Towards an Ethic of 'Social Flesh.'" *Feminist Theory* 8, no. 3 (2007): 279–98.

Berger, Teresa. *Fragments of Real Presence: Liturgical Traditions in the Hands of Women*. New York: Crossroad Pub. Co., 2005.

———. *Gender Differences and the Making of Liturgical History: Lifting a Veil on Liturgy's Past*. Burlington: Ashgate Publishing, Ltd., 2011.

Berlant, Lauren. "Sex in the Event of Happiness." Lecture presented at the "Strange Relations": Studies in Sexualities Graduate Student Conference, Emory University, January 24, 2013.

Betcher, Sharon V. *Spirit and the Obligation of Social Flesh: A Secular Theology for the Global City*. New York: Fordham University Press, 2013.

———. *Spirit and the Politics of Disablement*. Minneapolis: Fortress Press, 2007.

Biehl, João. "The Right to a Nonprojected Future." *Practical Matters*, no. 6 (2013). http://practicalmattersjournal.org/2013/03/01/nonprojected-future/.

———. *Vita: Life in a Zone of Social Abandonment*. Berkeley: University of California Press, 2005.

Bieler, Andrea, and Luise Schottroff. *The Eucharist: Bodies, Bread, & Resurrection*. Minneapolis: Fortress Press, 2007.

Book of Common Prayer. New York: Church Publishing Inc., 1979.

Brown, Karen McCarthy. *Mama Lola: A Vodou Priestess in Brooklyn*. Updated and expanded edition. Berkeley: University of California Press, 2001.

Butler, Judith. *Precarious Life: The Powers of Mourning and Violence*. Reprint edition. London: Verso, 2006.

Button, Mary. "Statement | Stations of the Cross: Mental Illness." Mary Button.com. Accessed February 7, 2016. http://stations2015.com/statement/.

Carey, Allison C., Liat Ben-Moshe, and Chris Chapman. *Disability Incarcerated: Imprisonment and Disability in the United States and Canada*. New York: Palgrave Macmillan, 2014.

Carvalhaes, Cláudio. *Eucharist and Globalization: Redrawing the Borders of Eucharistic Hospitality*. Eugene, OR: Pickwick Publications, 2013.

Chapman, Chris, Allison C. Carey, and Liat Ben-Moshe. "Reconsidering Confinement: Interlocking Locations and Logics of Incarceration." In *Disability Incarcerated: Imprisonment and Disability in the United States and Canada*, 3–24. New York: Palgrave Macmillan, 2014.

Cho, Min-Ah. "The Body, To Be Eaten, To Be Written: A Theological Reflection on the Act of Writing in Theresa Hak Kyung Cha's *Dictee*." In *Women, Writing, Theology: Transforming a Tradition of Exclusion*, edited by Emily A. Holmes and Wendy Farley, 183–206. Waco, TX: Baylor University Press, 2011.

Clare, Eli. *Brilliant Imperfection: Grappling with Cure*. Durham, NC: Duke University Press Books, 2017.

Cone, James H. *The Cross and the Lynching Tree*. Reprint edition. Maryknoll, NY: Orbis Books, 2013.

———. *The Spirituals and the Blues: An Interpretation*. Second revised edition. Maryknoll, NY: Orbis Books, 1992.

Copeland, M. Shawn. *Enfleshing Freedom: Body, Race, and Being*. Minneapolis, MN: Fortress Press, 2009.

Crow, Rosemary. "Weave." In *Chalice Hymnal*, edited by Daniel B. Merrick. St. Louis, MO: Chalice Press, 1995.

Davis, Lennard J. *Enforcing Normalcy: Disability, Deafness, and the Body*. London: Verso, 1995.

Edwards, Jonathan. *The Nature of True Virtue*. Reprint edition. Eugene, OR: Wipf & Stock, 2003.

Eiesland, Nancy L. *The Disabled God: Toward a Liberatory Theology of Disability*. Nashville: Abingdon Press, 1994.

Erevelles, Nirmalla. "Crippin' Jim Crow: Disability, Dis-Location, and the School-to-Prison Pipeline." In *Disability Incarcerated: Imprisonment and Disability in the United States and Canada*, edited by Liat Ben-Moshe, Chris Chapman, and Allison C. Carey, 81–99. New York: Palgrave Macmillan, 2014.

Farley, Edward. *Faith and Beauty: A Theological Aesthetic*. Aldershot, UK: Ashgate, 2001.

Fulkerson, Mary McClintock. *Places of Redemption: Theology for a Worldly Church*. New York: Oxford University Press, 2010.

Garland-Thomson, Rosemarie. *Staring: How We Look.* New York: Oxford University Press, 2009.

Garrigan, Siobhan. "The Spirituality of Presiding." *Liturgy* 22, no. 2 (2007): 3–8.

Guardini, Romano. *The Spirit of the Liturgy.* New York: Crossroad, 1998.

Haslam, Molly C. *A Constructive Theology of Intellectual Disability: Human Being as Mutuality and Response.* New York: Fordham University Press, 2011.

Jones, Serene. "Glorious Creation, Beautiful Law." In *Feminist and Womanist Essays in Reformed Dogmatics.* Louisville, KY: Westminster John Knox Press, 2006.

Kafer, Alison. *Feminist, Queer, Crip.* Bloomington: Indiana University Press, 2013.

Kavanagh, Aidan. *On Liturgical Theology: The Hale Memorial Lectures of Seabury-Western Theological Seminary, 1981.* Collegeville, MN: Liturgical Press, 1992.

Lathrop, Gordon W. *Holy People: A Liturgical Ecclesiology.* Minneapolis, MN: Fortress Press, 2006.

———. *Holy Things: A Liturgical Theology.* Minneapolis, MN: Fortress Press, 1993.

Luhrmann, T. M. *Of Two Minds: An Anthropologist Looks at American Psychiatry.* New York: Vintage, 2001.

Mingus, Mia. "Access Intimacy, Interdependence and Disability Justice." *Leaving Evidence* (blog), April 12, 2017. https://leavingevidence.wordpress.com/2017/04/12/access-intimacy-interdependence-and-disability-justice/.

———. "Forced Intimacy: An Ableist Norm." *Leaving Evidence* (blog), August 6, 2017. https://leavingevidence.wordpress.com/2017/08/06/forced-intimacy-an-ableist-norm/.

Minkema, Kenneth P. "Jonathan Edwards's Defense of Slavery" Massachusetts Historical Review, no. 4 (2002): 23–59.

Mitchell, David, and Sharon Snyder. "'Jesus Thrown Everything Off Balance': Disability and Redemption in Biblical Literature." In *This Abled Body: Rethinking Disabilities in Biblical Studies,* edited by Hector Avalos, Sarah J. Melcher, and Jeremy Schipper. Atlanta: Society of Biblical Literature, 2007.

Murdoch, Iris. *The Fire and the Sun.* Oxford: Clarendon Press, 1977.

Nakamura, Karen. *A Disability of the Soul: An Ethnography of Schizophrenia and Mental Illness in Contemporary Japan.* Ithaca, NY: Cornell University Press, 2013.

Osborne, Joan. *Relish.* Audio CD. Mercury, 2015.

Pinn, Anthony B. *Embodiment and the New Shape of Black Theological Thought.* New York: New York University Press, 2010.

Price, Margaret. "The Bodymind Problem and the Possibilities of Pain."
    Hypatia 30, no. 1 (2015): 268–284.

———. "Defining Mental Disability." In *The Disability Studies Reader*, edited by
    Lennard J. Davis, Fourth edition, 298–307. New York: Routledge, 2013.

———. *Mad at School: Rhetorics of Mental Disability and Academic Life*. Ann
    Arbor: University of Michigan Press, 2011.

Rembis, Michael. "The New Asylums: Madness and Mass Incarceration in
    the Neoliberal Era." In *Disability Incarcerated: Imprisonment and Disability
    in the United States and Canada*, edited by Liat Ben-Moshe, Chris Chap-
    man, and Allison C. Carey, 139–159. New York: Palgrave Macmillan, 2014.

Reynolds, Thomas E. *Vulnerable Communion: A Theology of Disability and Hos-
    pitality*. Grand Rapids, MI: Brazos Press, 2008.

Ruether, Rosemary Radford. *Many Forms of Madness: A Family's Struggle
    with Mental Illness and the Mental Health System*. Minneapolis, MN:
    Fortress Press, 2010.

Saliers, Don E. *Worship as Theology: Foretaste of Glory Divine*. Nashville:
    Abingdon Press, 1994.

Schmemann, Alexander. *For the Life of the World: Sacraments and Orthodoxy*.
    Crestwood, NY: St. Vladimir's Seminary Press, 1973.

Sedgwick, Eve Kosofsky. *Touching Feeling: Affect, Pedagogy, Performativity*.
    Durham, NC: Duke University Press, 2003.

Shain, Alan. "Comment from the Field: Perspectives on Comedy and Per-
    formance as Radical Disability Activism." *Journal of Literary and Cultural
    Disability Studies* 7, no. 2 (2013): 337–346.

Siebers, Tobin. *Disability Aesthetics*. Ann Arbor: University of Michigan
    Press, 2010.

———. "Disability and the Theory of Complex Embodiment—For Identity
    Politics in a New Register." In *The Disability Studies Reader*, edited by
    Lennard J. Davis, Fourth edition, 278–297. New York: Routledge, 2013.

Simmons, Andria, and Craig Schneider. "Lax Enforcement in Personal Care
    Homes." *Atlanta Journal Constitution*, May 22, 2012. http://www.ajc.com/
    news/news/local/lax-enforcement-in-personal-care-homes/nQT2J/.

———. "Perils in Personal Care Homes." *Atlanta Journal Constitution*, May
    9, 2012. http://www.ajc.com/news/news/local/perils-in-personal-care
    -homes/nQTgL/.

———. "Unlicensed Homes to Face More State Scrutiny." *Atlanta Journal
    Constitution*, May 31, 2012. http://www.ajc.com/news/news/state-regional
    -govt-politics/unlicensed-homes-to-face-more-state-scrutiny/nQWCr/.

Smith, Ali. *Artful*. Reprint edition. New York: Penguin Books, 2014.

Smothers, Ronald. "As Olympics Approach, Homeless Are Not Feeling at
    Home in Atlanta." *The New York Times*, July 1, 1996, http://www.nytimes

.com/1996/07/01/us/as-olympics-approach-homeless-are-not-feeling
-at-home-in-atlanta.html.

Snyder, Sharon L., and David T. Mitchell. *Cultural Locations of Disability*.
Chicago: University of Chicago Press, 2006.

Staff Writer. "Atlanta Preview '96: The Olympic Games Begin in 2 Weeks."
Fort Oglethorpe Press, July 3, 1996.

Swinton, John. *Resurrecting the Person: Friendship and the Care of People with
Mental Health Problems*. Nashville: Abingdon Press, 2000.

Taylor, Steven J. "The Continuum and Current Controversies in the USA."
Journal of Intellectual & Developmental Disability 26, no. 1 (2001): pp. 15–33.

Vacek, Heather H. *Madness: American Protestant Responses to Mental Illness*.
Waco, TX: Baylor University Press, 2015.

Vanier, Jean. *Becoming Human*. Second edition. Mahwah, NJ: Paulist Press,
2008.

———. "The Wisdom of Tenderness." Interview with Krista Tippett, *On
Being*, podcast audio, December 20, 2007. https://onbeing.org/programs/
jean-vanier-the-wisdom-of-tenderness/.

Walker, Pam. "Community Based Is Not Community: The Social Geography of Disability." In *The Variety of Community Experience*, 175–191. Baltimore: Paul H. Brookes Publishing Co., 1995.

"Warp." In *Merriam-Webster Online*. Accessed February 7, 2016. http://www
.merriam-webster.com/dictionary/warp.

Watts, Isaac. "We're Marching to Zion." In *Lift Every Voice and Sing II: An
African American Hymnal*, edited by Horace Clarence Boyer. New York:
Church, 1993.

Weil, Simone. "Forms of the Implicit Love of God." In *Waiting for God*. New
York: Harper Perennial Modern Classics, 2009.

———. *Waiting for God*. New York: Harper Perennial Modern Classics, 2009.

White, James F. *Introduction to Christian Worship*. Third edition. Nashville:
Abingdon Press, 2001.

Williams, Khalia Jelks. "Engaging Womanist Spirituality in African American
Christian Worship." *Proceedings of the North American Academy of Liturgy*,
2013, 95–109.

Williamson, Bess. "Access." In *Keywords for Disability Studies*, edited by Rachel
Adams, Benjamin Reiss, and David Serlin. New York: New York University Press, 2015.

Williams, Rowan. *Resurrection: Interpreting the Easter Gospel*. Revised edition.
Cleveland: Pilgrim Press, 2003.

Wright, Charles. *Appalachia: Poems*. New York: Farrar, Straus and Giroux,
1999.

INDEX

Page numbers in italic type indicate an illustration.

meals. *See* breakfast; shared meals; Wednesday supper
medical diagnoses, 132, 133, 137, 149–150
medical framework, naming in, 137–138, 148–152, 229n24
medicating practices, 103–104
medications, 137, 138
medieval seculars, 224n29
meeting God, 27
memories and connection, 111
mental difference, 13, 210
mental disability, 132–133, 210
mental health, 133
mental illness, 1, 10–13, 125–126, 132–159, 219nn27–28, 229n24
Mingus, Mia, 184
Minkema, Kenneth P., 201
miracle of modern medicine, 143
misnaming, 140–141, 142, 155
mistreatment in group homes, 176–180
Mitchell, David, 22, 142
modern art, 226n9
modern medicine, 143
money for cigarettes, 123
moral transformation, 202
motivations, 113–114
moving with bodies, 24
multiplicity, 31–38, 45, 54, 58
Murdoch, Iris, 196–197
mutuality, 14, 152–159

nail care, 45, 46, 118, 148
NAMI (National Alliance on Mental Illness), 46, 219n27
naming, 26, 39, 131–165, 229nn16,24. *See also* language
National Alliance on Mental Illness (NAMI), 46, 219n27
needs, 133, 137, 141–142, 147, 148
neglect in group homes, 176–180
neighborhood and neighbors, 16, 171–173, 218n17, 229n16
neurodiversity, 132
non-coercive nature of God, 199
noonday prayer, 30, 47–48, 117–118
normal and abnormal people, 219n28
normalcy, 12, 16–18, 54–55, 142–143, 147
North American society, 151
nurses, 46, 120–121, 148, 150
nursing students, 45, 46, 118, 148, 149

obliviousness, 24, 205, 232n23
offering, 96, 114
Olympics, 4–5
On Liturgical Theology (Kavanagh), 92–93, 95
one beside another, 76–78

open door, 2–3, 169
oppression, 21, 24, 201–202, 205
Ordinary Time, 227n17
Osborne, Joan: "What If God Was One of Us," 161
outings, 62, 184

paid (employed) congregants, 118, 119
painting, 5, 47, *64*, 161, 164, *194*, 195–196
parking lot, 42–43, 55
participant-observation, ix–x, 3, 6–10, 15
participation, *xvi*, 1–2, 14, 22, 40, 56, 73, 89–91, 95–96
passing of the peace, 82
pathologizing disability, 178, 179
patience, 50–51
patterns of identification, 132–137
peace, 32
peace, passing of the, 82
pedicures, 46. *See also* foot clinic; foot washing; nail care
"people first" language, 134
personal care homes. *See* group homes
philosophy and art, 196–197
Pinn, Anthony, 21–22, 24, 74–75, 93, 205, 225n19, 226n40; *Embodiment and the New Shape of Black Theological Thought*, 21
pity, 140, 160, 202, 209, 229n16
places, 24, 29
play, 94. *See also* holy play
pleasure, 84, 100, 109–115, 125–129, 205–206
pli, Holy Spirit as, 58–59
plurality, 3–4, 17–18, 58–59, 139
points of access, 25, 30, 31–38, 54
political action, 185–186
power, 15, 60, 122, 156, 162, 175, 184–185
prayer, 44–45, 75, 91–92, 141–146, 169, 206. *See also* common prayer; liturgy; noonday prayer
prayer books, *xvi*, 38, 48
prayer, common. *See* common prayer
praying without ceasing, 27
prejudice, 155–156
presence of God, 99–100, 207
Price, Margaret, 132–133
pride, 126
property values, 173
protest, social, 185–186
psychiatric disability, 11–12, 134
psychiatry, 133
public art, 21–22
public space, 39, 224n29. *See also* urban space

racial integration, 218n12
racism, 155

Rebecca F. Spurrier is Associate Dean for Worship Life and Assistant Professor of Worship at Columbia Theological Seminary.

CPSIA information can be obtained
at www.ICGtesting.com
Printed in the USA
BVHW030608200220
572802BV00028B/161

9 780823 285525